Build an Online Retail System for under $150

A Complete Step by Step Guide on how to use Shopify, Google AdWords, Helpscout, Chatra, MailChimp and Vimeo to build an On-line Retail Powerhouse.

A step by step guide on how to plan, build and run a complete Online retail system using low cost, Online tools including;

Shopify
Google AdWords, Analytics, Shopping, Merchant Center, YouTube and Apps
Helpscout
Chatra
MailChimp
Vimeo

Roger Butterworth
First Edition, February 2016

Roger Butterworth
2Piglets Press

Version 1.1
First Edition
Published in England, February 2016

Build an Online Retail System for under $150

A Complete Step by Step Guide on how to use Shopify, Google AdWords, Helpscout, Chatra, MailChimp and Vimeo to build an On-line Retail Powerhouse.
by Roger Butterworth

Copyright © 2016 by Roger Butterworth. All rights reserved. No part of this book may be reproduced in any form or by any electronic or mechanical means, including information storage and retrieval systems, without written permission from the author, except in the case of a reviewer, who may quote brief passages embodied in articles or in a review. Published in England by: Roger Butterworth, 33 Arlington Crescent, Wilmlsow, SK9 6BH, roger@rogerbutterworth.com

Every effort has been made in the preparation of this book to ensure the accuracy of the information presented. However the information contained in this book is sold without warranty, either express or implied. Neither the author, nor the publisher or any of it's distributors or retailers will be held liable for any damages caused or alleged to be caused directly or indirectly by this book.

Original and modified cover art by Roger Butterworth and CoverDesignStudio.com

All trademarks are acknowledged by the use of capitals where possible.

Chapter 1
Contents

Introduction	**Page 7**
2. About the Book	Page 8
3. About the Author	Page 11
Part One: Planning	**Page 13**
4. What can you sell on-line ?	Page 14
5. It's all About the profit	Page 16
6. Practical Considerations	Page 20
7. Shipping charges	Page 22
8. International Shipping	Page 24
9. Drop-shipping	Page 28
10. Logistics Processes	Page 32
11. Goods In Transit Insurance	Page 35
12. Platform Choices	Page 38
13. Limitations of Shopify	Page 42
14. Business Plan	Page 43
15. Funding	Page 46
16. The Financial Forecast Template	Page 48
17. About Domain Names	Page 50
18. Buy a Domain Name	Page 52
19. Payment processing	Page 59
20. Credit Card Rules	Page 63
21. PayPal	Page 64
22. Amazon Checkout	Page 66
23. Other Options	Page 68
24. International Payment Methods	Page 69
25. Protecting your on-line store	Page 73
26. Checking Orders	Page 74
27. Screening PayPal & Amazon Orders	Page 84
28. Preventing Attacks	Page 85
29. Denial of Service attacks	Page 87
Part Two: Setting up your store	**Page 89**
30. Set up a Google Account	Page 90
31. Setting up a Shopify Store	Page 101
32. Settings > General	Page 108
33. Settings > Payments	Page 110
34. Settings > Checkout	Page 117
35. Settings > Shipping	Page 120
36. Settings > Taxes	Page 128

37. Sales Tax and VAT	Page 133
38. Settings > Notifications	Page 140
39. Settings > Account	Page 142
40. Settings > on-line Store	Page 148
41. Google Analytics	Page 151
42. Adding Products	Page 158
43. Adding from a spreadsheet	Page 172
44. Product Variants	Page 180
45. Product Categories	Page 184
46. Choosing a Theme	Page 188
47. Modifying the Theme	Page 193
48. Color and Text settings	Page 195
49. Header and Logo	Page 202
50. Organizing the Footer	Page 208
51. The Slideshow	Page 214
52. Featured collections etc	Page 222
53. Product, Collection etc	Page 225
54. Integrating Social Media	Page 229
55. Checkout Page options	Page 232
56. Domain Name	Page 238
57. The Blog in Shopify	Page 246
58. Setting up Menus	Page 252
59. Static Content Pages	Page 259
60. Testing your store	Page 266
61. Communications	Page 267
62. Voice Over IP (VOIP)	Page 268
63. Customer Service eMail	Page 269
64. External e-mail addresses	Page 271
65. Set up your Helpscout Account	Page 277
66. Helpscout e-mail Forwarding	Page 282
67. Saved Replies in Helpscout	Page 294
68. Automated responses	Page 297
69. Helpscout notes	Page 301
70. On-line Chat with Chatra	Page 303
71. MailChimp eMail Marketing	Page 313
72. Cross-Over Integrations	Page 327
73. Other Shopify Apps	Page 346

Part Three Running your store — **Page 353**

74. Sales & Marketing	Page 354
75. Marketing Strategy	Page 356
76. Marketing Plan	Page 359
77. Google AdWords	Page 361
78. Google Shopping	Page 390
79. Notes about Google Shopping	Page 419

80. AdWords bidding strategy	Page 420
81. Google Analytics & AdWords	Page 423
82. Search Engine Optimization (SEO)	Page 426
83. Bing	Page 429
84. Facebook Marketing	Page 430
85. Setting up Facebook	Page 439
86. e-mail marketing	Page 448
87. Using Videos	Page 451
88. Integrating videos	Page 454
89. YouTube channel	Page 459
90. Pintrest	Page 468
91. Instagram	Page 469
92. Twitter	Page 470
93. Discount Vouchers	Page 471
94. In the box marketing	Page 476
95. Understanding Remarketing	Page 477
96. Google Remarketing Tags	Page 480
97. Facebook remarketing 'Pixel'	Page 489
98. Thoughts on Branding	Page 496
99. Making your web site sell	Page 499
100. Photography	Page 502
101. Text Content	Page 508
102. Reputation Management	Page 512
103. Product support	Page 517
104. Marketplace Web Sites	Page 521
105. Objectives	Page 522
106. Amazon	Page 524
107. eBay	Page 527
108. Other Marketplaces	Page 529
109. Accounting	Page 534
110. Business Considerations	Page 538
111. Overseas Staff	Page 539
112. On-Going tasks	Page 542
113. Taking a Break	Page 545
114. Logistics system	Page 546
115. Processing your first Order	Page 547
116. Taking orders over the phone	Page 550
Appendices	**Page 553**
117. List of Courier Options	Page 554
118. Template fraud screening e-Mail	Page 558
119. Checklist	Page 559

Thanks Mum

Introduction

Chapter 2
About the Book

This is a practical book, it explains the process of planning for, setting up and running an on-line retail store. In Part One, I will talk you through the process of creating a business plan for your on-line store, choosing payment processors, delivery partners and setting up your new business.
In Part Two I will give you step by step, illustrated instructions that show you how to set up your store using the market leading Shopify store builder platform, Google Apps, Google AdWords and Google shopping. I will also show you the best way to use low cost on-line applications for setting up a Voice Over IP phone system, on-line chat for your web site and a Help desk system for dealing with customer e-mails.
Then in Part Three I will talk you through the things that you need to do each day while you are running your store to maximize your profits.

This book is written for complete beginners, to use the information here you need to have basic computer skills, to be able to use a web browser to access on-line services and a spreadsheet to manipulate data, that's all, I will talk you through everything else that you need to know and give you detailed instructions to help you.

In bullet points, this book is for you if;

- You want to start running an on-line retail store, but you are not sure how to go about it and you want a thorough grounding in the basics of how to set up and run a store.

- You are not sure if an on-line store is the right way to sell your products and you want to know more.

- You have been given the job of setting up, building or improving an on-line retail store for your company, club or charity.

- You are interested in on-line retail and want to know more about what is involved in setting up and running a store of your own.

A note about the step by step instructions
All of the systems that are described in the book are on-line hosted systems that provide 'Software as a Service' (sometimes shortened to 'SAAS'). They are regularly updated by their owners so there is a chance that some of the processes could change at any time - please bear this in mind when working through the set up instructions.

What is on-line retail?
On-line retail is the process of selling things through the Internet. The first on-line retail order in the UK was taken in about 1995, back then setting up an on-line store could take a team of three or four skilled software developers three months. It was something only big companies or well funded teams could afford to do.
Today, in 2016 - if you have a reasonable level of PC skills you can set up you own on-line store in a day for less than £200 ($US300), if you pick your products carefully and run your store well it will become a small business that delivers an above average income for it's owner.
If you run a manufacturing business of any size, or a 'bricks and mortar' store then adding an on-line retail channel for your products is a thing that you really should do, it will give you extra revenue, better margins and closer contact with your end users - whats not to like about that?

Your on-line retail store will allow consumers to buy your goods or services over the Internet using a web browser. Your potential customers can use any web browser for their side of the transaction, it could be running on a PC in their home or office, a tablet like an iPad or on a smart phone.
Your on-line store will be available 24 hours a day and the customer's web browser can be anywhere in the world, the very best thing about on-line retail is that your web store can address a much bigger pool of potential customers than any bricks-and-mortar shop can possibly hope for. An on-line retailer based in the UK can easily sell to customers right across Europe, the USA, Canada and Australia. To sell into Europe you need to be able to transact in Euros and manage translations - but PayPal takes Euros, Google translate is free and pretty good, so why not?. Similarly an on-line retailer based in Chicago can sell to customers right across the English speaking world

An on-line shop does the same things that a physical shop (also sometimes called a 'bricks-and-mortar' retailer) does. It displays and explains the products and services that it has for sale and gives consumers easy ways to choose goods that they want to buy and pay for them. The only real downside to an on-line retail business compared to selling from a physical shop is that an on-line retail has to almost always deliver the goods that it sells using some kind of delivery service whether it's a commercial third party courier or an in-house delivery service run by staff employed by the retailer.

Who can run an on-line store?
Just about anybody can run an on-line retail store, the main qualifications that you need are a strong work ethic and the ability to use a PC, especially a web browser, and a spreadsheet program. It also helps if you can use a camera and photo editing software like Photoshop or Paint. All of those skills are easy to learn with a bit of time and practice.
Running a store, on-line or offline is not a get rich quick scheme, it takes dedication and hard work, but if you put in the work it will deliver an income, how big that income is depends on how smart your decisions are and how hard you work. On-line retail business make great family businesses, they are easy to fit around other responsibilities like childcare or care for elderly relatives and they generally pay better than doing similar work for other people.

Chapter 3
About the Author

You are probably asking yourself who wrote this book and why should you listen to him? - this chapter is aimed at answering that.

My name is Roger Butterworth, I have been selling products on-line since 1998

In 2000 I was one of the founders of eXpansys.com an on-line retailer of portable electronics, I ran eXpansys as it grew from a start up to a multi national business with turnover of over $100 Million, sales in 110 countries worldwide and and 6 international offices.

In 2007 I floted eXpansys on the AIM division of the London stock market before selling out and moving on in 2010. Since then I have helped to set up over 20 different web stores for companies big and small in a range of different industries.

Web sites that I have set up have sold over $1 Billion of product on-line, I have seen eCommerce from the inside of large corporations and from the point of view of a one man start up and I can tell you that today, with services from companies like Shopify, Google, Helpscout and Chatra available at a very low price there has never been a better time to start selling on-line and this book will show you how.

I have made a lot of money by selling products on-line, but I have also spent a lot on projects that did not work, I hope that by listening to some of my advice you can save yourself from a few of my mistakes and save yourself a lot of money in the process.

I wrote this book after a friend asked me to explain the process of building and running a Shopify store to her - it started off as an e-mail and grew into a book of nearly 600 pages - but I have tried to keep the tone of friendly advise given step by step, I hope that you appreciate it. Comments, corrections and questions are always welcome to roger@rogerbutterworth.com

Part One: Planning

Chapter 4
What can you sell on-line ?

Before you start to commit your cash and time to selling on-line it is a good idea to think about the products that you will be selling, even if you already have products selling through a bricks and mortar retail store or other channels you should read the points below to decide if you want to concentrate on a selection of your existing products rather than offering them all.
Some products work better than others on-line and there are other points to consider.

- **Are you an expert in your products, or do you know one?**

Do you or people on your team know the products that you are aiming to sell well enough to be considered an expert?
Giving advice and sharing knowledge in the form of product descriptions, blogs or user instructions as well as answering customer inquiries by e-mail, phone or on social media will be a big part of developing sales for your web site, if you can't do that it will hurt your chances.

Product expertise is also incredibly useful when it comes to selecting products to sell and deciding which items to invest in for stock.

I strongly recommend that you only sell a product that you have some kind of expertise in, however you can get round the problem by hiring someone with the expertise or if that is too expensive for your low cost start up plan you can fix it by simply educating yourself.

- **Can you communicate with the buyers?**

As a middle aged white guy from Cheshire I can not talk about fashion with a 17 year old black kid from Hackney in a credible or even understandable way - so I should probably not try to sell clothes to him, at the same time he would probably struggle to sell me fine wine. (although I'm pretty easy to sell wine to so maybe he would have a chance) These are extreme examples, but many hobbyists, social groups or even age groups have their own technical terms, slang or way of talking as well as channels of communication that are closed to outsiders. You need to be able to communicate with your buyers to sell to them effectively.

- **Do you like the products that you are planning to sell?**

You will be spending a lot of time thinking about, writing about, talking about and working with the products that you decide to sell - if they bore you, repulse you or scare you then you probably should not get involved with them. Make sure that you really want to spend a big part of your life working with the products that you sell.

One of the saddest people I know has a business making and selling coffins, his business is successful, but it makes him miserable, I'm pretty sure that he would be better off doing something else!

- **Can you get the products to your customers?**

On-line orders normally need to be fulfilled by a delivery service, products that are very large, very heavy or particularly fragile will need special handling that may cost a lot more or may even be impossible - you need to think about delivery method for your products early on.

- **Are there any legal restrictions on the products that you want to sell in the places where you want to sell them?**

There are legal restriction son the sale of some items on-line in countries where the same items can be legally sold in a retail store, the on-line sale of some drugs, knives, toy guns and cigarettes are all restricted in different parts of Europe and the rules on the sale of alcoholic beverages are quite complex in the USA. Check on the restrictions that apply to your chosen products in any countries where you think that you will want to sell one day so you know in advance.

- **Is there a big enough market for the products that you want to sell?**

When you sell on-line you are addressing a very large geographic area so it is possible to have a viable market on-line for niche products that could never attract enough interest to a physical store, but there are still limits, think about the market for your products, will there be enough potential customers out there to make your business viable?

- **Can you make money selling these products?**

If you can find a product set that meets all of these criteria then you may be on to a winner, but there is one last consideration and it is by far the most important - can you make money selling the products that you have chosen? We will work through that question in more detail in the next chapter.

Chapter 5
It's all About the profit

Assuming that you are thinking about getting into on-line retail to make money, then the main thing that you should consider is can you buy (or make) the products that you are planning to sell at a low enough price to make money when you sell them?

As a very broad rule it is much harder to make a success out of selling someone else's products on-line than it is to make money selling your own products, but it is easier to get orders selling famous brand items as long as you sell them at a competitive price. However I would strongly recommend that you do NOT set up a web store selling only other peoples famous brand products, it simply will not work in the long term unless you can maintain supply of goods at a much lower price than your on-line competition. Selling a mix of own brand items and famous brand items can be made to work but by far the majority of successful on-line retailers set up since 2007 have been successful by selling primarily items which they make, design or have some form of intellectual property in, even if the only major difference between their product and their competitors product is the logo.

The main reason for this is that your own unique products can be sold at a much higher profit as they only attract indirect competition, unlike the sale of famous brand items where an on-line retailer will be competing directly with many other retailers selling exactly the same thing. The second reason is that a lot of your competitors will be idiots. I know that sounds harsh and arrogant, and it is, but there is no other explanation for the way that many on-line retailers sell at prices below their own real costs. If you are selling only famous brand items that are available from many different stores you will almost always be facing competition from people selling below their real costs, perhaps without actually knowing that they are doing it.

Opening a store on-line is much, much cheaper than opening a retail store in a high street. And the costs of operation for the on-line store can be quite a bit less, but the costs of operation are significant, and it's important that you understand them when you come to set your prices.

When you run any business you can split your costs into three types of cost.

- Fixed costs or Overheads

The first group are your fixed costs or overheads, these are the costs that you pay every month regardless of what you do. Overheads are things like rent, wages for staff and line rental for your Internet connection.

- Direct Cost of Goods Sold

The second group are your direct cost of sales, these are the costs that you pay for the goods or services that you sell including things like the cost of materials used to make your products and the costs of items that you buy in to sell on.

- Revenue Related Costs

The last group are your revenue related costs - this is the group that people always under estimate when they set their selling prices, they are the costs that vary with the revenue that your company enjoys, they are separate from your direct costs because while the cost of an item is the same no matter what you sell it for the revenue related costs are always a proportion of the selling price.

The table below shows the typical revenue related costs that you can expect to carry when selling on line - these are just the costs that you get as a result of doing business, they do not include overheads or cost of sales.

Cost	% of Revenue	Notes
Payment Processing Charges	4%	* Charged on the total inc tax and shipping
Unrecoverable Shipping Costs	2%	* May be higher for lower priced or bulky items
Unrecoverable cost of Returns and Warranty	3%	* Can be 10% for clothing or electronics
Charge backs and Fraud	1%	* Try to make this zero, but budget for some costs
Advertising	10%	
Total	**20%**	

The numbers above are worse case numbers - and I make no apologies for that, these are the kind of numbers that you should be considering when you plan your margins - if you can get the cost of advertising or returns down then that is great - those savings will become extra profit, but do not set your business up with margins that are so low that you will lose money overall if you can't beat these estimates.

Remember that on top of these costs you need to add enough profit to cover your overhead costs like hosting, rent, wages etc and you also need to make allowance for sales taxes if you are based in the USA or sales tax's evil cousin VAT if you are selling in Europe.

Overall for a European on-line retailer to have a sustainable model you should be selling the items that you buy for about double the price you paid including taxes and shipping - so items that you buy for £50 should be selling at about £100 including taxes. For a US based business that could be a bit lower as VAT is not a factor but you will still need to be selling a $50 purchase for $85 retail. That is just not realistic if you are selling in many categories including famous brand electronics, most branded toys and games and many more besides which is why I am trying to steer you away from setting up a business selling that kind of product.

Remember that in Europe 'trade' cost prices are quoted excluding VAT while by law all retail selling prices must be quoted including VAT.

The next graphic shows for a UK based retailer paying VAT at 20% where the cash that you take for a £100 order goes if you are selling your purchase for double what you paid at trade price.

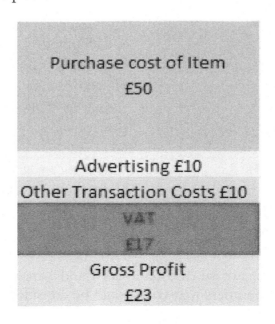

And remember that the £23 profit needs to cover all of your fixed costs like rent, wages, phone bills, web site hosting charges, accountants costs, corporate taxes, everything that you spend on your business and then just the bit left over will be your net profit that will contribute to your income as the business owner and go to build your business value.

So to cut to the chase, you should only even consider opening an on-line store selling items where you can buy the products that you sell (or make them) for about half of the selling price this is the golden rule for on-line retail in Europe - break it at your peril.

Chapter 6
Practical Considerations

One of the obvious differences between opening a small brick-and-mortar store and opening an on-line store is that most on-line retail stores need to deliver the goods that they sell to their customers.

Obviously this is not the case if you are planning to sell intangible or down loadable products or services like music, videos or on-line training courses, if that's the case then you can skip this chapter. But even if your main business is selling music downloads, wouldn't it be great to add in some tee-shirts, concert tickets and memorabilia? If so you need to figure out shipping as well so read on!

If you are shipping physical goods then before you can build your business plan you need to plan out the practical aspects of how you will deliver items to your customers. It is important to figure this part out in advance because knowing how you will deliver your goods to customers, how long it will take and how much it will cost is a big factor in your business plan.

For smaller, lighter items that are robust enough to stand shipping by post or a normal courier service, postal services like Royal Mail in the UK, USPS in the USA and Australia Post or standard courier services from big names like UPS, FedEx and DHL are normally the best choice, it is almost always worth having a contract with your national post office as many customers prefer their service, it covers remote areas well and normally offers reasonable value.
You will need at least two courier options, one for regular deliveries and one to offer a premium service, and it makes sense to have more options if possible. The List of Courier Options in the appendices contains a list of delivery couriers along with some notes about their strengths and weaknesses.

If you are shipping larger items like furniture or fragile items including any kind of liquid in glass bottles or containers or even if the items that you want to sell are considered dangerous by couriers then you will need to consider making alternative arrangements for shipping. There are specialist couriers who ship larger items, palletized deliveries and dangerous items, but they can be very much more expensive than regular couriers so make sure that you get binding quotes in advance as you will need them to set your prices.

Courier prices vary quite a bit and the higher priced ones do not always offer a better quality service, shop around and make sure that you have multiple options. It pays to have multiple delivery options.

You should also consider the value of the items that you will be shipping and think about insurance for your goods in transit. Most couriers offer insurance schemes and while they are not great value you should think about building insurance into your selling prices. If you base your insurance charge on a couriers own scheme you will have the option to shop around later and get a better deal that will let you cut the cost and make more profit in due course.

Chapter 7
Shipping charges

Many people will tell you that you should offer free shipping in order to help persuade customers to buy from your web site - I have carried out scientific analysis of customer buying behavior using chargeable shipping and free shipping and I can tell you with absolute certainty that free shipping does NOT increase sales by enough to cover the cost of the shipping.

There you go - this book just saved you more than it cost!

I think that there are two big reasons why that is the case, firstly people value intangible services like shipping based on what you charge for them, the assume that a $10 delivery option is twice a good as a $5 option and that a free one is worthless. Secondly, if you offer free shipping and you want to remain profitable you have to build the cost into your selling price. A retailer selling a product with free shipping who includes the shipping cost in the selling price will be charging more for the actual product than a retailer who charges for shipping separately. Some customers are smart enough to work out the total cost when comparing prices from one retailer to another, but a surprising number of customers just look at the headline rate - they will mostly end up buying from the retailer who charges separately for shipping.

Shipping is an important cost to most on-line retail businesses for a business with average order value of £100 shipping items that average 1Kg the cost of shipping will be about 5% of revenue - that's a substantial cost and not one that you should ignore or give up on.

Almost all successful on-line retail businesses that ship goods charge for shipping, Amazon, Tesco, Argos all charge for shipping only eBay (who don't actually ship anything themselves) insist on free shipping - customers are happy to pay for shipping as long as the charge is reasonable. In the UK market I feel that a reasonable shipping charge is between 4% and 7% of the purchase price, so £6.99 to ship a £100 item is OK but that's at the top end of what people will pay - as you can see from the data in Appendix 1 (Courier Options) you can get DPD to deliver an item of 30kg in the mainland UK with a premium service with on-line tracking for just £5 so you should be able to cover your shipping and handling costs.

As a rule I suggest that you try to cover your shipping costs with what you charge customers for shipping - they will be able to see that is reasonable (by getting shipping quotes on-line if they care enough) and it will not cost you in sales as a result. Trying to make a profit on shipping will probably backfire and offering free shipping simply does not work.

Adding a free collection offer
I recommend that you always offer a 'Free' collection option if you have the facility to allow customers to collect from your warehouse, some customers prefer it and they don't have to collect themselves, they could send their own chosen courier if they like. However I would recommend that you don't do this if you are working from home.

One last note:- Shipping is the only cost that is is acceptable to recover from customers with an additional charge, in the past airlines and others have tried to add in charges to cover the costs of credit card processing, printing tickets etc - in most cases customers react badly to these charges and go elsewhere if they can, I would recommend recovering shipping costs only in this way.

Chapter 8
International Shipping

Your new on-line retail business can offer it's products for sale to customers more or less anywhere in the world (but be sure to read the section on on-line credit card fraud before you pack up those orders from the guy in Indonesia and his mate in Nigeria!)

To make the most of the opportunity to sell your products around the globe you need to make sure that you have a way to ship goods to customers all over the world, and that you understand the costs so that you can price international shipping. I recommend that you get a relationship set up with just one international courier to start with - for On-Line retailers based in the UK I recommend DHL and for those based in the USA, Canada or Australia I recommend FedEx

You also need to understand when international shipments attract customs charges and how to work out in advance how much they will cost you.

Thanks to the European single market, if you are shipping from the UK or any other country within the European Union then there are no customs barriers preventing you shipping goods to customers in any of the other EU states.
The EU states are Austria, Belgium, Bulgaria, Croatia, Republic of Cyprus, Czech Republic, Denmark, Estonia, Finland, France, Germany, Greece, Hungary, Ireland, Italy, Latvia, Lithuania, Luxembourg, Malta, Netherlands, Poland, Portugal, Romania, Slovakia, Slovenia, Spain, Sweden and the UK.
For customers in these countries you just need to charge the appropriate rate for shipping - you can get a rate table from DHL which will show the cost of shipping for each country in 0.5Kg increments, as long as you have accurate data on how much each item that you are selling weighs and what size it is then you should have no problem pricing delivery for these countries. But remember that if you are based in the EU you will be expected to collect VAT on sales to retail customers in any EU state.

When you ship goods across an international border there will normally be additional costs for taxes and duty which the government of the country to which the goods are being sent will charge to allow the goods into their country.

For shipments of goods from inside the EU to customers outside the EU (including customers in the states that are 'semi detached' from the EU like Switzerland, Norway, Iceland and Liechtenstein) and for on-line retailers based in the USA, Canada and Australia shipping goods to customers in any other country there will be a customs charge applied on top of the shipping cost. There are also requirements for extra paperwork with international shipments which can be quite time consuming.

The customs charges are made up of three components.

1. VAT, GST or other sales or use tax.
This is calculated as a percentage of the value of the goods shown on the 'Commercial Invoice' (or 'CI') which you include with the goods.

2. Duty.
This is a separate tax levied on products depending on what type of goods they are, the rate can be zero or it can be higher than 100%, it is calculated based on the 'Commodity Code' that you show on the commercial invoice accompanying the goods. The commodity code is used to identify the type of goods shipped, this tells the customs officer what percentage of duty to apply to the value of the goods shown on the Commercial Invoice.

3. Admin fees.
Most couriers will pay the duty and taxes over for you as they move the goods into the country and clear them through customs for you, but they typically add a fee to the costs to cover the work that they do to deal with the customs authorities.

As a rule VAT and other sales taxes tend to be levied at a more or less flat rate on all goods - but of course there are a range of exceptions to that rule, duty is much more variable. You need to figure out what the typical duty rates are for your type of goods and find out if there are any countries that charge unusually high duty and tax rates on the products that you sell. the UK government has some really helpful information about tariff codes at https://www.gov.uk/finding-commodity-codes including a guide to help you find the right codes for your items at https://www.gov.uk/trade-tariff/sections.

Who pays the duty and taxes?
When you ship goods to a customer in another country somebody is going to have to pay the duty and taxes charged by the government of the country that the goods are imported into, this can be paid either by you as the shipper (When you

do this you are shipping the goods on the basis that they are 'Delivered Duty Paid' or 'DDP') or you can hand it off to the customer and require them to pay it (This is called shipping the goods 'Delivered Duty Unpaid' or 'DDU').

Both options have downsides, if you include the costs in the price you could lose sales by being too expensive, but if you expect the customer to pay then the courier will hold the goods at the border while they contact the customer and the customer will have the option to simply refuse the delivery and then claim the payment back from you through their credit card company or PayPal, since you will not have proof of delivery for the parcel you will not have a leg to stand on when contesting the 'charge back' and you may or may not get the goods back depending on the destination and the courier that you use. You will always end up paying the freight charge regardless.

My Recommendations for your International Shipping policies

I strongly recommend that you build the cost of duty and taxes into the price that you show on your web site and ship to your customers Delivered Duty Paid (DDP) as this is the best way to ensure good customer service, Although it will cost you some orders. If you get an international order on your site where the price paid by the customer is not enough to cover the cost of the goods plus shipping and taxes on import then you should hold the order and contact the customer to ask them to pay the extra cost of taxes for their country, if they refuse simply cancel order and refuse or refund the payment.

You do not need to show the full price paid for the goods on the commercial invoice that you include with the goods, in fact if you are charging a price that includes delivery and duty paid 'DDP' then you must not show the full amount as you will then pay extra taxes and duty on the portion of the price which is there to cover taxes and duty.

When you decide what value to declare on the commercial invoice, it is perfectly legal to deduct the following costs from the actual price that the customer pays to you for the order;

- The value of taxes and duty that you have collected in order to pay them on import
- The value of any services provided, as an integral part of the transaction, outside the destination country (such as set up, pre-loading software, picking and packing etc)
- The cost of the delivery service from your warehouse to the border (but

not the part paid for delivery from the border to the customer)

You may need to have documentation to show how you worked out any deduction as you could be required to prove how it was calculated, but in my experience this is unlikely unless you are very aggressive. It is quite normal to declare around 50% of the transaction value as the value for customs purposes.

NB - I am not qualified to give you formal tax advice, the information above is anecdotal and it is based on my experience only.

Chapter 9
Drop-shipping

I was quite tempted to title this chapter of the book 'Drop-shipping - DON'T DO IT' but I decided that was too harsh, as with most things in life the decision on how to use drop-shipping is not quite so black and white.

For those of you that don't understand what drop-shipping is here is a brief explanation from wikipedia;

"Drop shipping is a supply chain management technique in which the retailer does not keep goods in stock but instead transfers customer orders and shipment details to either the manufacturer, another retailer, or a wholesaler, who then ships the goods directly to the customer"

Many wholesalers offer drop shipping services, they will allow you to place an order for a single item and have it shipped in a plain box directly to you customer. This has several advantages for you as a retailer but also some very important disadvantages.

On the plus side;

- **There are cash flow benefits to drop-shipping**

Drop-shipping is great for your cash flow, you can set up your web site's payment processing systems so that customers pay you when they place their order and you can then use that cash to buy stock from your suppliers. Some suppliers may even allow you to have a credit account so that you can pay them 30 days later and the customers cash can stay in your account (or be used for something else - as long as you can get it back in time to pay the supplier) until then.

- **Drop-shipping orders is easy**

Drop-shipping is also great for a start up e-Commerce business because it takes up very little of your precious resources, the supplier handles the picking, packing and shipping of the order and they choose, pay for and get the package to the delivery service, although they probably charge a fee for all of that.

But on the negative side;

- **Drop-ship stock is out of your control**

You can never be 100% sure that your supplier has the stock that your customer needs, or if they have it you can't be sure when they will ship it, so you can never give your customer an accurate delivery time and customers care about when they will receive their order. In fact accurate predictions are more important to customers than faster deliveries, so customer service is negatively affected by drop-shipping. Even if you link your web site systems into your suppliers stock control systems there will still be a delay updating your site when the distributor sells their last stock of a hot item which could leave you with orders that you can not fill and unhappy customers to deal with.

Also a new, small customer will struggle to get priority for 'in demand' items, very few distributors operate a strict 'first come, first served' system for hard to get stock, you run the risk of being 'gazumped' for stock by bigger customers.

- **Drop-ship deliveries are out of your control, but you are responsible for them**

You do not know for sure what the supplier shipped to your customer, regardless you are responsible for it even though you can never be sure that the correct item was sent. If your customer says that they received the wrong item or even that they received an empty box you will find out pretty fast that a retail customer paying by credit card or PayPal has a lot of power in their relationship with a retailer, while a small retailer buying from a large drop-shipper or distributor has no power at all.

This is because your relationship with the customer is governed by consumer rights law and your agreement with PayPal or your credit card processor which ALL favor the consumer while your deal with your supplier is governed by business to business contract law which is based on the terms and conditions that you agree to when you set up your account with the distributor, that will probably be controlled by the distributor to favor them, as a result you leave yourself open to getting squeezed between the customer and the distributor which can be very painful.

- **Returns are a pain when you drop-ship orders**

When you drop-ship stock you are still responsible for returns and warranty claims from the customer, goods returned to you by customers who are entitled to a full refund may not be in a good enough condition to return to your supplier or sell as new (remember the customer has a lot of power over you, but you have very little over your supplier in these relationships)

- **Competition**

Drop-Shipping is fast and easy, so everyone is doing it. When you drop ship you will struggle to find any kind of unique selling point, your drop-ship partner will sell to all you competition and they will probably have employees who are tasked with finding and developing more competition for you.

- **Your payment processor hates drop-shippers**

Your credit card processing company will charge you higher rates, keep a bigger retention and may even refuse to deal with you at all if you are drop-shipping. PayPal HATES drop shippers and they will treat you as a high risk customer if they know that you are drop shipping. This is because over many years of dealing with customers who use drop shipping services to build eCommerce businesses that have discovered that for all of the reasons above this kind of arrangement leads to serious customer service issues for the retailer which ultimately lead to credit card charge-backs and customer disputes.

You will also have problems with sales through marketplaces like Amazon and eBay if you are drop-shipping them.

My Recommendations on how to use Drop-Shipping effectively

- **Make Drop-Shipping a small part of your business, use it to add extra items to your portfolio, not as the main part of your business.**

As you can see above there are more negatives than positives with drop shipping, so on balance I recommend that you use drop-shipping services as an incidental part of your business, don't set your business up to rely on drop shipping.

Every business that I know that has set up to use drop-shipping as their only way to deliver goods to customers has failed. It's a great way to bulk out your product set with some extra items that make your store look more complete, but the items that you drop-ship should not be the core focus of your business.

- **DO NOT sell Drop-Shipped stock on marketplaces.**

Don't sell drop shipped stock on marketplaces like Amazon and eBay, it simply does not work. It is a fast way to get yourself banned from the platforms due to poor customer service.

- **DO NOT tell your payment processor that you are drop shipping (even if you are)**

Try really hard not to lie, but under no circumstances should you tell your credit card processor that you are drop-shipping.

- **Consider just in time purchasing as an alternative to drop-shipping**

Just in time purchasing is a great alternative to drop shipping, it takes a bit more work, but it gives you back the control. Instead of sending your supplier an order for each order that you receive from a customer you order once each day 'just in time' to get the stock shipped to your office next day - then you send the goods out to the customer. The cash flow is almost as good and the customer just waits an extra day, as long as you tell them up front what to expect in terms of delivery, most customers are OK with that. Costs are often lower as most distributors charge a lot less for a bulk delivery than a drop ship delivery and you are in charge of the service used to ship to the customer, and you don't need to lie to your payment processor.

Chapter 10
Logistics Processes

To ensure that you able to react quickly to customer needs and to be able to handle short term issues quickly I think it's vital that every on-line retailer has some in house logistics capability, even if you are working from home you should have an area set up where you can unpack deliveries, break down large batches of stock and re-pack them into smaller customer deliveries.

All you need for that is an area set aside for the purpose with room to unpack boxes and pack up orders, some room to store supplies like tape, bags and bubble wrap and set up with a PC connected to the Internet a printer, separate label printer and a bar code scanner.

If you are expecting deliveries on pallets get yourself a pallet truck, they make it a lot easier to handle large batches of stock.

A large desk with some space around it is perfect, if you are working from home to start with a domestic single garage is the perfect size for this kind of facility, if you have an office set up to run your business from, dedicate a corner to this area.

For a small on-line business shipping orders is a very important job as it directly affects customer satisfaction, which drives word of mouth recommendations and on really busy days it is not uncommon for a small on-line retailer to have every single person in the business stop what they are doing and spend some time helping to pick, pack and ship orders. Thats how Amazon operated until quite recently and it works really well.

However, while relying on everyone in the business to pull together is a great way to deal with demand peaks in your start up phase it is not a long term solution to your logistics needs.

When you start up an on-line retail business, either as a solo entrepreneur, as a family business or as a department of an established business it is likely that you will be short of resources in one way or another, people will have to take on multiple responsibilities. Regardless, you should do your own logistics for as long as possible while you grow.

If you can do all your own logistics for ever then you should. In house logistics is ALWAYS better than outsourced logistics. Even if your business needs to use someone else to handle logistics in the long run you should still do your logistics in house to start with - understand the processes in detail and document them before you consider outsourcing. You should also keep a logistics capability in house and use it when you can.

You will need to consider outsourcing part of your logistics in the long run if;

- Demand for your products is highly variable due to seasonal spikes, product release cycles or just the vagaries of the market.

- You are shipping goods made overseas to customers in countries where you have no physical presence - for example a UK based company having products made in China who then sells them in the USA would be well advised to outsource pick pack and ship services to a company in China or Hong Kong for their US based customers.

- Your logistics processes are very simple because you have a small product set and you sell a lot of each item.

- If you sell the majority of your product through Amazon then using Fulfillment By Amazon (FBA) is a great option, because products stored in Amazon warehouses get a boost in Amazon search and they are eligible for free shipping to customers who pay for Amazon Prime which is very helpful to sales.

Here are my key recommendations for logistics processes

Every on-line retail business needs a packing area.
Every on-line retail business must have a capability to handle some logistics in house, by that I mean the ability to receive deliveries from suppliers, send packages to customers and accept customer returns.

Do all of your own logistics in house if you can.
It's as simple as that, in house logistics is ALWAYS better than outsourcing. Sometimes in house logistics are more expensive than outsourcing, sometimes they are not MUCH better, but they are always better.

Even if you have to outsource in the long term, do your own logistics until you are sure that you have the processes working perfectly.
Manage your logistics yourself to begin with, do each process with your own hands, not just for an hour or two, but for days. Refine the processes, document

them and try to find an outsourcing partner who can take them on in full. Changing processes that have been outsourced is much harder than changing them when you are doing them in house.

Here are the contact details for some businesses that can help you if you need to outsource some of your logistics, with a few notes about what they do.

Shipwire
Shipwire is a division of Ingram Micro, one of the biggest distributors in the world, it is a fully on-line service that you can use to handle all of your logistics or to handle just a part, the system is very comprehensive and reliable.
http://www.shipwire.com/

Floship
Floship is a Hong Kong based company that specializes in helping companies deliver products made in China to customers in the USA and Europe as efficiently as possible.
http://www.floship.com/

Fulfillment by Amazon (FBA)
Fulfillment by Amazon is a storage and logistics service provided by Amazon. It is mainly used by people who are selling their stock through Amazon because it offers better placement in Amazon search results than the same items would get if they were shipped by a third party. FBA is quite expensive for shipments outside of Amazon.
http://www.amazon.com/

Chapter 11
Goods In Transit Insurance

If you ship goods to customers using postal services or commercial shippers like the post office or even the international professional couriers like DHL you will suffer losses in transit from time to time. However you should not panic, in my experience loss rates with the top grade couriers like DHL, FedEx and Royal Mail are very low, typically in the order of 1 loss every 5,000 to 10,000 shipments, (0.02 - 0.01%).
Many couriers use sub contractors to deliver to remote areas, these tend to be more prone to losses.

For a small on-line retailer it can be tough to decide whether to insure your shipments or not and if you decide that you need to there are a number of options available, on balance the insurance offered by most couriers is a flat out rip off, costing 10 times or even 100 times the real cost of losses and even the blanket insurance policies offered by commercial insurance brokers are not good value and they typically come with very restrictive terms and they have high deductibles or excess clauses on each claim which reduce their value significantly.

If you take sensible precautions and use reputable services for your shipments then you should not need insurance for the majority of your deliveries. You will make a few losses on goods in transit but they will probably be a lot less expensive than the cost of insurance would be.
So I recommend that you budget for small losses on regular customer deliveries at the rate of about 1 per 1,000 shipments (0.1%) this should be a very conservative estimate and that you only pay to insure large shipments.
The definition of a large shipment that warrants insurance is up to you - but I think it's best defined as a shipment, who's loss would cause serious harm to the business, any shipment worth more than 10 times the average order value is another way to look at it.

Sensible precautions to avoid making your packages a target include not branding the outside of the boxes or wrappers if you are known for selling high value items. In a test that I conducted a few years ago parcels marked with the name of a famous jeweler and those marked with the name of a famous brand of high end electronics went missing from Royal Mail post batches at a rate almost 20 times higher than plain parcels sent to the same addresses!

One last point on this - your deliveries from suppliers will normally be of much higher value than your deliveries to customers as in many ways an on-line retail business is a business that breaks down large batches of stock into single units for delivery to end users, so it is much more important to make sure that your inbound deliveries from suppliers are insured, you may be able to persuade your suppliers to pay for the insurance as a part of the deal, but they will probably not do so unless you ask. If they won't you should either pay extra for it or get a commercial insurance policy to cover the value of inbound shipments.

Lastly, if you are buying stock in from suppliers overseas note that commercial air-freight services, especially the cheap ones that go via hubs in the middle east or third world are very vulnerable to losses. It is rare for a whole shipment to be stolen but very common for items to be taken from the batch, in fact it is almost the norm. And it's impossible to hide what is in these shipments as they need to be accompanied by customs paperwork with the details of what is in the boxes.
Avoid this as much as possible by making sure that your freight forwarder uses direct services where possible and make sure that high value deliveries are wrapped with security film (like cling film wrap but opaque and tougher).

So here are my recommendations on goods in transit insurance

DO NOT take out blanket insurance on all shipments
It's just not good value if it costs you more than the losses that it protects you from, and it will.

DO insure specific high value shipments, including inbound shipments from suppliers
Do that with a commercial policy or get your suppliers to include it in their delivery charge, but remember if they don't explicitly say that your deliveries are covered they probably are not.

If you are selling high value goods, DO NOT brand your packaging
Branding your packaging is a great marketing idea, but it is not sensible if you are known for selling expensive items that are vulnerable to pilferage or if you plan to be!

Shipping insurance on international shipments
It is useful to remember that in most cases the maximum payable under your goods in transit insurance will be the value declared on the Commercial Invoice for tax purposes.

Chapter 12
Platform Choices

This book is all about how to set up a store using Shopify as the core on-line retail platform. Shopify is a fantastic store platform but it is not the only one available. Now that you know what you are going to sell and how you are going to deliver it to your customers it's worth spending a few minutes making sure that Shopify is the right platform for you.

The market for on-line retail platforms is huge, there are many different ways to build a website and start selling your products on-line, the choice can be confusing and it is a crucial decision, one that you have to get right if your store is to be a success.

There are three main types of system for setting up a web site. Fully hosted web store systems, configurable shopping cart software and bespoke web sites built from scratch.

FULLY HOSTED WEB STORE SYSTEMS
Fully hosted web store systems are the easiest systems to set up and use, they are usually the safest and most secure as well. However this makes them less flexible and usually less capable overall than the other two choices.
Fully hosted systems are usually the cheapest to set up by far and the cheapest to run overall for order volumes up to around $US 8Million (£5Million) per year
Fully hosted web store systems include

Shopify - www.shopify.com
Volusion - www.volusion.com
Big Commerce - www.bigcommerce.com
2Checkout - 2checkout.com

My recommended choice of fully hosted web store system is Shopify, because the costs of set up are in line with all the other systems listed, the feature set is very good and the system is easy to use - but primarily the choice is obvious for one very simple reason Shopify is the market leader in this segment with more customers than the next 2 systems combined and stability of the business running your fully hosted web store is key. In the last year two significant businesses offering fully hosted web stores have closed (Magento Go and Amazon Web

stores) this has caused serious disruption for the on-line retail businesses using those platforms and you do not want it to happen to you. Shopify picked up a lot of customers from these platforms as they both recommended it as the best replacement.
Shopify also has an excellent App store and an open API system that allows you to add apps to connect Shopify to ERP systems, chat software systems and help desk software as well as marketing systems like Google shopping.

Using Shopify a reasonably competent person can set up a great web store in a weekend, detailed instructions for doing that are included in section 2 of this book.

Setting up a Shopify store with a custom URL, help desk system for 2 people, on-line chat, corporate e-mail and will cost you around £100 and running it will cost you about £75 per month

CONFIGURABLE SHOPPING CART SOFTWARE
Configurable shopping cart software is software that you can install on a server that you own and control or on a virtual server in a cloud based system like Amazon Web Services. If you install it on a real server that can be installed at your office or in a hosting center.
An on-line retail store built using configurable shopping cart software is intermediate in cost between a fully hosted web store and a truly bespoke system.

My recommended choice of Systems built using configurable shopping cart software is Magento Community Edition 2.0, Magento has been the market leader in this segment for around 5 years, mostly because it is free and it runs well on Linux servers using the Apache web server with My SQL for a database system and uses PHP for web scripting. All of which are also free to use (Linux, Apache, MySQL and PHP are often referred to by the acronym term 'LAMP'). But don't let the fact that you don't pay for the software required to set up a Magento web store make you think that it's a free ride.

The cost of having a Magento based web store set up for you by an expert will be between £2,000 and £10,000 depending on the partner that you appoint to do the work and the complexity of the job. Of course if you understand Linux and web technology like HTTP and CSS then you can set a store using Magento yourself and save a lot on the cost of set up, but be warned setting up a secure, stable and high performance web store using Magento is a complex and skilled job, I strongly recommend that you get a professional to do it for you unless you have done it before, your first DIY built Magento store will probably be awful!

Before you can appoint a developer to build a Magento based store for you it is important to specify the store in detail, the specification will tell the developer how you want the store to look and how you want it to work. Specifying the store win detail is a complex job that takes time, it's the downside of great flexibility.

Setting up a good Magento based store will take a good developer between two and four weeks, when it is complete a Magento based web store can look amazing, the front end can be customized in almost any way that you want, in fact you can build a completely bespoke front end on the Magento platform for a fraction of the cost of a fully bespoke web site. Magento is also widely supported with integration tools to connect it to ERP systems, chat systems and helpdesk software as well as other essential tools like Google shopping.

Apart from it's flexibility, Magento has one other big advantage over Shopify, it has the ability to run multiple web stores each in a different language and currency as part of a single store platform - this is something that you need to set up multiple Shopify web stores to achieve.

There are a couple of downsides to Magento based sites that you should know about.

Firstly because Magento is the most popular shopping cart software in the world, so it is subject to the most security breaches because hackers focus on it - because they can get more from a Magento hack than they can from hacking any other system, so you need to make sure that your security set up is top notch if you use Magento.
Secondly Magento is slow in terms of page load speeds for your customers, it needs more capable hardware or better cloud resources to run at an acceptable speed than a fully bespoke system would require.

BESPOKE WEB SITES BUILT FROM SCRATCH
A Bespoke web site built from scratch is the best possible solution for a professional on-line store, if you absolutely have to have the best looking, fastest and most perfect web store then a bespoke web store is the best way to get it, but the downside is cost, both the cost of set up and the on-going maintenance cost are significant.

The cost of a bespoke web store for you business will be between *£10,000* and *£ 100,000* plus monthly maintenance cost of between *£ 5,000 per month* and *£ 20,000*.

If you choose to commission a bespoke web site then you will be able to define how it connects to your other systems and integrate it directly to systems like Google shopping.

If you decide to commission a bespoke web site then you will need to specify it in even more detail than for a system based on a platform like Magento.

The downsides of a fully bespoke system are the price for set up and maintenance and the time that it will take to specify and build a bespoke store - which will typically take three to six months.

Chapter 13
Limitations of Shopify

There are a few limitations to Shopify stores that you should know about before you commit to using the system for your store.

The biggest limitation is that a Shopify store can only transact business in one currency, you can show the equivalent prices in different currencies, but you can only actually charge credit cards in one currency per store. In practice that means that if you want to have stores selling in several currencies you will need to set up a store for each currency. That means that you will pay at least $US30 (£20) per month per store and if you want to link the stores together to share a stock and order management system you will need to pay extra for a system like StoreFeeder to manage that.

The minimum cost of running 5 stores in this way will be around $US400 (£275) per month plus transaction fees, this still compares well with the cost of running a similar multi site store on Magento.

Shopify stores charge a commission on all of your sales, the starting rate is 2.2% - this covers both credit card processing and commission so it is not unreasonable - but it can be a significant cost if your store really takes off. You can pay extra to get the rate reduced, if you pay $US79 (£55) the rate falls to 1.9% and if you pay $US179 per month (£120) the rate is reduced to 1.6%. If you are selling more than £5Million (US$8 Million) per year through your store then Shopify may be more expensive to run than a hosted Magento store.

Lastly, although there is no technical maximum number of products that you can have in a Shopify store, the system does not work well with more than about 2,000 items - if you want to carry a bigger portfolio than that you will need an external stock and content management system like StoreFeeder and you may be better off with a Magento based platform.

Chapter 14
Business Plan

According to Wikipedia 'a business plan is a formal statement of business goals, reasons they are attainable, and plans for reaching them. It may also contain background information about the organization or team attempting to reach those goals' A key part of a business plan is the financial plan or forecast, a spreadsheet that shows how the business will perform at different levels of revenue, how the cash flow will respond to different levels and types of sales and how much funding the business will need to reach it's goals.

Your business plan will have two parts, one is the text part where you explain what is special about your business, how you will make it work and, if you are trying to raise funding for your enterprise, you explain to funders why you are more likely to be successful than the next guy. You are more or less on your own with this part of the plan, but I do have a template to get you started and make sure that you don't miss anything important, you can download it at www.rogerbutterworth.com
The second part of your business plan will be a financial forecast, here I can help you more comprehensively, this book comes with a license to use my on-line business plan forecast system also available at www.rogerbutterworth.com.
You can use this as a part of your overall business plan to raise funding for your business or to better understand what you are spending your own money on. It will help you to produce a comprehensive financial forecast for your on-line business.

There are many reasons why you should have a complete and comprehensive financial forecast as a part of your business plan, but in my opinion the main reason that you need a financial forecast is to try to understand how your business will work at different revenue levels. A really good business plan spreadsheet will help you to understand the way that your business will respond to different levels of sales, this is called 'running contingencies'. By running contingencies you will better understand what you need to do when your sales increase and what to expect when they decrease and most importantly you will be able to use your business plan spreadsheet to predict how much funding you need to make your business work.

The business plan template that I have provided with the book provides works based on weekly numbers. I think that this is very important - forecasts that use monthly data are inherently awkward as they struggle to take account of the way that months have different numbers of days, some months have 8 weekend days in them, others have 9 or even 10 and in all businesses the trade that you can expect on a weekend day is different from that you would expect on a weekday. Weekly forecasts are much easier as almost every week is made up of 5 weekdays and 2 weekend days, some weeks contain public holidays, but these are easy to look up and forecast for.

It is very, very important to recognize that the data you put into your financial forecast is part careful research and part complete guesswork. The parts of the forecast that you can get perfectly right are usually the costs - you can research in advance how much you will be paying for the items that you sell, what rent, server hosting and salaries will cost you, but you can only guess at what your sales will be in the first week that you operate. Most business plans are set up for at least 3 years, sometimes a far out as 5 years, predicting your revenue in week 150 after set up when you have not yet taken your first real order is close to impossible. But you have to try.

A good business plan is not a fixed thing, it is updated and developed regularly in response to data gained from the real world and changes in the way that you plan to run the business. A good financial forecast is updated more often, you should update your financial forecast each and every week, updating the forecast with the actual numbers for the performance of the business in the last week and adjusting the forecast data based on any new insights that you have gained. In this way the financial forecast will be refined over time and get closer and closer to being accurate.

My recommendations regarding your business plan

You MUST have a business plan
Even if you are setting up the business with your own money, or if you have been told to set up a web store for your employer you should still go through the process of setting up a business plan and a financial forecast, it will help you think through the process properly and to be able to judge the success of your sales on an ongoing basis.

Be realistic in your financial plan, if you are not sure then be conservative (pessimistic)
If you can be sure what something will cost then of course you should put the exact number into your business plan, but for both sales numbers and costs if you

are making an estimate be realistic or even pessimistic. So that means that you should over estimate costs and under estimate sales. That way you will build in some tolerance in you business plan for unexpected costs or unexpectedly lower revenues.

If the financial forecast shows that your business will not work then don't start it!
It might seem a bit silly to say this, but it is really important to treat the plan as a test, you are using it to check your assumptions about the business in a 'virtual' world If your plan shows that the business will lose money even if you hit your sales forecasts or if it shows that it needs more money to be successful than you can raise then do NOT start running the business.

I have broken this rule, thinking that I would figure out the problem down the road, it was a disaster, be smarter than me - don't do it !

Chapter 15
Funding

All businesses need funding. By that I mean that all businesses need to start off with some money or resources that will be consumed by the business in order to get business.

This is a practical guide to setting up and running your store rather than raising funds so we can only cover the options in brief, there are loads of good books on fund raising for business and some great new options involving crowd funding, I recommend that you read one or two before deciding how to proceed. You should also consider getting professional advice on how to raise funding if it's available.

One of the main reasons why you create a financial forecast for your business is so that you can understand how much funding you will need in order to get your business up and running. You can also use the financial forecast to explore ways to minimize the funding requirement, because all funding has a cost.

There are basically 4 ways that you can fund a business set up. You can take out a loan, You can take equity investment from other people where they buy a share in your business for cash, you can use either way to invest you own cash - which is the same thing - the business is just borrowing cash off you or taking investment off you instead of someone else.
Lastly you can find a way to start a business that is cash positive - meaning that it has more income each day than outgoings, usually this is because customers are paying you before you have to pay your costs leaving you with a positive bank balance at all times, this is sometimes referred to as 'boot strapping' the business, short for 'pulling the business up by it's own boot straps'. This is a popular way to get a small web business going, but it is risky.

Getting a Business Loan
Loans are easy to get for established businesses that can show a profit, they are almost impossible to get for a startup unless you are able to provide some sort of security to the bank making the loan. But they are usually the cheapest and least risky way to fund a business, you should talk to your bank and to other banks about the terms that they can offer for loans before you look at raising funding elsewhere.
There are a number of new crowd funded options for business loans, look around

for them, in the UK http://www.fundingcircle.co.uk is a great option.

Getting Outside Investment in your Business

The normal process to get investment for a start up business is to raise cash in a number of batches or 'rounds' as follows.

Firstly the founder or founders invest their own cash to get the business going, then they look outside the people working in the business to find relatives or close friends who may like to invest in the business to support the founders (the so called 'friends and family round') Then they look to professional investors or Venture Capitalists (also known as 'VCs') to raise further rounds of funding.

Raising funding in this way is a great way to build a big business, it's that way that huge companies like Amazon, eBay, Facebook and twitter were built. But it does not suit small businesses that will always be nice players as with each round of funding the founders of the business give up more of their share of the business.

For smaller businesses funding through an 'Angel Investor' according to Wikipedia and Angel investor, also known as a business angel, informal investor, angel funder, private investor, or seed investor is an affluent individual who provides capital for a business start-up, usually in exchange for convertible debt or ownership equity.

Angel investors are often able to offer business help to he founders, especially if they have experience in the type of business that you plan to run. Angel investors are a very good option for fund raising for a new business.

Loaning your Own Cash to Your Business

Investing your own cash in your business is usually done as a loan from you to the business or as an investment in the form of a purchase of shares. It's best to do this formally and it can be a very powerful way to demonstrate your faith in the business to a bank or an investor if you make your investment at the same time and under the same terms that they make theirs.

'Bootstrapping' Your Business Through Cash Flow

Funding your business through your business cash flow can be a great way to get your business going. If you choose to do that it's a great way to build a business in the short term and get it going, but it is really just another way of borrowing money to fund your business, you are borrowing it from your customers and suppliers rather than from a bank or investor, but never lose track of the fact that you are borrowing money just the same - and from people that probably don't know that they are funding your business and may be quite upset if they find out!

Chapter 16
The Financial Forecast Template

Before you can start to use the business plan template you will need to download a copy from http://www.rogerbutterworth.com

Before staring work on your financial forecast remember the works of master statistician George Box who once said: "All models are wrong but some are useful." The Forecast is a model, it can help you understand a lot about how your on-line business is likely to perform, but it is just a model - the actual performance numbers are more important.

The Financial Forecast Template spreadsheet has tabs for Variables, Weekly P&L and Weekly Cashflow, It has been been set up using Microsoft Excel as a part of office 365, it is fully unlocked and editable, you can change it, modify it or develop it in any way, feel free to send me your updates and I will make them generally available to other readers, I will also try to update it over time if I can so don't be surprised if there are multiple versions available with more tabs etc.

To set up the spreadsheet as a simple forecast just fill out the yellow fields on the 'Variables - fill this out first' tab, each yellow field can be edited and will affect the results shown on the other tabs, they are all set up with default values that you can over wright or keep as you see fit.

These numbers are used to build a basic P&L and cashflow forecast on a weekly basis for the next 5 years in the other sheets.

Once you have set the variables in the first sheet the basic P&L and cashflow forecasts will be automatically created - but I'm afraid that this is not the end of the job, you will need to double check all of the data and make adjustments to the way that the sheet works to make it more accurately reflect the way that you plan to run your business. Spend some time on the sheets and really get to understand them, getting your financial forecast right is really important, change a few of the variables to see what happens if your sales are lower or higher than you think that they will be.

The 'Weekly P&L' sheet provides a Profit and Loss forecast week by week for the first 5 years of your business. The P&L includes a forecast of costs, revenue and profits for your business.

The 'Weekly Cashflow' sheet provides the same for cash flow in and out of your business, this will tell you how much funding you need for your business based on the rules that I have set up and the data that you have entered, remember that these numbers are forecasts, they are not 100% guaranteed, but they will give you a good idea of what you need.

You can edit any of the cells on the revenue line by hand to see what that does to the cash flow and the other results fields.

When you create your business plan it will be based on a lot of assumptions, some that you are pretty sure are true, some that you got from this book and some that are not much better than wild guesses. Once it is complete the business plan should become a dynamic tool to help you plan the future of your business, it should be updated every week in response to the actual performance of your business, you can change the forecast numbers to actual results and use them to fine tune the prediction or keep both the forecast and actual number separate for comparison.

Over time you will replace the assumptions and guesses with hard data gained from experience and the plan will improve and get closer to reality, it's really important to make sure that you update the forecast every week and check the cashflow consequences of the changes.

Chapter 17
About Domain Names

Before you go ahead and buy your domain name you need to know a bit about Domain Names, what they are and how they work.
Every web site needs a domain name. Your web stores domain name is the 'human friendly' Internet address for your store.
In truth there is a lot more to Domain Names than that, you can find out all the details by reading the excellent wikipedia article here;
https://en.wikipedia.org/wiki/Domain_name

However, back on a practical level, before you set up your store It's a good idea to decide on the domain name that you will use and secure it.

To secure your domain name you need to pay a domain registration company, they will register the domain on your behalf with the Internet Corporation for Assigned Names and Numbers (ICANN) or one of their regional authorized agents.

You need to choose a reputable company to act as your domain registrar.
I recommend that you use the market leader, GoDaddy. www.goddady.com

The system works like this;

You create an account with GoDaddy, set up a way to pay them (credit card of PayPal is best) and then you can ask them to register as many domain names as you like to your account.

Of course before you can register a domain name you need to make sure that it is not already registered to someone else, GoDaddy provide search tools to allow you to find which domains are registered and which are not.

To pay GoDaddy a registration fee for the domain and it's yours for a fixed period of time (usually one to three years) at the end of the period you get the option to renew the registration for a further fee or you can let the name 'expire' and somebody else can pick it up if they want.

While the name is registered to you you can tell GoDaddy how the domain should be used if it is requested by a web browser or targeted by an email - in effect you tell them where the domain name should 'Point'. This is set using a service called 'Domain Name Service' or DNS which you administer through your account with GoDaddy.

But before we can get into the detail of how to do that you need to choose which type of domain name or names you want to register.

From your own use of the Internet you probably know that there are a lot of different types of web address each with a different ending, for example

www.amazon.com,   www.amazon.co.uk,   www.amazon.de

As you can see if you point your web browser to the addresses in the example above, Amazon uses different regional domain names to direct users to it's different regional stores, this is considered by purists to be the 'correct' way to use international domain extensions.

International domains
If you plan to open a number of international stores then it makes sense to register all of the domains at the same time to prevent someone else seeing your success in your home territory and registering overseas domains to either copy you or hold them hostage and demand a payment to release them to you.
However you need deep pockets to register some regional domains and for others (like '.ie' for Ireland or '.com.au' for Australia) there are residency requirements.
To register a representative suite of domain names for Europe, North America and Asia will cost you about $US1,000 (£650), by contrast to just register a '.co.uk' and a '.com' will cost about £50 (US$75)

In Early 2015 a huge number of new domain endings become available, you can now register a host of domains with geographic or business type endings '.london', '.club', '.pub' and many, many others, some are quite expensive and as far as I can tell from a brief survey none of them have yet been used for successful stores.

My Recommendation
I recommend that if you are setting up a small store in your home country register your local domain and the same name with the '.com' extension, so for a UK based store register '.co.uk' and '.com', for a French store register '.fr' and '.com'. If you are running a store in the US then just a '.com' will be enough.

Chapter 18
Buy a Domain Name

How to choose and buy a domain name for your site
The first part of buying a domain name for your on-line store is deciding what domain name you want to use. The biggest factor in the name that you choose will unfortunately have to be availability, so you will need to have a couple of options available.

To buy your domain you will need a pen and paper for taking notes and your credit card to pay the charges (minimum £10, US$15)

Start the process by listing out a few names that you think would work for your store.

The name should be;

Easy to type, without any confusing or difficult spellings.
Easy to say.
Easy to remember.

Length is not such a big deal, but shorter names are still better than long ones.

If you can include the name of the type of item that you sell in the domain then that will help for SEO, so it's worth it if you can.

Avoid Symbols, Your domain name can't contain symbols, such as $ # or @, you can include hyphens if you want, but they are not ideal especially for typing on a smartphone's on screen keyboard.

Lastly if you have an intention to extend your business to stores in none English speaking countries then you need to be a bit more careful, a store name that works really well in the English speaking world might be meaningless or even worse, offensive in Spanish, German or French. Of course the other choice is a name that is meaningless everywhere until you spend the marketing money required to give it a meaning (like 'GoDaddy' for example).

I like simple names that make the store purpose obvious, if you are a guy called

Steve looking to open a shop selling horse tack, why not try names like

steveshorsetack.com
horsetackbysteve.com
horsetackstores.com
horsetackstore.co.uk
tackandfeed.co.uk

GoDaddy has a great search feature where you can look through to find a domain name or names that you like, but before you can use that you need to set up an account.

Once you have a few ideas point your web browser at www.godaddy.com - GoDaddy uses different web sites for different regions so you may find your web browser loads a site like https://uk.godaddy.com, it should look something like the page below, but don't worry too much if it is bit different, they keep their homepage fresh with regular updates.

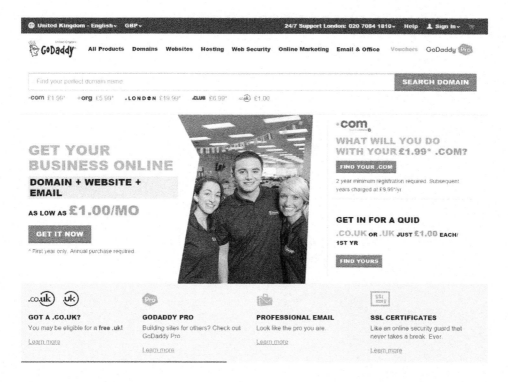

To create your account first click on the 'Sign In' button at the top right, a pop up

will open

Click the green 'CREATE MY ACCOUNT' button and a short form will pop up

- Use your personal e-mail address for the sign up (an @gmail, @live or similar) as you will need to have access to your GoDaddy account outside of any business domains that you have set up.

- Pick a user name - this needs to be unique, the system will show you if it is available or not so you can alter it if needed, then pick a password in line with the rules.
- Your password for your GoDaddy account is the key to your domain, which will become very important to you if your store is a success, I recommend choosing a very secure password and not re-using it elsewhere.

Tip - Investigate a secure password storage system like Passpack (www.passpack.com) to help you generate and securely store complex passwords
- Finally choose a 4 digit PIN for use if you call tech support.

Then click the green 'CREATE ACCOUNT' button to complete the process, you will see a screen like the one below

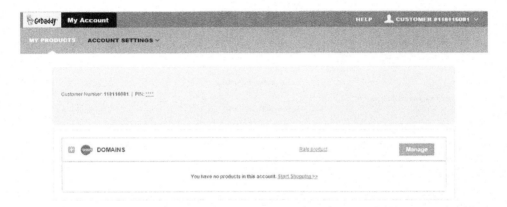

Now you have an account set up with GoDaddy - make a note of your customer number on the top right of the page, it's worth writing this down.

Click on the 'Start Shopping' link in the center of the page to look for your domain name.

Enter the name that you would like for your store in the search box and press 'search' you should see a page like the one below with your search results

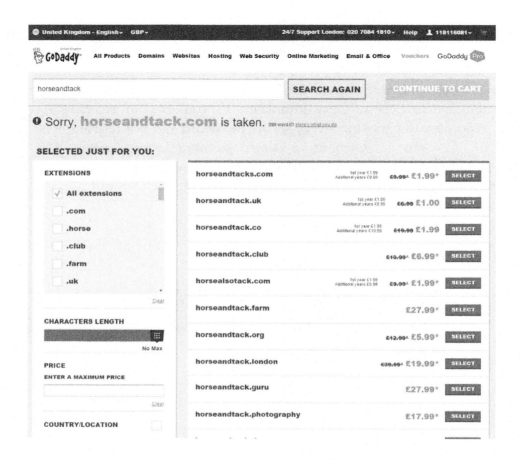

I searched for 'Horseandtack' as my example store will be a store selling horse accessories, unfortunately as you can see 'horseandtack.com' is taken, GoDaddy helpfully suggests a few alternatives that are available, but I don't like the look of any of them, I am setting the store up for Steve so I will try a search for 'steveshorseandtack'

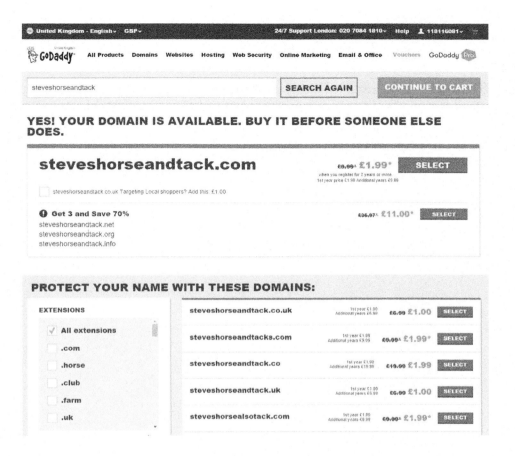

This looks good - I'm going to buy the '.com' and the '.co.uk' so I will tick the box to add the '.co.uk' then select to add the two to my basket, then press the big oranges 'CONTINUE TO CART' button

Beware of the add on's that they try to pile into the basket as you go through the checkout process, also note that the prices that you see on the search page are the registration charges.

Shopping for domains on GoDaddy is just like buying things in an on-line store so I won't insult your intelligence by going through a step by step, but note that the price you see in bold on the site is the registration fee, there are also annual charges to pay and by default GoDaddy will add extra years annual fees on to your purchase, great if you want them, but they add up to a lot if you accept them, you can just take a year and renew when it ends if you prefer to keep the initial cost down.

Accept the terms and complete the purchase by entering your credit card details.

I'd recommend allowing GoDaddy to save the card details for future automatic renewals.

You now own your domain - well done

Chapter 19
Payment processing

To build a successful on-line business you need to be able to get paid by your customers through the internet. Most people who buy on-line use a credit or debit card to make their purchase, other payment systems like PayPal, Amazon Payments and Google Wallet are also available but only PayPal and credit cards have become 'Must Have' payment methods for the average on-line retail store.
Many people have a preferred payment provider or a credit card that has a special rewards scheme that they like, many of these such as American Express charge more for the privilege of taking payments from their card holders, but if you want to build a successful on-line store it is worth taking them.

There are billions of credit cards in the world and they are issued by tens of thousands of different banks, through multiple card schemes like Visa, MasterCard and American Express, you could not possibly reach an agreement with each of them so in order to take credit cards you will need an agreement with a company that already has a deal with them so that they can process the payments with any card holders bank on your behalf - for obvious reasons this kind of company is called a 'Payment Processor'

The payment processor will charge you a fee for each transaction that you make, it is usually a combination of a small percentage of the transaction and a flat fee. In the UK typical rates for a small card processor taking payments on-line are around 2.5% of the transaction value plus 20p. The rates charged for processing cards for on-line retailers based in Europe are usually lower because they are legally regulated, for on-line stores based in the USA and Asia they are usually higher. If you already take cards in a retail store you will notice that these rates are a lot higher than the normal rates charged for taking a card in a store, that is because the card processors believe, with some justification, that transactions taken on-line are much riskier than those that take place in a store where the card and customer are together and a PIN number is usually required.

Payment processors use the fees that you pay to cover the costs that they are charged in turn by the card issuers and (obviously) they add on a bit to allow them to make a profit.
The fees that the card issuers charge to the credit card processors are very complex and if the card issuer is in a different country to the payment processor then they

get even more complex as cross boarder fees are added on and exchange rates become a factor in the calculation. If you want to know more about the way that the system works you can find out here
https://en.wikipedia.org/wiki/Interchange_fee

Some card payment processing companies will share the rates that they are charged for different types of transaction and offer you a different rate for each, others charge a flat fee for all transactions. For a startup business or even a medium sized business I think a flat rate is much better as it gives you certainty, so the processors that I will recommend here all offer that. But when your business reaches a turnover of £1Million (US$1.5Million) per year or more you may be able to make a significant saving by negotiating a better deal with more complexity.

There are loads of credit card processors offering their services in the market as well as several companies offering alternative payment systems. I recommend that to begin with you sign up with two dedicated credit card processors and with PayPal, and that you also allow customers to pay in advance by bank transfer. This will allow most people who come to your store a reasonable payment method and the majority of people will be able to use their favorite payment method to pay you through your store.
If you plan to sell your products through the Amazon marketplace as well as through your own web store, it is also worth adding Amazon Checkout.

You should also know that payment processors are inherently unreliable, they can have technical issues, commercial problems or they may decide that they want to make your terms worse because of customer service issues or a change in their policy towards particular products. They can do this at any time without consulting or even warning you.

To get started taking payments for your on-line store I recommend that you set up three payment processing accounts, one with Shopify payments, another with PayPal and lastly an account with SagePay. If you are also going to be selling on Amazon you might also want to consider using an Amazon payments account as well - but that's optional.

Shopify Payments
Shopify payments is closely integrated into Shopify, you should set up your Shopify store to take credit cards with Shopify payments, this will get you paid 7 days after order with a fee of 2.4% which is deducted from your payment. It's a great way to

start, fast and easy to set up with simple acceptance terms and integrated management of payments as part of your Shopify store.

Shopify payments is run by Stripe, stripe is a new entrant into the credit card processing space, they have taken the space by storm using a web based, retailer friendly model. You can learn more about Stripe here https://stripe.com/about.

Shopify Payments is quick and easy to sign up for, to set it up you just need to enter your bank details and you are ready to go. It works well to get you started, but the 7 day payment cycle and quite high fees make it less attractive for high volume merchants, however it's good to have a backup system and Shopify Payments has great rates for American Express cards so I recommend you set up an account there even if you will use another method as your primary credit card processor.

PayPal
PayPal is a very popular payment method in the UK, USA and Germany, you should sign up for a PayPal business account. Do this even if you already have a personal PayPal account - it helps to keep them separate, although PayPal will know that you are working on both accounts.
Sign up for PayPal Business here
https://www.PayPal.com/uk/webapps/mpp/merchant.
There is more information about setting up a PayPal account below.

Sage Pay
Sage Pay is a direct competitor to Shopify Payments, however it has two advantages over Shopify Payments, the first is that it supports 3D Secure for Shopify stores .3D Secure is also known as Verified by Visa and MasterCard Secure Code, it is a very important function to have if your site is selling high value items that are a target for credit card fraudsters. The second advantage of Sage Pay over Shopify payments is that it pays you faster which will help your cash flow significantly.
I think that it is really important to have two credit card processing options available, because credit card processing is vital to your store's revenues.

Amazon Payments
Amazon Payments is a useful add on if you plan to also sell on Amazon - if not then it could more trouble than it's worth. This system allows customers to pay you with the credit card details that they already have stored in their Amazon account - it does not open you up to any new customers as everyone who could

pay with Amazon must have a credit card that they could use through Stripe or Sage Pay but it does make paying you faster and more convenient for some customers.

Integrating Amazon payments into a Shopify store is very easy, there are more details about Amazon Payments below

Chapter 20
Credit Card Rules

Before you start taking payments on credit card or PayPal through your web store you should clearly understand the rules that surround them, some may surprise you.

Fraudulent use of credit cards
The first surprise to many people who are new to on-line retail is that the retailer is liable for the costs of all fraudulent use of credit cards on their store. If you process a transaction that has been placed by someone using another persons card without their permission and you send the goods then once the misuse of the card is reported to the card holders bank the transaction will be 'charged back', the funds will be recovered from you by your card processor and they will likely also charge you a significant fee on top. You need to check your orders carefully to make sure that you do not ship goods to someone using stolen card details.

Customer Service
Many credit card companies also allow their customers to reclaim funds that are paid over to retailers if the customer is not happy with the goods, usually the retailer will have an opportunity to put their side of the case to the credit card company, but if the customer is unhappy with the goods they will almost always get a refund. This is one of the reasons that it is usually better to take returns quickly and with minimum fuss.

Timescales for charge backs
Most charge backs on credit card transactions come through within 45 days from the transaction, with orders using cards issued in the same country as the merchant coming through faster than those from overseas cards - but remember that a fraudster could be using a foreign card without you knowing. The normal limit for a charge back is 180 days from order, but customer service charge backs can be made up to a year after the order has been placed.

Chapter 21
PayPal

You will need a PayPal account
PayPal has become a must have for on-line retail stores over the last 5 years as it offers consumers a fast, easy way to pay for on-line purchases.

Setting up a PayPal account for your business is quick and very easy, you can sign up at www.PayPal.com.
I recommend that you do not use a personal PayPal account for your business, it is much better to sign up for a new account in the companies name.

When you set up your PayPal account you link it to your company bank account and PayPal will be able to both transfer funds into your account and take them out - essentially it acts as an extension of your bank account.

Once you have signed up for an account you can add PayPal as a payment method in Shopify very easily, it is as simple as entering your PayPal user name and password.

PayPal charge a fee for receiving cash from your customers of around 4% so it is more expensive than accepting credit cards, but the funds paid to you will normally be available for withdrawal to your bank account on the same day so cash flow is better with PayPal.

PayPal Payments Pro
PayPal also offers a credit card processing service called PayPal Payments Pro which can be integrated into Shopify but I would not recommend it unless you can not use Shopify payments for some reason as it is more expensive overall.

Managing PayPal orders
One of the best things about PayPal is their seller protection program. When a customer pays you via PayPal, you will be told whether or not the order is eligible for seller protection and if it is, as long as you follow the rules and send the goods by a tracked service with a signature on delivery you are protected from claims for non delivery. Orders that are eligible for seller protection can be shipped without further checks, however orders that are not eligible should be checked in the same way as credit card orders.

PayPal Customer Service Rules

The PayPal system enforces a high standard of customer service, you are obliged to take any return requested by a PayPal customer within 14 days of shipment and PayPal has a dispute resolution system that you will be obliged to use. If a customer is unhappy with the item that they have purchased from you using PayPal then they can raise a 'dispute' with you through PayPal. In most cases when a customer does this you will have the option to either offer to accept the goods back or offer the customer a partial refund. It is not uncommon for unscrupulous customers to use the dispute system in PayPal to try to get a post sale discount, I'd recommend that you don't use the partial refund option unless you are sure that it is the best option.

You are able to put your case to PayPal and ask them to decide the case, but they almost always find in favor of the customer.

Like a credit card charge back, a dispute on PayPal can be raised up to 180 days after the transaction.

Braintree

Braintree is a credit card processing system that competes with Stripe and Shopify payments, but is owned by PayPal and integrated with their system, however in a Shopify store it offers no advantages over Shopify payments.

Chapter 22
Amazon Checkout

About Amazon Payments (previously known as Checkout by Amazon)
If you are a regular user of Amazon you will know that Amazon has a system for processing payments which stores your credit card details and address so that you can checkout using their patented 'one click' system. This means that as an Amazon customer you do not need to enter your credit card details, address and so on every time that you buy something, which is really convenient for customers and increases conversion as a result.

Amazon payments allows customers to use the details that they have stored in their Amazon account on your web site. This is convenient and it WILL increase your conversion ratio as well and integrating Amazon payments into a Shopify store is very easy and Amazon handle all of the fraud screening so you can simply ship every order that is validated by Amazon.

However there are a couple of downsides that you should know about before you rush ahead to install amazon payments on your store

- Amazon payments is just another way of using a credit card – it is more convenient for some customers, but it does not remove a barrier to using the store, it just makes it easier.

- Amazon in the UK charge 3.4% plus 20p per transaction for the use of Amazon Payments at the time of writing - that's about 1% more than if the user was to just use their card with Braintree or Stripe.

- You do not get any marketing data for the customer if they use amazon payments – the customer is Amazon's and you are just 'borrowing' them.

- You have to abide by Amazons customer service policies and rules if you use Amazon Payments. This means that you must take returns for any item regardless of condition for up to 180 days after purchase and Amazon can withdraw the account at any time for any reason. As a rule if more than 1% of your customers makes a complaint or gives you a bad review they will suspend your account – this is no problem if you have lots of orders going through Amazon and Amazon Payments and you give a good standard of service, but if you only do 50 orders through Amazon Payments 1 complaint is 2% - which will cause a problem so beware.

I recommend only using Amazon Payments if you also intend to sell on Amazon.

Chapter 23
Other Options

Bank Transfer
Setting your site up to take payment for orders by bank transfer is really easy, some customers especially corporate customers buying larger volumes prefer to pay by bank transfer and it's more or less free to do, although there may be a small fee from your bank for receiving cash from overseas customers you can usually ask the customer to pay that.

Skrill
Skrill (formerly known as MoneyBookers) is an alternative to PayPal and one of Europe's largest on-line payment providers in it's own right, offering it's clients more than 100 payment options in 200 countries and territories. It is easy to integrate with Shopify and the set up and operation processes are simple.

Skrill's payment solutions are used by over 140,000 on-line merchants around the world. In 2015 Skrill partnered with Yandex in Russia, integrating with Yandex-money which is one of the most popular payment methods in Russia, which makes Skrill a good fit for retailers targeting the Russian speaking markets.

Bitcoin
It is now possible to set up your Shopify store so that customers can pay through Bitcoin, but personally I think it is a bit early in the life of Bitcoin as a currency to be using it as a payment method in a small store so I would not recommend it until it becomes a popular payment method with your customers and the long term value of bitcoin is clearer.

Google Wallet
Google Wallet is a stored value system and credit card processing system from Google. Currently it is not possible to use Google Wallet as a payment method for a Shopify store.

Chapter 24
International Payment Methods

When you start to expand your store to target the markets in Europe you should bear in mind that different European countries have a range of different payment methods that are popular in specific areas, if you want to maximize sales in each of these territories as well as translating your web site into the local language you need to use the payment methods that customers prefer.

The five leading economies of the Western Europe totaled 80% of the region's $230 billion in on-line commerce in 2013. It is anticipated that from 2014 to 2016, Western European eCommerce will expand by around 12% per year and will continue at similar pace after that.

Credit and debit cards tend to be king across the five largest Western European on-line economies: the UK, Germany, France, Spain and Italy. Other on-line payment methods most notably bank-to-bank transfers in Germany and PayPal nearly everywhere are very common. In some countries, including Spain, cash on delivery remains the most preferred payment method.

Below you will find a short guide to the different payment methods in use around Europe on a country by country basis, there are a lot of other payment methods that you should consider accepting if you want to get the most out of the European markets.

The United Kingdom and Ireland
The UK is the largest, most developed, most advanced on-line retail economy in Western Europe. I think that the UK has the most competitive on-line retail market in the world, having the highest share of GDP globally transacted on-line (13% compared to 12% in the US).

Credit and debit cards have a high penetration rate in the UK with about 2.4 cards per capita so more or less all of the population of eCommerce market consumers would be able to pay by credit or debit card if they choose to do so. For a foreign retailer to accept local debit cards, a local entity must be established, or a payment service provider that can provide a local UK banking relationship must be used. There are 23 million PayPal accounts in the UK, which covers about three quarters of the market.

In the United Kingdom and Ireland credit cards are the most frequently used payment method for on-line purchases. About forty percent transactions in the UK are paid by credit card. Debit cards account for thirty five percent and PayPal is used for about another twenty percent. These three represent ninety six percent of the on-line payment market in the UK with bank transfer payments accounting for another two or three percent so the rest of the payment options here are not really worth worrying about.

Germany and Austria
In Germany cash and debit cards are the most popular payment methods for purchases in shops, however Germans tend not to use debit cards when purchasing on-line.
The most popular on-line payment method in Germany is offline bank transfer so you should definitely offer this option when selling in Germany, just under half of all on-line purchases are completed this way in Germany. You will need a German bank account or at least a Euro denominated account in a Euro zone country for this. Allied Irish Bank (AIB) in Ireland can be very helpful for this as they are inside the Euro Zone but they speak good English.

Germany has a range of micro-payment services which account for about a third of on-line transactions. They include ELV, GiroPay and PayPal.

ELV is a direct debit payment method that acts as a credit card on-line as banks do not check if the shopper has sufficient funds in their account. EPS is a similar system used in Austria, with over 3 million end customers signed up, EPS is the most popular on-line banking payment scheme in Austria. Through the system's standardized technical interface, transactions are authorized by the end customer using the common PIN / TAN process.

Giropay is a similar payment system based on on-line banking allowing consumers to pay for on-line goods using direct on-line bank transfers, eighty percent of all German customers who bank on-line use Giropay. Giropay offers immediate payment processing with the highest level of security and a payment guarantee for transactions up to € 10,000. Transactions are authorized by the consumer through the a PIN / TAN process. Payment through mobileTan or chipTan is also supported by this system.

France
In France many on-line customers use Carte-Blue to pay for their purchases on-

line. This is a debit card, that can also be used as a credit card. Other popular credit cards are MasterCard and American Express. PayPal is also quite popular in France.

Like in many developed countries, credit payments are the most preferred payment method in France, with 57% of consumers choosing it as their preferred payment method. The most popular credit cards are Visa, co-branded with Carte Bleue, private label cards, and MasterCard. PayPal follows in popularity with 25% of consumers using it as their preferred payment method.

The Benelux Countries
The Benelux consists of three countries, Belgium, The Netherlands and Luxembourg. In the Netherlands a lot of people pay on-line with iDEAL. iDEAL is similar to the German ELV system and it processes more than half of the payments made on-line in the Netherlands. They are the preferred payment method and make it easy for customers to make on-line payments directly from their bank. Since the introduction in 2005 more than 400 million transactions have been completed with iDEAL. Belgian customers primarily use cards and on-line bank payment method to pay on-line, while in Luxembourg customers use credit cards, like Visa, MasterCard, American Express and JCB as well as PayPal.

Scandinavia
Swedish on-line customers like to pay by credit card, with MasterCard and Visa being their most used cards. on-line bank transfers are also popular as they are used by three in ten on-line customers. Almost the same amount of people prefer to pay per invoice cards. In other Scandinavian countries like Denmark, Norway and Finland, debit and credit cards are also the preferred payment methods. In Denmark Dankort is very popular: a hybrid card which can be used as a debit card and as a credit card.

Spain
In Spain credit and debit cards account for more than a third of on-line transactions. Another very popular payment option in Spain is 4B, a payment method owned by various Spanish banks. Cash on Delivery is the next most popular payment method accounting for about a quarter of transactions. The COD preference may be a response to the relatively higher rates of on-line fraud in Spain compared to other EU countries. PayPal is also popular in Spain.

Italy

In Italy, credit cards and PayPal are the dominant on-line payment methods, but credit cards are the most important with three quaters of transactions paid that way. About twenty percent use PayPal making Italy very similar to the UK in the choice of payment methods.

Outside of Europe Credit Cards are still the most popular payment methods, but there are a few other things that you should consider.

Australia: Credit cards are the most popular followed by PayPal

Canada: Credit cards are popular, then PayPal then Debit cards

China: Many people use Alipay (provided by Alibaba), a third pay by cash

Japan: Credit cards are most popular followed by cash.

South Korea: Credit cards are the most popular

Latin America: DineroMail and MercadoPago are popular

Brazil: Brazil has a native stored value system called Boleto

Chapter 25
Protecting your on-line store

When you put your business on-line the most brilliant thing is that you make everybody in the world with a credit card or a PayPal account into a potential customer, but the downside is that open your store up to the attentions of a lot of other people with more sinister motives who want to steal from you.
The main ways that people will try to steal from your site are

1. Placing orders on your site using stolen credit card details
All sites are vulnerable to this kind of activity and you need to protect yourself from it by checking every order carefully - I'll explain how to do that in the next chapter.

2. Making attacks on your site to steal customer data stored there or to intercept credit card details when customers place their orders. Shopify sites are protected from this kind of activity by Shopify, it's one of the great things about Shopify.

3. Denial of service (DOS) attacks
All web sites are vulnerable to this kind of attack, sometimes they are combined with blackmail, Shopify does a lot of work to protect your store and their systems from this kind of attack but you should be aware of it.

Chapter 26
Checking Orders

Protecting yourself from Fraudulent Credit Card Orders
As I mentioned above, a retailer who takes any fraudulent credit card order is always responsible for the costs of the goods sent to the fraudsters and for the fees levied by the credit card processing company in connection with the fraud. So if you are going to trade on-line you need very robust fraud screening processes to avoid loosing a lot of money.

The purpose of this section of the book is to provide you with information about the fraud screening tools available to you and give you a recommended fraud screening process to start you off.

Balance between putting off real customers and shipping fraudulent orders
The key to an effective commercial process for screening your inbound orders for fraudulent activity is to strike a balance between putting off real customers with unusual circumstances and shipping fraudulent orders, you need to approach every order carefully and have clear rules that you always enforce.

Set the fraud filters on your card processing system to enforce address verification system (AVS) checks and card verification value (CVV) number checks.
Both Shopify Payments and SagePay have the ability to provide you with the results of address verification and card verification value checks. You can also set them to refuse orders that fail either of these checks automatically.

Address Verification System (AVS)
What is an Address Verification System (AVS) check?
The address verification system is an optional system that credit card issuers can enroll in, it allows retailers to check part of the customers address against the records stored by the credit card company to confirm that they are correct.

Knowing that you are shipping goods to the address that the customer has on file with the credit card company is very helpful for fraud prevention, and even if you allow customers to ship goods to a different address it is still very helpful to confirm that they know the address where the card is registered - however there are a couple of problems with the AVS system that you should know about when using it's results.

The first problem is that the AVS system only checks the numbers in the first line of the address provides and the post code (or zip code) it does not check any other part of the address, this creates two problems - the first one is that to the AVS system 44 Acacia Avenue, London EC2A 5BW is the same address as 44 Smith Street, Manchester M2 5GD,

The second problem is that addresses that have a street number and a flat number often produce an AVS failure when they should not because the address entered has to match the address on file exactly. For example the system would see 'Flat 1, 44 Acacia Avenue' as different from '44 Acacia Avenue, Flat 1'

Thirdly there are countries that have ridiculously strict data protection rules which prevent the AVS system from working for cards issued there, the most notable offenders are Australia, Ireland and France. The AVS system will report 'not checked' for these countries.

Normally the system should tell you separately if the address matches and if the zip code (post code numbers) match or not or have not been checked.

Set your AVS system to allow, but record orders that do not match
I recommend that you set the AVS system to automatically reject orders where the billing address given by the customer does not match the postcode on file with the issuing bank, but to allow orders to be placed where the first line of the address does not match, you can then check these manually.

But you should note that this will still allow orders to be placed where the details can not be checked - you should be able to see that the address was not checked however so that you can screen the order manually.

Card Verification Value (CVV)
What is a Card Verification Value (CVV) check?
Card Verification Values were added to credit cards from around 2005, they are the 3 digit number at the end of the signature strip on a Visa or MasterCard and the 4 digit number on the front of an American Express card.

Your credit card processing system will check these to make sure that they are correct and that they match the main card number.

Refuse orders that fail the CVV check.
I recommend that you make passing the CVV check mandatory for any order to be placed on your web site. There is no valid reason why the CVV given by a customer should not match.

To change the security settings on your Shopify Payments system navigate to Settings > Payments

And click the 'Edit' button to open out the settings box.

The two tick boxes circled above can be used to set the system to decline charges that fail CVV verification and to decline charges that fail Postcode verification both of which I recommend for all stores.

Once you have ticked the boxes press the blue 'Save' Button to save the settings.

3D Secure
What is 3D Secure?
3D Secure stands for 3 Domain Server, this is the name for the most up to date fraud prevention scheme set up by the credit card industry to protect on-line retail stores that process credit card transactions.

It allows shoppers to create and assign a password to their card that is then verified whenever a transaction is processed through a site that supports the use of the scheme. There are 3 parties that are involved in the 3D Secure process, hence the name, they are

- The on-line store that the purchase is being made from.
- The Acquiring Bank (the bank of the company)
- VISA and MasterCard (the card issuers themselves)

The scheme is also known as Verified by VISA (VBV) and MasterCard Secure Code (MSC) depending in the card type being used, 3D Secure is the collective term for these two schemes.

The main benefit to companies using the 3D Secure scheme is the availability of a liability shift for a successfully verified transaction. This offers protection by the card issuers against charge-backs, this shift of liability is widely advertised by the card companies, but I have personal experience and I have heard from many merchants that the liability shift is not guaranteed. Charge backs can still occur as liability shift is decided at the discretion of the banks processing the transaction so you still need to be careful when accepting payments that have passed 3D secure if they are obviously fraudulent. That order for 10 diamond rings for shipping to a parcel drop off shop in Lagos, Nigeria IS fraudulent and your credit card processor expects you to know that and refuse it even though the thief had the 3D secure code !

Use 3D Secure if you sell high risk items
3d Secure is vital for on-line stores selling items which are easy to convert into cash or with and average order value of more than about US$100 (£65) you should enable it for any on-line shop that sells items like that. If your orders are under that level or if you do not feel that you will attract a lot of fraudulent orders because of the nature of your products then you could do without it because there is no doubt that 3D Secure does put off some legitimate customers as it adds quite a bit of hassle to the placing of an order.

Regardless of your other checks, review every order manually
This is my key fraud screening recommendation, regardless of the value and of the other security processes that you have in place you should review every order manually.

When you do the review, the objective is to place each order into one of 3 categories. The three categories are Definitely Good, Definitely Bad and Needs More Info

- **DEFINITELY GOOD**

An order that you are 100% sure is legitimate and can be passed directly to be shipped as soon as possible, 'Verified and Confirmed' PayPal orders will go into this status as will Credit Card orders where everything matches and there are no 'Red Flags' to worry about. You can leave definitely good orders as they are in Shopify and then ship them as soon as possible.

- **DEFINITELY BAD**

An order that you are 100% sure you will not be shipping either because there are too many 'Red Flags' or because the address (or country of delivery) is on your black list.
When you place an order into this status you should cancel the credit card authorization or refund the card right away then cancel the order and archive it in

Shopify - if you don't you could get a charge back and all the associated costs right away which is really annoying when you have already spotted the fraud.

- **NOT SURE - NEEDS MORE INFO**

Every order that you can not put into the Definitely Good or Definitely Bad categories needs to go into this status. When you put an order into this status you send the customer an e-mail politely explaining that you have been unable to verify their details and that you need to see more information in order to ship their order.

There is a template for the e-mail to send requesting further information in the Appendices to the book you should set this up as an saved mail in your HelpScout system so that you can send it quickly and easily when required.

Once you have sent the e-mail you need to tag the order in Shopify to make sure that it is not shipped while you are waiting for a response from the customer. You will see how to do that in Section three of the book.

After sending the e-mail it can also help to call the customer, if the number that they have provided is not connected then that is a very bad sign that will push that order over to definitely bad. If the customer answers explain that some details of the order do not match and ask the customer why, with experience you will be able to tell the difference between a genuine customer and a fraudster who is trying to trick you, consider the name on the order and the accent of the person on the phone, do they sound right? If you need to leave a voice-mail then do so, ask the customer to call you back.

Send a second copy of the e-mail 24 hours after the first, if you do not get a reply 24 hours after that then cancel and refund the order.

Shopify will help you to check which orders are good, Shopify places orders into low, medium and high risk based on their own criteria, these can be used to help guide your decision making process, but you need to decide yourself which orders should be shipped and which should not. Here are a few notes to help you decide.

Notes on how to decide which status an order should be in

1. Check the e-mail address provided
Fraudsters tend to use untraceable free e-mail addresses, they do use gmail and hotmail addresses, but these take time to set up and they need to use them over

and over so they tend to set up addresses that do not contain real names - compare the order name to the e-mail address and ask yourself if a person with that name would have that e-mail address, if not then that's a red flag. For example

Customer name = James Smith, email address = billy2945@gmail.com

Corporate email addresses are usually a good sign especially if they are attached to an order for delivery to an address that you can verify as linked to the company even if it's not the billing address.

The following e-mail address domains are known to be associated with a lot of on-line fraud and should be an automatic red flag

@usa.com - Automatic red flag
@mac.com - Automatic red flag

The following domains are free email accounts that are not automatically a red flag, but they are not automatically good either

@yahoo.com
@outlook.com
@live.com
@gmail.com
@hotmail.com

Personally I have never had any problems with customers using these domains - they are paid for and traceable so **PROBABLY** OK

@btinternet.com
@talktalk.com

Of course, just because they entered the email address, it doesn't mean it's an active email account, you need to send a message to the address and get a valid reply to know that it is active, but even that does not prove that the address is being used by the real owner rather than someone who has stolen the username and password!

2. Check the delivery address CAREFULLY
Firstly compare it to the billing address, if they are the same then check that the

AVS response shows a match for zip code and address. If the AVS matches and the shipping address is the same as the billing address then the order is Good.
When the "bill to" and "ship to" addresses are different and the customer is asking for expedited shipping, there's a high risk of fraud. Different billing and shipping addresses are not always a sure sign of fraud as delivery to work is quite common, but in that circumstance check that the work address is close enough to the registered billing address to be realistic.

One of the great things about the Internet is that you can check out the address before you ship through Google maps, it's just like making a drive by visit. Simply go to Google maps and put in the shipping address and check it out on street view. You may need to do a bit of searching to find the exact house listed, but it's worth it. When you see the house, does it match the order?
If the address looks like a house in multiple occupancy - that's a big red flag.

Most countries have some kind of directory service that you can use to try to match the customer to the address, use whitepages.org or anywho.com for the USA, www.192.com is great for the UK, Zillow and ZabaSearch can also help.

You should also maintain a blacklist - Never ship to the following countries

Nigeria, Ghana, Indonesia, Algeria, Morocco, Libya, Romania, Bulgaria, Albania, Egypt.

Credit card fraud is the national sport of Indonesia and Nigeria is the world capital of all kinds of Fraud.

Be very careful of orders from

Lithuania, Belarus, Ukraine, Philipines, All of Africa, Serbia

Beware of orders that say they are from Singapore, it's pretty common to put Singapore at the end of an Indonesian address to try to make it look legitimate.

Another common fraudsters trick is to 'break' the address by using a zip code or post code and an address that do not match - they will then try to collect the parcel from the courier depot when the delivery fails - be very wary of delivery addresses that do not resolve when you put them into a zip code or post code checker. (www.royalmail.co.uk for uk addresses)

3. Check the items in the order and the shipping method

Is the order realistic? Will the items on the order work together or are they just a mix of the most expensive things from your on-line store?

Are they paying more for faster shipping? It isn't the fraudsters money and the quicker they can get the goods before the card is canceled, the better for them. Check for the ratio of money spent on shipping versus the value of the goods. Would a "real" customer pay £30 to ship £50 worth of merchandise?

4. Check the phone number provided

The Phone number is not too diagnostic by itself, you can check if the area code matches the billing address but that's not really proof either way.

The phone number comes in if you are not sure about the order, if that's the case then call the number, if it is not a real number then that's a big red flag, similarly if the person who answers sounds wrong, for example a male voice when the name indicates a female customer then that's a red flag too.

If you get through say ' I'm calling about the order that you placed with us on-line' - if they reply 'Which one' then that's a bit of a red flag too, fraudsters work a numbers game placing lots of orders.

A voice mail service from a pre-paid service is a bit of a red flag too.

5. Check the IP address that the order was placed from

Use a reverse IP address lookup tool on-line (I like http://mxtoolbox.com/ReverseLookup.aspx) if that doesn't work just try searching for 'reverse IP lookup tool'.

What is an IP address?

Acording to wikipedia 'An Internet Protocol address (IP address) is a numerical label assigned to each device participating in a computer network that uses the Internet Protocol for communication. An IP address serves two principal functions: host or network interface identification and location addressing.'

Unfortunately for us when we are fraud screening orders for our On-Line stores the IP address that we see for the customer does not usually tell us which exact device the order was placed from, it usually just tells us about the ISP that was used, so we may find out that the IP address is registered to an Egyptian ISP, but the billing address is in the USA - and that's a big red flag.

Check your own IP address by going to 'www.whatismyipaddress.com', now do the same from your web browser on your phone - you will start to understand how it works...

Check all orders regardless of value
Don't assume that a low value order isn't fraud. Fraudsters will place small orders to test your defenses or just because they want the item. They obviously want to get as much from a store as they can before the stolen card is shut down, if they have figured out that you ship all orders under £20 they will exploit that - and they are a repeat customer!

6. Check for failed transactions associated with the order
Your credit card processing system should show you how many times the customer tried to process the order before getting it through. If you are using Shopify payments then you will see a list of attempts at the bottom of the Shopify order processing screen. If the customer has tried multiple times with different cards then that is a big red flag.

Conversely if a customer has tried two or three times with the same card and then got the order through that can be a good sign, because they corrected a post code or CVV error.

7. Remember fraud comes in waves
Fraudsters will try to get as many orders through your store as possible if they find a way to get through your system so if you get a sudden increase in orders that look dodgy it could be a sign that you have passed a bad order - re check anything that was 50/50 from the last day or two, maybe you can catch an order before it ships or even stop it in transit.

8. 3D Secure Orders
3D Secure orders with liability shift are ALMOST always good, just check the delivery address and the product for obvious fraud, remember you are still liable for obvious fraud committed through the 3D Secure system, you just can't ship those diamond rings to Nigeria and claim for them.

Chapter 27
Screening PayPal and Amazon Orders

PayPal
Fraud screening of PayPal orders is made very simple by PayPal, but remember that you can still be liable for obvious fraud committed through PayPal.

When you get an order paid through PayPal you will be told if the user's identity is verified by PayPal and whether or not the delivery address has been confirmed by PayPal, if the user is verified and the address is confirmed then you should qualify for PayPal seller protection so you only need to check these PayPal orders to make sure that they are not obviously fraudulent and you can pass them directly as definitely good.

If the user is not verified or the address is not confirmed then you need to be more careful and treat it just like a credit card order and ask for more information if required.

Amazon Payments
The big advantage of Amazon Payments is that Amazon handle all of the fraud screening - you can just ship approved Amazon orders with no further checks.

Chapter 28
Preventing Attacks

Protecting Customer Data
As I write this book in January 2016 news of the theft of customer data from the web sites of companies like Talk Talk and Hyatt Hotels is in the headlines.
If someone can access the credit card information used by customers on your web site they can sell them through the black web to people who will use them to place fraudulent orders or they can try to use them directly - either way your customers cards will get used inappropriately and you could lose your ability to process credit cards. You need to protect yourself and your customers against these risks, they are very real.

Shopify
First the good news - Because Shopify is a hosted platform it is protected against data theft by Shopify, and your customers card details are encrypted and protected. The cost of doing it is included in your Shopify fees, but you do have some extra responsibilities, you need to make sure that any credit card details that you take from your customers over the phone are not written down or stored anywhere and you need to make sure that customer data is never stored outside of a secure system like Shopify, HelpScout or MailChimp.

Always use a secure password for your access to your Shopify store, don't write it down and don't share it with other people. I recommend that you set up a free account with Passpack (www.passpack.com) You can set up extra users accounts very easily in Shopify and restrict their access to sensitive data.

Problems with Magento based Sites
It is interesting to spend a couple of minutes thinking about the issues faced by people running Magento stores or bespoke stores and how they compare with people running Shopify stores.
Magento is a real target for this kind of activity, as it is the most popular platform for medium size web stores it attracts a lot of attention from hackers and thieves. As standard Magento does not store credit card details, it just passes them directly to your payment provider for processing and then stores the results of the charge that come back with reference numbers etc.

One Magento based store that I worked with was compromised by the insertion of a piece of code into the Magento set up which copied customers credit card details as they were entered, making them available for download by the thief at a later date.

The result of this activity was that many customers had their card details stolen, the retailer was forced by their credit card processor to pay £7K for a check of their systems by an approved forensic expert and they lost a huge amount of customer trust.

Bespoke Sites

Bespoke sites are less likely to be attacked than Magento based sites as they are all different, however they can still be attacked both from outside the organization and inside, both Talk Talk and Hyatt hotels had bespoke systems which were compromised..

Recommendations on how to protect Magento based and bespoke sites

1. Always update your Magento installation with the latest security patches on the day that they are released.
2. Never store credit card details on your server or in your database.
3. Always encrypt all customer information that you do store in your system in any form.
4. Use complex passwords and user names, I recommend www.passpack.com for storing, sharing and creating complex passwords, it works very well.
5. Make sure that your admin log in for the site is NOT at www.yourdomain.com/admin which is the default location for Magento and hence gets hit a lot by thieves and hackers.
6. Make sure that your site is protected against SQL injection attacks through the search box (your developer will understand that)
7. Install a site screening tool to check for compromises and nip them in the bud if they occur, I recommend Forgenix Vngo http://www.foregenix.com/fgxweb.php it costs about £45 per month.

Chapter 29
Denial of Service attacks

When you pay Shopify for your store each month, even though the price is really quite low you are getting the same class of protection against attacks on your web site that major sites like Amazon have, but you should still know about the threat of a denial of service attack.

A Denial of Service (DOS) attack is actually a very simple form of attack where your website is sent thousands of requests for web pages every second to overload it and stop it working for real users. The site will still be there and probably still working, but it is simply unable to cope with the volume of requests that it is receiving.

Your server host or ISP can help you block simple DOS attacks that come from a single PC, however there is a much more vicious form of denial of service attack, the Distributed Denial of Service attack (DDOS) where a large number of PCs that are being remotely controlled by a master machine all attack together - it is almost impossible to defend against a DDOS attack, even the FBI web site was recently taken offline by such an attack. The only good thing about a DDOS attack is that it will end eventually because it costs the attackers money and resources to keep it up.

I must emphasize that it is very unlikely that an attacker would bother to organize a DDOS attack on a small retailer, but you should be aware of the possibility.

Blackmail
A denial of service attack is sometimes associated with a blackmail attempt, the attackers demanding a payment to not do it again.
Of course you should NEVER pay blackmailers, it just encourages them. Report any attempt to the Police.

Part Two: Setting up your store

Chapter 30
Set up a Google Account

Once you have decided what you will be selling, worked out a business plan that shows that you can make money through an on-line store you are ready to start the fun part of setting up your store. Your Google Account for your store gives you a range of Apps including your own e-mail on your own domain. You bought your domain name for your store back in chapter 18 your next job is to set up a Google Apps account for your business, this will take about 30 minutes and you will need a pen and paper for taking notes and your credit card to set up the payments for your account (a minimum of £3:30, US$5 per month)

Setting up a Google Apps account will give you access to a wide range of products and services from Google. The main one that you will use is Google Email (like GMail but without the ads) but you also get Google Calendar, Google Docs, Google Talk (Chat), Google Mobile and Google Sites. All of these web applications offer an on-line alternative to traditional office suites.

More importantly your Google Apps account will be your gateway to important free services like Google Analytics and Google AdWords as well as handy tools like Google+, Hangouts, Blogger and more.

To get started with the sign up process go to https://apps.Google.com/

Next, click the green 'Get Started Now' button to start setting up your account

Fill out the form with your first name, surname and put your personal e-mail address into the 'Current email address you use at work' box

Tell Google your store name, for my example I'm Using 'Steves Horse and Tack'

Select one employee for now, you can add more later. And put in your phone number, I recommend that you use your cell phone number as Google can use it to text you recovery information if you forget your password.

Once the form is complete press the blue 'Next' button.

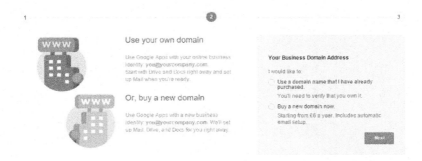

As we already have a domain ready select 'Use a domain name that I have already purchased' and then enter your domain name in the box that opens up.

Then click the blue 'Next' button

Choose your user name, pick this carefully as when it is combined with @your-domain-name it will create your e-mail address. Since there are no other e-mail addresses in your new domain you can have any address that you like, I'd recommend that you just use your first name.

Then choose your password - again this one is very important, make it secure and unique, if in doubt use Passpack (www.passpack.com) or a similar service to generate and store a secure password.

And then type in the number in the photo to prove that you are real and accept the 'Google Apps for Work agreement', you can also sign up for the Google email newsletter if you like. It's a good idea as they often send out free Google AdWords vouchers and other offers which you will be able to use later.

Then press the blue 'Accept and sign up' button to complete your account set up.

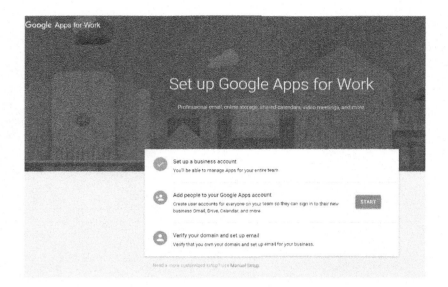

Next you can add any extra users to your account, remember that Google charges 'per user per month' for this service so each extra user costs $US5 (£3:30) per month, even if you don't want to add extra users you still need to tell Google so regardless click the blue 'START' button next to 'Add people to your Google Apps account' this will open out the section shown below.

As it says in the window group e-mail addresses like info@steveshorseandtack.com or sales@steveshorseandtack.com can be added later at no additional cost so do not add them right now.

I don't want to add any extra users so I have just ticked the box to say so.

Then click the blue 'Next' button.

The next step is to verify that you own your domain, this should open up a new section as shown below.

Verify your domain and set up email

Before you can use Google Apps with domain **steveshorseandtack.com**, we need to contact your domain host to verify that you own it. Doing this helps ensure that no one can pose as you on Google Apps and send email from your domain. Learn more

After your domain is verified, we will set up Google Apps email for your users on **steveshorseandtack.com**. This will automatically re-route your emails to Google Apps. Learn more

We have detected that **steveshorseandtack.com** is hosted at **GoDaddy.com**. If you're having trouble, try to verify your domain here.

> **Note:** Before you route email to Google Apps, make sure that you create a user on Google Apps for each person receiving mail at steveshorseandtack.com

VERIFY

 Need help? Search the Help Center or call us.

As you can see Google can check to see where your domain is registered, GoDaddy is integrated into Google which makes it much easier to complete this step, all you need to do is click the white 'VERIFY' button at the bottom

This will open up a new window where you can log into your GoDaddy account to confirm that you own the domain, simply enter your GoDaddy user name and password into this window.

Log in to your GoDaddy.com account

Sign in to allow Google to verify with GoDaddy that you own steveshorseandtack.com.

Username or Customer #:

Password: Forgot Password

Secure Login

VERIFIED & SECURED

GoDaddy is a Google registrar.

Then press the Orange 'Secure Login' button to see the screen below.

Confirm Access

Google is requesting permission to make changes to your DNS For **steveshorseandtack.com**.

Clicking **Accept** allows Google to submit changes on your behalf to the DNS records for **steveshorseandtack.com**.

When you click the Orange 'Accept' button Google and GoDaddy will verify that you are the domain owner and configure your DNS records to make sure that your e-mail account works properly and the pop up window will close.

You can do this manually if you have a different domain registrar, but that's a long winded job - this way is much faster and easier.

The automated process takes a few minutes so this is a great time to get a cup of tea or coffee, when it's finished the Google apps window will show this message.

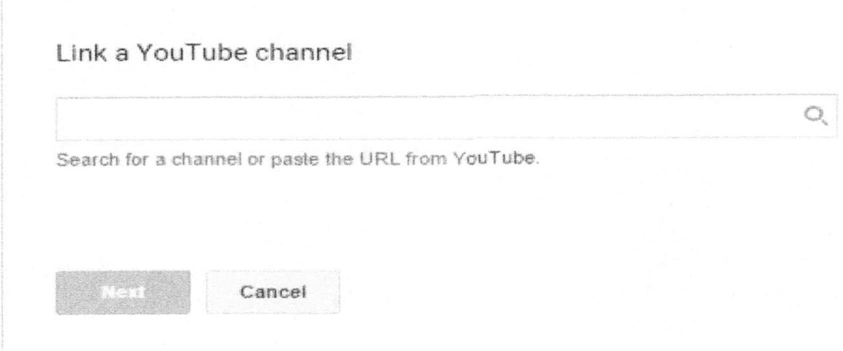

Link a YouTube channel

Search for a channel or paste the URL from YouTube.

Next   Cancel

Click the blue 'Next' button to go on and see the window below, all you need to do now is set up a payment service.

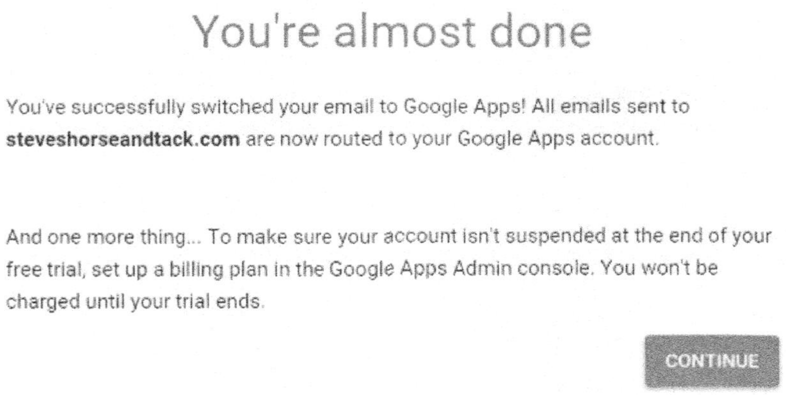

You're almost done

You've successfully switched your email to Google Apps! All emails sent to **steveshorseandtack.com** are now routed to your Google Apps account.

And one more thing... To make sure your account isn't suspended at the end of your free trial, set up a billing plan in the Google Apps Admin console. You won't be charged until your trial ends.

CONTINUE

Click the blue 'CONTINUE' button to go on to set up billing.

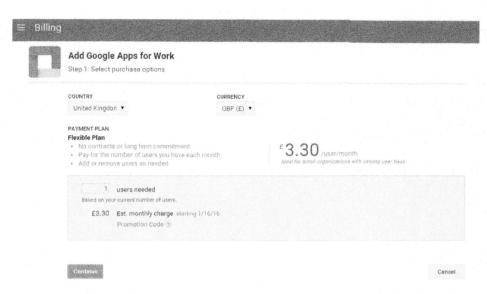

Choose the country where your card is registered and the currency that you want to pay in. I recommend that you use the same currency as you use to pay your credit card bill to avoid currency conversion charges from your card issuer, then click the blue 'CONTINUE' button to go on to finish your purchase and enter your credit card details.

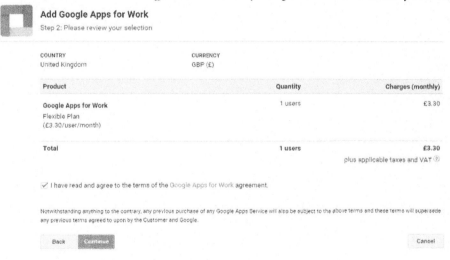

Agree to the terms and conditions then click the blue 'CONTINUE' button which will take you to a normal checkout page where you can fill out your details and add your credit card payment details. Your card details will be stored and used to pay for your account every month.

Your Google account including your company e-mail is now set up, to log back into your admin page at any time simply point your web browser to https://admin.Google.com , there you can add new users, set up e-mail groups and aliases as well as changing your billing details.

To access your new company e-mail go to https://mail.Google.com, you should go there now and complete the set up process by adding an e-mail signature and a profile image for your new account and if you are not familiar with Gmail you can click on the 'Learn how to use Gmail' link to go through their tutorial.

Next we will move on and start to set up your store on Shopify.

Chapter 31
Setting up a Shopify Store

You are now ready to set up your Shopify store, the initial set up will take about an hour, you will need a pen and paper for taking notes and your credit card to pay the charges (minimum £20per month, $US30)

It will help a lot if you have the details of your first few products to hand, including some digital photos.

To get started point your web browser at https://www.shopify.co.uk/

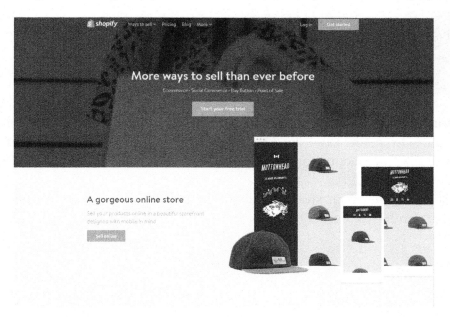

You should see a page like the one above, but don't worry if it's a bit different, Shopify regularly update their page to keep it fresh. Click the 'Get started' button or the 'Start your free trial' button to begin setting up your store. The short form below will pop up

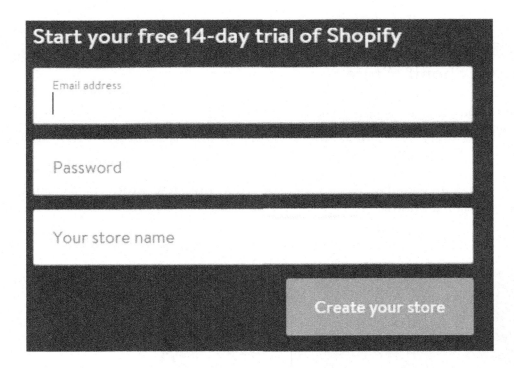

Fill in your new company e-mail address, create a unique and secure password and add your store name in plain English. Once again this is a really important password, make sure that it is secure and unique.

The name that you put in the 'Your store name' will be used to create your Shopify store name so type it carefully!

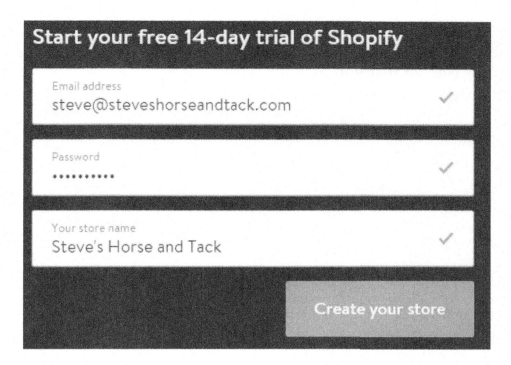

Press the green 'Create your store' button and Shopify will spend a minute setting up your store.

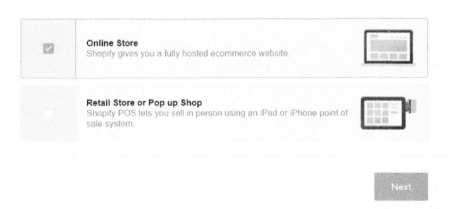

Shopify can be used both for on-line stores and to sell using an iPad in a physical store, the next step is to decide if you want to have the physical stores option enabled, it costs extra and is not part of this book, but if you want it tick the box and press 'Next', if not just press the green 'Next' button to move on.

The next step is to fill out your business details so that Shopify can configure the currency and tax rates for your store.

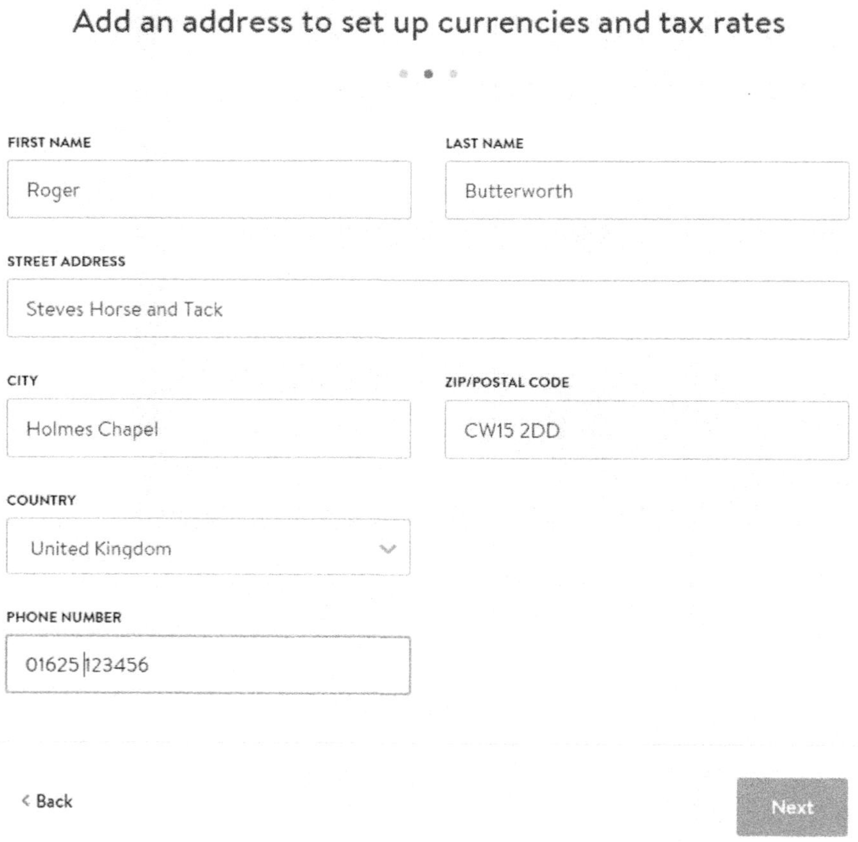

Add an address to set up currencies and tax rates

FIRST NAME

Roger

LAST NAME

Butterworth

STREET ADDRESS

Steves Horse and Tack

CITY

Holmes Chapel

ZIP/POSTAL CODE

CW15 2DD

COUNTRY

United Kingdom

PHONE NUMBER

01625 123456

< Back

Next

Finally tell Shopify where you are up to with your store by selecting from the two drop downs offered, this helps Shopify tailor the store to your needs.

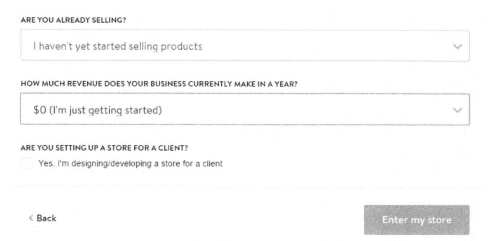

Then click the 'Enter my store' and your store set up is complete. Your store home page will load up, it should look a bit like the image below, but it won't be identical.

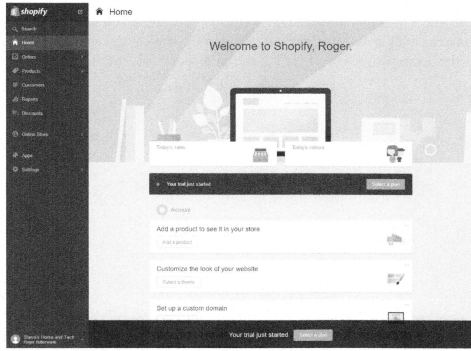

Check the URL bar at the top of your browser

Here you will find your store's Admin URL - you can see that it has been made up from your store name that you entered in the first stage and the url 'myshopify.com/admin'

This is the URL that you will come back to in order to make changes to your store, check for orders, add products etc - it's the engine room of your on-line store, make a note of it and add it to your stored favorites in your web browser so that you can get back here easily.
If you want to take a break in the setup process you can come back by just pointing your web browser to this address, entering your Shopify user name and passwords and then you can pick up where you left off.

There are some important parts of the page that I need to tell you about.

The black bar down the far left hand side of the screen is your main menu. The names are clear and I will explain what they do in more detail later on. The four choices that have a small arrow to the right all open up sub-menus when you click on them like the example below showing the sub-menu of the 'On-line Store' menu choice;

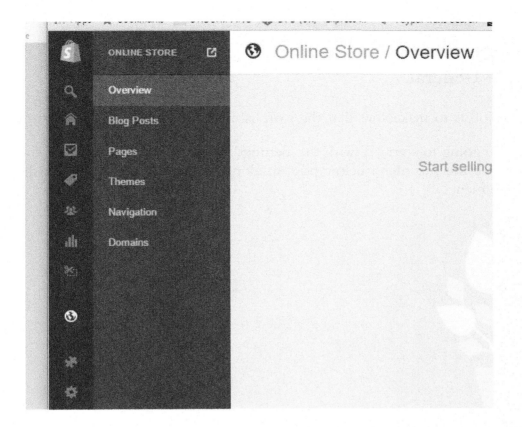

As you can see the sub menu obscures the name of the main menu options on the left, but you can still see the icons.

Chapter 32
Settings > General

As our first job is to make sure that the store is correctly set up with all of your details we are going to start off with the 'Settings' ⚙ menu choice, select it and you should see the sub menu below pop up along with the main screen for the 'General' sub menu.

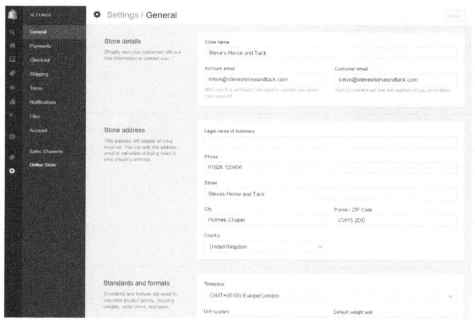

Some of the fields in the form are filled out with the information that you entered in the set up process, however there are a few things missing so you need to make some updates.

Firstly put in the legal name of your business, this will be used on your invoices and order confirmations which are sent to clients. If you are a sole trader put your trading name in there.

Next scroll down to see the 'Standards and formats' section

Set the time zone for your main office, this will be used to time stamp orders and e-mails, it helps a lot if this is also the time zone for most of your customers.

Next, choose the imperial or metric system for measurements and set the default weight unit accordingly - these are mainly used for calculating shipping costs. If you don't have a preference I recommend that you use metric and Kilograms, because, honestly they make more sense!

The store currency will have been set based on your country as defined in the initial set up.

Next set a prefix for your order reference numbers, you don't want to have your first order to look like your first order so add a 4 number prefix here like 2015, your first order will then be '#20151001'

Once that done click the blue 'Save' button (note - there are two, one at the top right and one bottom right of the page, they do the same job)

Chapter 33
Settings > Payments

The next job is to set up the payment options for your store, click 'Settings' , then 'Payments'

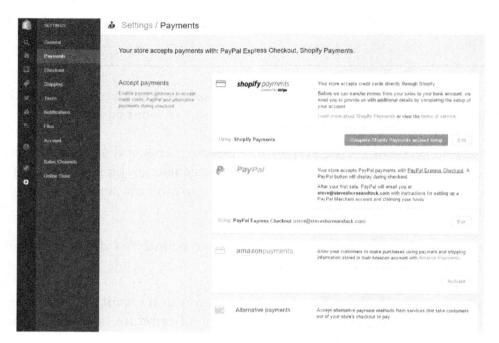

By default your store will be set up to use Shopify payments and PayPal to take money from customers when they order, but the set up is superficial, you need to finish it off and I would recommend that you add in a bank deposit payment method as well.

Lets start by completing Shopify Payments, but before you complete the setup of Shopify payments you need to confirm that the items that you are selling are allowed to be paid for through the Shopify payments scheme.
At the time of writing (January 2016) Shopify payments is only available to stores based in the USA, Canada, the UK, and Australia and the following items are not allowed to be paid for through Shopify Payments (although the list is not complete, it is the main items that cause problems)

1. Mobile Phones
2. E-cigarettes and Vaping supplies
3. Weight loss pills and supplements
4. Adult products
5. Travel services

If you do not qualify to use Shopify payments I recommend that you try Braintree and Sage Pay, both of which are less restrictive.

As long as you qualify to use Shopify payments, click on the blue 'Complete Shopify Payments account setup' button to bring up the page where you can enter your details

You should of course fill out the form accurately, but as a start up you may be providing forecasts as answers to some of the questions about your business, so bear the following points in mind while completing the questions;

- Higher average order values are considered to be more risky.
- Stores that take longer to ship orders will probably be paid more slowly for the transactions that they process.

Scroll down the form and fill out all of the fields, you will need to tell Shopify about all owners of the business that have more than a 25% share in the business.

Of course it's very important that you get right down to the bottom of the page and fill in your bank details so that Shopify can send you your payments when they are ready!

Once that's all done you can press the blue 'Complete account setup' button to save your details, this will take you back to the payments page in the settings section - now that Shopify payments is fully set up you should see this section at the top for Shopify payments. This is how you know that the set up is complete.

You are nearly done, but not quite - click the 'Edit' button in the corner of the box to change the security settings, a box like this will open out.

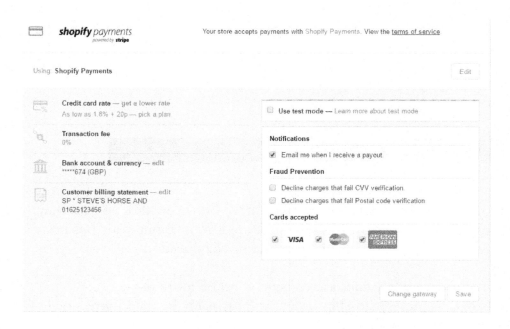

Not every region has the same options, these are the options for the UK test store.

I recommend that you tick the box that makes Shopify payments decline all charges that fail CVV verification - there is simply no good reason why a real customer would not have the CVV for their credit card.

You should also seriously consider turning on the function to Decline charges that fail Postal code verification (or ZIP code) where it is available - that WILL reduce your orders a bit, but it will reduce fraudulent orders a LOT.

The way that Shopify payments handles rejection of orders that fail these tests is quite good, customers are told why the order has been rejected and given a way to fix the problem, if they have made a simple typo 99% of customers will just fix it.

When you are done - click save.

PayPal

The next step is to check the PayPal setup. By default your store will have been setup to accept PayPal express checkout payments using the e-mail address of your store as the PayPal payment address - this can be an issue especially if you have just set up the email account. If you just leave it then when a customer pays by PayPal you will get an e-mail from PayPal asking you to set up your account to claim your funds, this can take a while to do, it is much better to get set up in advance.

If you want to use a new company PayPal account then you can leave the default setting as it is and go to PayPal to set up a new account using your company e-mail address. Go to www.PayPal.com and click the 'Sign Up' button, follow the instructions and set up your new PayPal business account.

If you prefer to use your existing PayPal account you need to first cancel the default setup. To do that click the 'Edit' button in the PayPal payments box shown below, then click the 'Deactivate' button in the box that pops up.

| P PayPal | Your store accepts PayPal payments with PayPal Express Checkout. A PayPal button will display during checkout. |
| | After your first sale, PayPal will email you at steve@steveshorseandtack.com with instructions for setting up a PayPal Merchant account and claiming your funds. |

Using: **PayPal Express Checkout** (steve@steveshorseandtack.com)　　　　Edit

This should take you back to the main payments setup screen with no PayPal payment system activated. This box will be shown for PayPal

If you click the 'Select a PayPal method' drop down you will see this list of choices

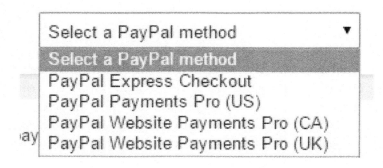

PayPal Payments Pro is a credit card processing system run by PayPal.
Any PayPal account can be used for PayPal Express Checkout but PayPal Payments Pro requires a separate agreement with PayPal to upgrade your account to accept credit card payments.

You can have PayPal express checkout and Shopify Payments active at the same time to give customers the choice of either PayPal or credit card payment, but you can not have Shopify Payments and PayPal Payments Pro active at the same time.

Check out the section on payment processing for a more complete discussion of payment processing options, but if you just want to get set up and running I recommend that for most stores a combination of Shopify Payments and PayPal Express Checkout is the best solution to begin with, if you want this just select PayPal Express Checkout from the drop down and login to your PayPal account to complete the set up.

Add a Bank Transfer Payment option

It's worth having the capability to take orders by Bank Transfer, it is free to you to use and it can be more convenient for some customers.

To set that up scroll down to the 'Manual payments' section and click the 'Activate a custom payment method' drop down menu.

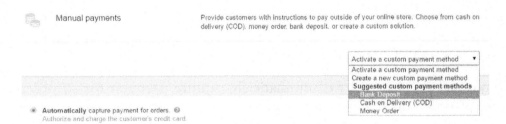

Select 'Bank Deposit' and two new boxes will pop up as shown below, the top one is the short bit of text displayed on the checkout page as the name of this payment option, the lower one is the instructions provided to the customer after they checkout to allow them to make the payment, the boxes below show the kind of information that you should put in each box.

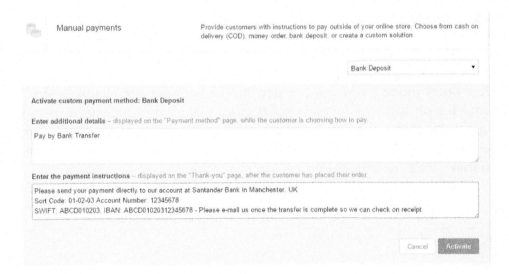

You can customize the text to suit your own taste and location. The bottom box scrolls if you add extra lines, make it as comprehensive as possible and the more info there is better, the text in the top box should be short and to the point, six words or less so it's fits on the checkout page.

Once you are finished click the blue 'Activate' button to complete the set up.

Cash collection Options - known as 'Payment authorization settings'

The last part of the payments system to set is the Payment authorization settings.

By default your store will be set to Automatically capture payment for all orders when they are placed. This works well if you are shipping items from stock, but it can cause problems if you are making to order or if you need to get stock in before you can ship and there is a chance that you may not be able to complete every order, in these circumstances I'd recommend switching to 'Manually capture payment for orders' as this will allow you to check each order first before capturing the payment.

If you choose to manually capture payments you should either capture the cash or release the authorization within 7 days of the order being placed as some cards do not guarantee that you can collect after 7 days, most will be OK, but not all.

You can of course refund orders that you can not ship - but that is bad for two reasons, firstly it costs money, you will not get the fee back for the charge and you will pay a refund fee on top which is not good. Secondly card processing accounts that process a lot of refunds are considered risky and you could lose your card processing deal if you do too many refunds, so choose the manual option if you think that you may not be able to ship every order reliably.

Chapter 34
Settings > Checkout

Once the Payment options are set we need to complete the checkout settings which deal with how your checkout page will be presented and how it will work.

The first setting is the 'Customer accounts' I recommend that you set this to 'Accounts are optional', this allows customers to create accounts for regular shopping if they wish to but it does not force them to have one.

Note: - If you select 'Accounts are required' your store will not be accessible to customers without an account which you need to create for them - you should use this for 'trade only' stores but not for retail stores.

Next you can decide which fields are required in order to allow a customer to order from your store, I recommend the following

1. Require first and last name, this is important for fraud checking
2. Make Company name optional
3. Make Address line 2 optional
4. Require every customer to enter a Phone Number. The customer's phone number is important for fraud screening and some delivery services require it.

Next, scroll down to see the rest of the checkout options

While the customer is checking out
- ☑ Use the billing address as the shipping address by default
  Reduces the number of fields required to check out. The shipping address can still be edited.
- ☐ Require a confirmation step
  Customers must review their order details before purchasing.

Collecting consent to send promotional emails to customers from your store
- ⦿ Customer **agrees** to receive promotional emails by default
- ○ Customer **does not agree** to receive promotional emails by default
- ○ Disable and hide this field

After an order has been paid
- ○ Automatically fulfill the order's line items
- ⦿ Do not automatically fulfill any of the order's line items

After an order has been fulfilled and paid
- ☑ Automatically archive the order

Additional content and scripts
Any additional instructions or scripts you'd like to appear on the order status page of the checkout. Use this for things like ROI/conversion tracking codes and partner tracking systems.

Make the following changes

1. Set the system to use the billing address as the default shipping address, the customer can still add a separate shipping address, but it makes it easier for them if they choose not to.
2. Check the 'Customer agrees to receive promotional emails by default' button, this makes collecting customer newsletter subscriptions much faster.
3. Check the 'Do not automatically fulfil any of the order's line items' button
4. Check the 'Automatically archive the order' button - this makes order processing a lot easier

Scroll down, past the section where you can change the checkout language (I assume that you are using English) and down to the section below where you can set up your Refund policy, Privacy policy and Terms and Conditions (Terms of service)

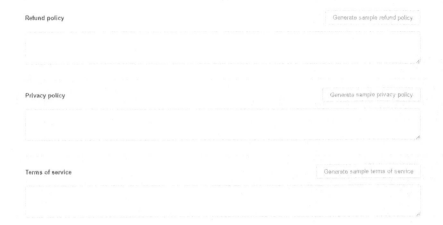

It's a condition of advertising on Google and a condition of most payment processing services that you have a reasonable policy for each of these areas and Shopify makes this really easy.

For each one of these, just click the 'Generate sample' button which will add a sample policy in each area - you will need to review them later and maybe make some changes, but the samples are good enough to get you started.

Press one of the blue 'Save' buttons to save these settings

Page 119

Chapter 35
Settings > Shipping

Setting up the different shipping choices that you will offer to customers through your Shopify store is very important, you need to get this part right or customers may not be able to place orders. Shopify has a very powerful shipping model that allows you to create as many, or as few shipping rates as you need while making sure that only the relevant shipping choices are shown to each individual customer.

You can even integrate your Shopify store with selected couriers to get them to calculate the shipping cost for each order as it is placed, this feature is called 'carrier-calculated shipping at checkout' but it is only available on the 'Unlimited' plan which costs $US179 per month (£120).

For smaller stores using the standard shipping engine Shopify allows you to create a hierarchical system of shipping rates. First you create as many geographic 'Shipping zones' as you need, then within each zone you set up the prices for shipping which Shopify calls 'shipping rates'. Shipping rates are based on either the weight of the items in the order or on the price of the items in the order.

By default you will have two zones set up, one called 'Domestic' for your home country and one called 'Rest of world'.

Within the Domestic Shipping zone you will have a 'Standard Shipping' rate and a 'Heavy Goods Shipping' rate set up, in the Rest of World zone you will have a single rate called 'International Shipping'

To get you started these may be good enough, but you may also want to set up a more complex set of choices, especially if you are selling heavy items like furniture which are expensive to ship over long distances. You may also like to edit the prices, weight bands or names of the default rates.

Following my example store for Steve's Horse Tack, I want to do the following.

1. Add heavier weight bands for my bigger items
2. Add more expensive rates for the remote areas and islands that form part of the UK (Scottish Highlands, Isle of Man, Jersey etc)
3. Add rates for shipping to Europe.

The following section will show you how I'm setting up the shipping settings for 'Steve's Horse and Tack'.

Firstly I want to change the prices and weight bands in the default shipping rates, to do this you simply select the shipping rate name to open up an editor window for the rate, first I will change the Standard Shipping rate by clicking on it

I'm going to change the name to 'Small Item Shipping'. This will be my postal shipping rate for items from 0 to 1kg at a cost of £3.99, once the changes are done I will press the blue 'Save' button.

The page updates and I can see that the rate has been changed.

Note - This is a dangerous position for the settings to be in, because without a valid shipping rate for items from 1Kg to 2.266Kg Shopify will not allow anybody to place an order for a basket of items in that weight range. We better fix that quickly so I will add a new shipping rate by clicking on the 'Add shipping rate' link directly to the right of the Domestic (United Kingdom) shipping zone name, that will open up a blank form where I can create a new shipping rate.

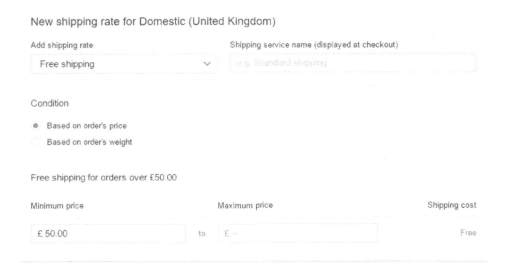

I will set the rate to be 'Based on order weight' in the drop down in the top left, and give it the name 'Medium size parcels by courier'

My agreement with DPD gives me a rate of £5 ($7.50) for next day delivery on items up to 30kg - but I want to make a small margin to cover packaging and warehouse costs, and I'm not 100% sure that the recorded weights in my product database are perfect so I'm going to set the minimum to 0kg and the maximum weight to 27kg - giving a 10% margin for error, and the price to £6.99.

Then I press the blue 'Save' button and I have a new rate set up.

Now customers with a UK address ordering an item or items weighing between 0kg and 1kg in total will be offered two choices of shipping method on checkout, one at £3:99 and one at £6:99.

The Heavy Goods Shipping obviously needs updating so I will do that by clicking on the blue 'Heavy Goods Shipping' link and changing the weight range to 25Kg to 100Kg and the price to £49.99, I'm going to call that 'Palletized Delivery - 5-10 days'. I think it's important to set a delivery expectation in the customers mind that is conservative and my Pallet delivery service normally delivers in 5 working days.

Shipping zones   Add shipping zone

    Domestic (United Kingdom)   Edit zone   Add shipping rate
    Small Item Shipping
    0.0 kg - 1.0 kg   £3.99

    Medium size parcels by courier
    0.0 kg - 27.0 kg   £6.99

    Palletized Delivery - 5-10 days
    25.0 kg - 100.0 kg   £49.99

Next I will add the separate shipping zone for remote areas of the UK and for shipping to the republic of Ireland, it's a new zone rather than a new rate because it covers a different geographic region.

First I click the blue 'Add shipping zone' link in the top right hand side of the main 'Settings > Shipping' window

A shipping zone can be made up of any one or more of the pre-defined 'countries' set up by Shopify. These match the countries that your customers select on the checkout page when they place an order so the system is consistent.

If a country or region has not been set up then you can't create a zone using it, but the list is updated from time to time and if it really matters to you, you can e-mail Shopify support to have them make changes for you.

The areas that I want to add to my new Zone are Jersey, Guernsey and the Isle of Man as well as Ireland, to select these I start typing the first name in the search box,

As you can see even one letter is enough to produce a drop down list of regions that start with that letter, I am going to select Jersey, then I will type 'g' for Guernsey and select that from the list and now I have two regions added to my new shipping zone

I will add the Isle of Man and Ireland and then the zone is complete, I just need to give it an internal name in the box to the right

And then I can press the blue 'Save' button and I have a new shipping zone

Shipping zones		Add shipping zone
🇬🇧 **Domestic** (United Kingdom)	Edit zone	Add shipping rate
Small Item Shipping 0.0 kg - 1.0 kg		£3.99
Medium size parcels by courier 0.0 kg - 27.0 kg		£6.99
Palletized Delivery - 5-10 days 25.0 kg - 100.0 kg		£49.99
🌐 **JGIOMEIRE** (4 countries)	Edit zone	Add shipping rate
You need to add at least one shipping rate to accept orders from customers in this shipping zone.		
🌐 **Rest of world**	Edit zone	Add shipping rate
International Shipping -0.002 kg - 9.074 kg		£20.00

But before my customers can use this zone I need to add at least one shipping rate, I'm actually going to add 3, I can't ship really heavy items t
o customers in these places so I will be quite restrictive.
I click 'Add shipping rate' next to my new zone to add the first rate and then go through the process above, making sure that there is no rate for items over 40Kg as I have no way to ship items that big to customers offshore.

🌐 **JGIOMEIRE** (4 countries)	Edit zone	Add shipping rate
Postal Shipping 0.0 kg - 2.0 kg		£10.00
Offshore Courier 2-5 days 0.0 kg - 20.0 kg		£34.99
Offshore Pallete 10.0 kg - 40.0 kg		£99.99

Lastly I'm going to remove the 'rest of world' zone as I can't ship my items to the rest of the world

I will start by clicking the blue 'Edit zone' button next to the 'Rest of world' shipping zone name

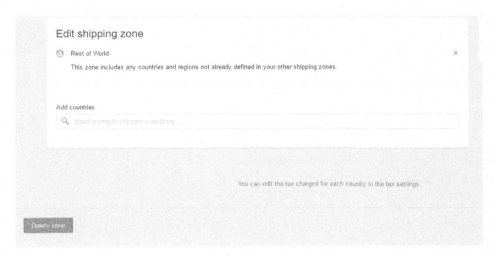

Then I will press the red 'Delete zone' and confirm the deletion in my pop up window and my zones are complete.

However this means that my site can not take orders from customers who are not located in one of the Zones that I have set up - for my example store this is fine, but you may want to be able to take orders from anywhere, if that is the case you need to keep the 'Rest of World' zone and set it up with rates that are appropriate for your items.

Chapter 36
Settings > Taxes

Once you have set up your shipping zones you then need to tell Shopify what tax rates should be charged for each zone.

Shopify only needs to know the tax rate for the regions that you have set up as shipping zones, so in the case of my example store for Steve's Horse and Tack, when I navigate to Settings > Taxes I see this screen

The most important field here is the one at the top

✔ All taxes are included in my prices
If selected, all taxes will be calculated using this formula:
tax = (tax rate * price) / (1 + tax rate). For example: £1.00 at 20% VA

This tick box affects every price on your site.

If you have it ticked (which is the default) then every price that you enter when you set up your products will be shown on your site as the complete price including any taxes. If you un-tick that box then all prices on your store will have the appropriate tax added onto the price that you set at the checkout. Shopify has to do it this way as it does not know for sure where the customer is until they select their region on the checkout page.

For stores based in the EU I recommend that you leave the box ticked and include the taxes in your selling prices, this is a legal requirement in most EU countries and it's the 'normal' way to do things, adding taxes on top of the selling price at checkout puts EU customers off and it will lead to a lot of customers failing to complete the checkout (The technical term for this is 'cart abandonment'). For stores based in the US it is a lot more normal to add taxes at checkout, but it does still create a barrier to purchase that you should avoid if you can.

You should also tick the 'include taxes on shipping rates' box - that's a legal requirement almost everywhere. Once you have ticked that box you will notice that the 'Save' button turns blue, click it to save the change.

Once that's done you need to set the tax rate for each of the countries to which you are shipping. To do that you click on the country name to open up the tax rate editor, I will start with Ireland because Guernsey does not have VAT so the default rate of 0% is correct for Guernsey.

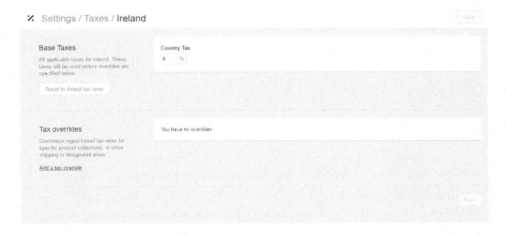

Shopify has a database of the default tax rates for most countries built in, if you want to just set the tax rate to the 'normal' sales tax rate for the country you can just hit the button marked 'Reset to default tax rates', this produces a pop up window.

Page 129

Click the red 'Reset taxes' button to set the tax rate to the default.

The standard rate of VAT in Ireland is 23%, this is now set.

If you choose you can also override the tax rate for particular categories of product or for some delivery areas within the country. This is mainly for countries like the USA that have different local tax rates that may or may not apply to your business.

But note that because we have decided that our prices are inclusive of tax nothing that we change here will change the actual selling price of the item, it just changes that proportion of the sale that is reported as tax on the invoice issued to the customer.

We will cover changing the tax rate on a particular category of item when we cover setting up a product category later.

Now I can click on the 'Settings > Taxes' menu choice again to see the main page.

As you can see the Irish tax rate has been updated.

I now need to change the Isle of Man tax rate to 20% by clicking on the name 'Isle Of Man'.

I will then select the 'Country Tax' box and type in '20' as the tax percentage.

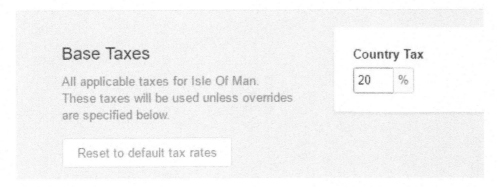

Then I press the blue 'Save' button then click the 'Settings > Taxes' menu choice to see that my tax rates are correctly set up

Chapter 37
Sales Tax and VAT

Some notes about Sales taxes and eCommerce
The issue of sales tax is very complex for on-line retailers, because as technology has developed new ways of selling, the government bodies that manage taxes around the world have failed to keep up in any meaningful way. On-line retailers are left to try to comply with outdated tax laws designed to deal with the world as it was twenty five or even a hundred years ago. Regardless of this we need to try to navigate the web of international taxes if we want to sell our products on-line and develop our businesses, so here are some practical tips to help you.

Almost every country in the world levies some kind of sales tax, in most countries it is levied at a national level. In Europe it is called Value Added Tax (VAT), in Australia and Canada it is called Goods and Services Tax (GST) and in the USA it is called simply Sales Tax and it is levied by a confusing array of state and local authorities. Wikipedia has a great article about US sales tax https://en.wikipedia.org/wiki/Sales_taxes_in_the_United_States.

As an on-line retailer you will need to deal with sales taxes every day, this book is not a tax guide and the tips below do not constitute tax advice, I am neither qualified nor authorized to give formal tax advise anywhere - they are simply notes from my experience that a new on-line retailer might want to bear in mind when dealing with taxes and international shipping.

Shipping goods internationally
When you ship goods across an international border there will normally be additional costs for taxes and duty which the government of the country that the goods are being sent into will charge to allow the goods to be imported into their country. These taxes and duties will normally be charged as a proportion of the value of the goods that you declare on the 'Commercial Invoice' or 'CI' which you will be required to include with the goods.

The Commercial Invoice is a document that accompanies each shipment that you send internationally, most couriers who ship provide international delivery services will require you to print off at least 3 paper copies of the Commercial Invoice and attach them to the outside of the parcel in an open documents wallet so that copies can be taken out by the various admin staff that handle the package. I recommend printing 5 copies to make sure that there are plenty to go around. Some couriers like DHL and FedEx have systems to help you create a Commercial Invoice which is both printed and stored electronically in their systems which are integrated into many countries import tax systems - if you can use these systems then you should as they can speed up the process of clearing customs and also avoid unnecessary delays due to lost physical paperwork.

Normally a CI should also include the 'harmonized tariff code' for the items in the shippment. The harmonized tariff code is a system for the classification of goods that most countries around the world have agreed. It allows them to define products and to set different tax and duty rates for different kinds of goods.

The UK government has some really helpful information about tariff codes at https://www.gov.uk/finding-commodity-codes including a guide to help you find the right codes for your items at https://www.gov.uk/trade-tariff/sections. The cost of duty is based both on the declared value of the goods and the commodity code for them.

For small parcels with a declared value of under £270 (US$400) that can be sent by international post you can attach a small sticker to the box instead of including a full commercial invoice, this is called a 'CN22' and looks like this

In practice small items sent by post with a CN22 are almost never checked by customs as the time and effort to do so is simply not worth the small amount of extra tax that can be collected, so the CN22 system is widely abused. Similarly it is very common practice to declare a lower value on a commercial invoice than the price that the customer has paid to you so that the tax bill on import is reduced. The strict legal requirement is for the commercial invoice to show the value of goods that are being imported, that will almost never be the same as the total transaction value as some part of the price paid will be for shipping and handling or services provided overseas which can not be imported.

Many on-line retailers, especially those based in the far east selling mainly through marketplaces like eBay and Amazon have been exploiting this loophole for many years and declaring very low proportions of the selling price on their Commercial Invoices, so in many countries the customs officials check these quite carefully. Customs officers have the right to hold up a parcel if they think that the CI is wrong and request further proof or documentation from the sender, this can take weeks and it really annoys customers, so I recommend caution when deciding what to declare on a CI, by all means deduct a reasonable proportion of the sale and allocate it to the services that are provided in the warehouse, but make sure that you could defend the value shown on the CI if you have to. As a rule of thumb declaring less than 50% of the actual sale price is likely to backfire in the long run, declaring more than 80% is wasteful.

Shipping insurance is linked to the value declared on the Commercial Invoice

It is useful to remember that in most cases the maximum payable under your goods in transit insurance will be the value declared on the Commercial Invoice for tax purposes.

Import taxation thresholds

Most countries have a threshold level where they consider the duties and taxes on an import to be uneconomic to collect if the value is below that level. But the levels vary wildly across the world, here are a few examples. You should get to know more about any countries that you plan to ship to regularly, your courier should be able to help you find out more.

- Australia

Shipments valued below AUD 1,000 (FOB) are given a duty and tax waiver, although as I write in early 2016 this is under review with a view to reducing it.

This excludes tobacco products and alcoholic beverages.

- Canada

Although shipments valued under CAD 20 are not dutiable or taxable, Canada uses the full cost of both goods and shipping for this determination so in effect all shipments will be subject to duty and GST/PST.

- Hong Kong

Hong Kong is a duty free destination. No duties or taxes are collected.

- India

There is effectively no duty/tax free threshold and most shipments will be subject to a range of duties and taxes.

- Europe

Goods costing less than EUR 150 (or equivalent) are duty free. As individual EU countries have control of their own tax regulations, this exemption will not necessarily apply to VAT/sales tax. VAT is chargeable on the value of the goods + the duties payable.

- Malaysia

Customs duty and sales tax may be payable on imports. Customs duties are generally below 10% and are assessed on the value of the Cost of the goods + Insurance + Freight (CIF value).

Sales tax is payable on imported goods although there are some exemptions. Currently, there are three rates: 5%, 10% and 15%, with the applicable rate depending on the specific goods. The tax is assessed on the CIF + duty value.

An exemption for customs duty and sales tax exists in certain limited circumstances. For shipments entering through designated international airports (KLIA, Penang) duty/tax is not applied to goods below a value of MYR 500

- Philippines

The limit is officially set at PHP10.00 of duty amount payable. In practice shipments valued under USD 75 and under 10 kg in weight receive duty free clearance.

- Russian Federation

Duty and tax depend on an individual's monthly import activity. The monthly allowance is currently a total value of 1,000 Euro (CIF value = value of goods + shipping) or a total weight of 31 kg. Duty and tax are payable at a combined rate of 30% of the value in excess of 1,000 Euro, although nothing is payable if the duty and tax are 2 Euro or less. For items exceeding a total of 31 kg, duty and tax are payable on the excess at a rate of 4 Euro per kg.

- Singapore

There is no duty payable on most products except alcohol, tobacco products, motor vehicles and petroleum products (but see list of Prohibited Items).

A Goods and Services Tax (GST), currently 7%, is imposed on the cost of the Cost of the goods + Insurance + Freight (known as the 'CIF value'). The GST is waived if the total CIF value is below SGD 400.

- Turkey

Shipments valued under EUR 75 are duty free.

- United Arab Emirates

Shipments valued under 500 AED enter free from duty and tax.

- United Kingdom

Goods costing less than £100 are duty free but VAT is charged on all shipments over £17

European VAT rules

If you are based inside the EU you should understand the VAT rules as enforced in your country in detail, check the web site of your tax office carefully and ask them directly if you don't understand as the system is complex. If in doubt pay for professional tax advice.

Registration for VAT in Europe

Every country in Europe requires businesses based in it's territory to register for VAT with their own national tax authority if they transact business above the countries VAT registration threshold which is usually one hundred thousand Euros for larger countries like the UK, France, Germany and Italy or thirty thousand euros for smaller countries. Countries that do not use the Euro convert the limit into their local currency each year.

Companies that are registered for VAT are required to keep track of the VAT that they charge their customers and the VAT that they are charged when they buy stock and business supplies, they then report those figures monthly or quarterly and pay over the difference to the government.

If you can avoid being registered for VAT it will probably be financially beneficial for you, but the penalties for not registering when you should have are usually quite severe. It is possible to make a nice profit on sales under the VAT threshold in your home country along with additional sales in other countries.

VAT payments are based on your declarations, you are required to make a declaration and to make it as accurate as possible, but the detail is entirely up to you - the government tax office have a right to audit you and check your numbers, but they do not cross check your reports as a matter of course.

Basic rules on Cross Border VAT within Europe for European retailers
When you ship your goods from one of the EU member states you can ship goods to any other EU country without any customs delays or checks on the goods between your warehouse and your customer, you do not need to include a CI with these shipments either. When you do this you are required to charge VAT when selling to consumers but you do not have to do so if you sell to another VAT registered business, you are however required to get the customers VAT registration number and check that it is valid, you can do that here http://ec.europa.eu/taxation_customs/vies/.

Additionally, you are required to register for VAT reporting and payment in each European country where you sell more than the local VAT registration threshold, so if you sell across Europe you could end up managing thirty different VAT registrations in different languages.

Sales made through marketplaces like Amazon and eBay count towards your total sales in each country.

There is a lot more information about European VAT here http://europa.eu/youreurope/business/vat-customs/cross-border/index_en.htm#

In practice it is very hard for European tax authorities to be sure that you have exceeded the tax threshold in their region so you can realistically be quite cavalier with the VAT registration limits and get away with it. Remember that once you are registered it will put you on the country in question's tax list and it will be impossible to get off.

Once your sales are at a significant level (two or three times the 'actual' registration limits) the risk of not registering probably exceeds the benefit of not doing as breaking tax related laws tends to carry draconian punishments. This is one of the reasons that I recommend you to trade through a limited company rather than as a private individual when you sell on-line.

Shipping goods into Europe from outside
When you Ship goods into Europe from outside the EU the situation is in many ways much simpler, the goods that you send will be taxed at the point of entry into the EU based on the value that you declare on the CI and the tax rate of the country that you import through.

Chapter 38
Settings > Notifications

Notifications is the generic name that Shopify gives to the confirmation emails that the systems sends to your customers after they place and order, create an account or interact with your store in another way.

You can edit the standard email templates in Settings > Notifications, but for our purposes you do not need to edit any of them as Shopify does a great job of setting up these mails.
Please note that editing the standard e-mails requires some knowledge of HTML and basic coding.

This page of the settings does however require one change in my standard set up. I want to get an email to my personal gmail whenever we get an order through the store, just so I know and can make sure that it is shipped. By default Shopify has set it's self up to mail me at my work address as you can see below.

To add the extra mail to my set up I click the 'Add and order notification' button which produces a pop up window where you can add the extra e-mail address.

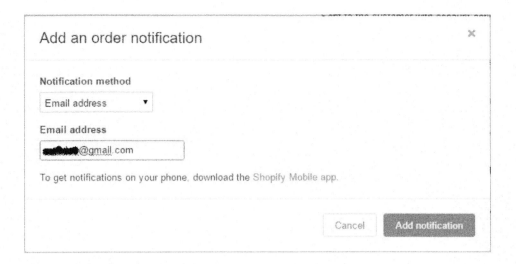

Simply add your e-mail address to the box and press the blue 'Add notification' button to complete the process

You will then see your new email listed to receive a copy of any new notifications.

Chapter 39
Settings > Account

The next thing to do to set up your store is to choose a Shopify plan, enter your payment details and set up login details for any other members of staff that you want to be able to use the site, you do these things in the Settings > Account section of your store.

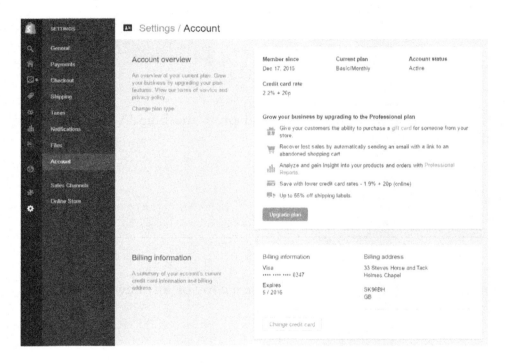

Shopify is paid for on a monthly basis, in order to charge you for your store, Shopify requires that you have a credit card or debit card on file with them, you can use a Visa, Mastercard, Amex or Discover card.

You will be charged a monthly fee from $US29 to $US179 based on the plan that you choose plus a percentage of the revenue through your store for the credit card fees. These charges will be made to your card on file each month so make sure that the card that you use has enough limit for the charges - if the charge fails your store could be suspended.

This card will also be charged for any themes or chargeable apps that you buy

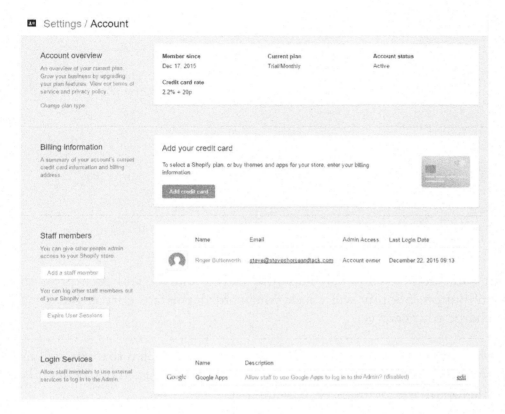

First of all enter your credit card details, click on the blue 'Add credit card' button and the pop up below will appear

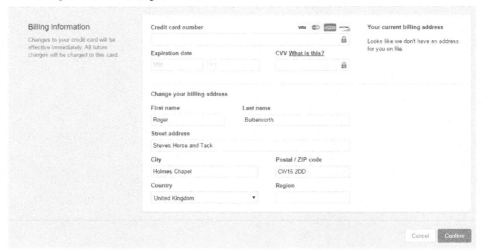

Simply fill in your credit card details and your billing address and then press the blue 'Confirm' button. Shopify will check your card details are correct but it will not actually charge your card yet.

Once you have entered a credit card you can then choose the plan that you will use for your store, there are 4 options for this, to see them click on the 'Change plan type' link at the top of the 'Settings > Account' page.

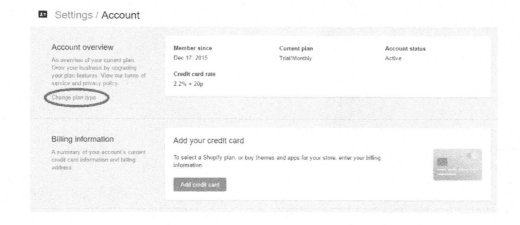

This will bring up the plan choice window

Page 144

I recommend that you start out with the Basic plan ($29 per month (£20) plus 2.2% of sales at the time of writing), this gives a good mix of features at the best price to get you started. You can upgrade your plan at any time or pay for a longer period, but before you do that lets be 100% sure that the store is running correctly.

Just for your information, to get economic benefit from the reduction in card fees charged by the more expensive plans you need to have sales of

$US 16,700 per month (£11,000) for Professional

$US 25,000 per month (£16,500) for Unlimited

To confirm the plan of your choice simply click 'Choose this plan' on the button below the price and then confirm your change on the next page.
Shopify offers discounted plans if you pay for a whole year or even for two or three years in advance. Based on which of these options you select it also lets you know when you will be charged, how much you will be charged and the period that the charge will cover, see below.

◉ Bill me once a month for $29.00
◉ Bill me once a year for $312.00 and save $36.00 every year
◉ Bill me every two years for $558.00 and save $138.00 every two years
◉ Bill me every three years for $783.00 and save $261.00 every three years

Your credit card will be charged for the monthly basic plan of $29.00 USD on 2015-12-31. This will cover your Shopify subscription from: December 31, 2015 to January 30, 2016.

Shopify lets you add multiple staff members who can work on your store at the same time, this means that multiple people can login to the store at the same time to update products, check for orders etc

By adding extra users with their own user name and passwords you do not need to share your own log in details if you want to get a bit of help with the day to day running of your store from time to time. As the store administrator you can always check who did what and when if you need to.

Extra users are added through the ' Staff members' section of the 'Settings > Accounts' menu choice.

To add an extra user you click the 'Add a staff member' button shown above and a box will pop up.

Simply fill out the first name, Last name and Email address of the new user and press the 'Send invite' button which will turn blue once there is data in each box.

The new user will get an e-mail inviting them to become a new user at your store, with a link to the web page where they can complete the sign up process by creating their own password.

Chapter 40
Settings > on-line Store

The last page that we need to complete in the Settings tab is the 'on-line Store' page. This is a bit of a mixed bag of settings that don't really fit anywhere else.

To get to these fields go to 'Settings' on the main menu and then choose 'on-line Store' from the pop out sub menu, it's a bit confusing as there is also an 'On-line Store' option on the main menu which we will deal with later. For now we want the sub menu of 'Settings' then 'On-line Store', the page should look something like this.

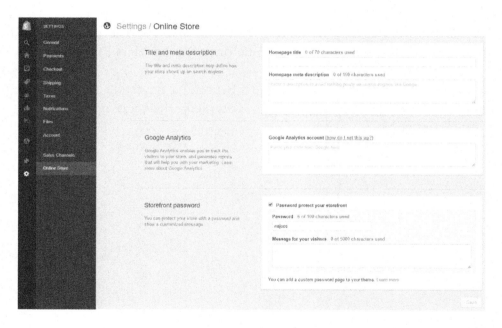

We need to deal with all three sections of this page, we will tackle the easy one first. By default Shopify blocks your store from new users with a password, that can be a bit of a pain when checking things out so I recommend removing it now.

To remove the password simply click on tick box next to the words 'Password protect your storefront' to remove the tick.

Then click the blue 'Save' button

The next part that we need to set up is the title for your homepage and the homepage meta description to improve SEO for your store. The meta description is used to tell Google and other search engines who you are and what you do, you can simply type the description that you want into the two boxes at the top of the page shown here

There is a section of this book about Search Engine Optimization for your web site, so I won't repeat it all here, but understand that the text that you put here is really important, think carefully about it.

Homepage Title
The homepage title is the text that pops up when you hover your cursor over a tab of your web browser when it is showing your site's homepage - this is meant to be read by humans and as you can see it's only allowed to be up 70 characters long.

Try to find a way to explain to someone what your store does in this length of text, imagine you are explaining what you do to a friend.

Homepage Meta Description
The Homepage meta description is a longer version of the same thing, but the key difference is that it is intended to be read mainly by Google, it is important to include phrases that you expect people to search for on Google in this section.

The text that I have entered for my example store is here

Try to use all the characters that you are allowed, include common mis-spellings of your key item names if you think that they will be used by customers.

Don't forget to press the blue 'Save' button when you have done.

Chapter 41
Google Analytics

Set up a Google Analytics account and integrate it with your Shopify store

Google Analytics is a web analytics service offered by Google. Web analytics is the process of tracking and reporting website traffic, allowing you to see where your traffic is coming from and what users are doing on your web site. This is very important as it helps you to track the results of your web advertising activity, to understand how customers are finding your store to make sure that you are getting value for money from your advertising on-line.

Google launched the service in November 2005 and it is now the most widely used web analytics service on the Internet. And the really good news is that it's free - although you can pay for extra features the basic features that you will need to get started are all free.

To set up an account with Google Analytics for your Shopify store you should first open a new tab in your browser, then point it to http://www.Google.com/analytics/ .
Make sure that you leave the tab with your Shopify store in it open as well. You will need it later to cut and paste the Google tracking code back into your Shopify store settings page once your Google Analytics account is set up.

Then click the 'SIGN IN' menu choice in the top right hand corner to bring up this drop down

Google Analytics

Google Analytics Premium

Google Tag Manager

Adometry by Google

Choose 'Google Analytics' and as long as you are still logged into your Google account you should see a page like this

If you are not still logged in you may need to log in using your Google account credentials.

Click the Grey 'Sign up' button to bring up a form where you can tell Google what you are trying to track

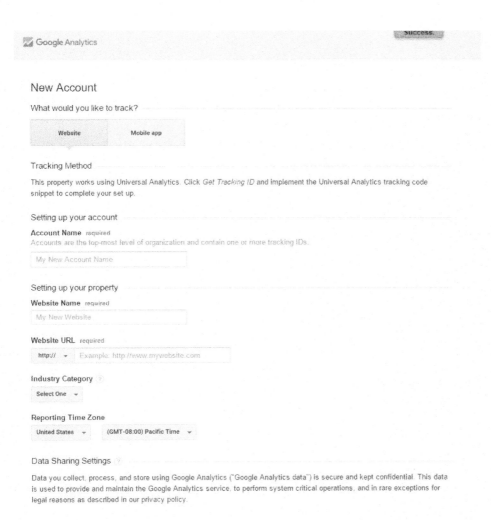

Google Analytics can be used to track multiple web sites, you can have a number of Accounts set up in Google Analytics each with many Websites to be tracked in them but we will just be setting up one account with one web site in it, so set the 'Account Name' to 'My Retail Stores' then Set your Website Name appropriately and then enter your website domain in the box marked Website URL.

Select your Industry Category from the drop down and set the reporting time zone to the home time zone for your target country, this is important to match the reports to the local time recognized by your customers.

The settings for my example store are shown below

Don't forget the 'www' in your store URL

Next scroll down and make sure that all the Data Sharing options are ticked, then select the blue 'Get Tracking ID' button

Data Sharing Settings

Data you collect, process, and store using Google Analytics ("Google Analytics data") is secure and kept confidential. This data is used to provide and maintain the Google Analytics service, to perform system critical operations, and in rare exceptions for legal reasons as described in our privacy policy.

The data sharing options give you more control over sharing your Google Analytics data. Learn more.

☑ **Google products & services** RECOMMENDED
Share Google Analytics data with Google to help improve Google's products and services. *If you disable this option, data can still flow to other Google products explicitly linked to Analytics. Visit the product linking section in each property to view or change your settings.*

☑ **Benchmarking** RECOMMENDED
Contribute anonymous data to an aggregate data set to enable features like benchmarking and publication that can help you understand data trends. All identifiable information about your website is removed and combined with other anonymous data before it is shared with others.

☑ **Technical support** RECOMMENDED
Let Google technical support representatives access your Google Analytics data and account when necessary to provide service and find solutions to technical issues.

☑ **Account specialists** RECOMMENDED
Give Google marketing specialists and your Google sales specialists access to your Google Analytics data and account so they can find ways to improve your configuration and analysis, and share optimization tips with you. If you don't have dedicated sales specialists, give this access to authorized Google representatives.

Learn how Google Analytics safeguards your data.

You are using 0 out of 100 accounts.

You will need to accept the terms and conditions for the use of Google Analytics, then you should see a page like this

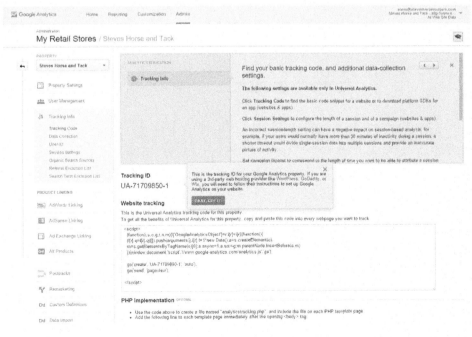

Page 155

Get rid of the pop up window in the middle of the screen then you need to select the Website tracking code shown in the middle of the screen so that you can cut and paste it over to your Shopify store.

Luckily Google is clever enough to make that really easy, just click anywhere in the window showing the tracking code and the whole code should be highlighted, then you can right click in the box and select 'copy' from the drop down menu.

Switch back to the tab with your Shopify store in it, that tab should still be pointing to the Settings > On-line Store page which should look like this

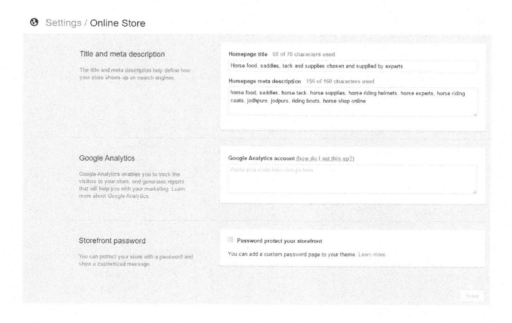

Page 156

Right click in the window for the Google Analytics account, where it says 'Paste your code from Google here' and select Paste from the drop down menu

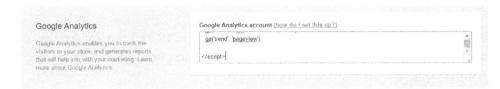

Don't worry that you can only see a bit of the code, just hit the blue 'Save' button, Shopify should go off and check that the code is correct and as long as it is you should see the Google Analytics section update to something like this

Cross check the Google Analytics account number shown in Shopify - it should be the same as the number shown on your Google Analytics page.
Make a note of this number, you will need it later.

Chapter 42
Adding Products

Now that the settings have been properly completed, the next step in setting up your store is to create your product listings and your catalog structure so that users can navigate round yous site and buy things from you.

There are two ways to add products to your Shopify store, you can add them one by one using the manual product editor, or you can add lots of them at the same time through a product upload.
Adding products manually takes about 2 minutes per product if you have the details such as the product descriptions and images prepared in advance, in contrast to this, uploading hundreds of product's details from a spreadsheet to Shopify takes just a few seconds - but of course you need to have the product details sheet prepared in advance to do that.

Preparing the details in advance is the key to getting your products looking good on your website because your whole site will look much better if your product names, images, prices and descriptions are consistent. Before you start adding products, get prepared.

I recommend that you use a spreadsheet to list out your product details, it will help a lot if you have experience of using a spreadsheet system like Microsoft Excel or Google Sheets to set up all a spreadsheet containing all of your product details and then save it as a '.csv file' to be uploaded into your Shopify store. The product upload feature in Shopify is very flexible, you can upload as much or as little of the product record as you like, the minimum required is that you upload a product name, if you like you can just upload that and then manually add all of the rest of the product details.
However, don't worry if you don't regularly use spreadsheets, you can prepare your details on paper and then set up products manually using your web browser if you prefer - it just takes a bit longer that way.

Here is my recommended process for setting up your products in your Shopify store

1. Set up a spreadsheet listing your product details
Write all of your product details out in a spreadsheet one product per row, making

sure that the names, descriptions and prices are consistent, it helps a lot if your product names have consistent format and capitalization. Add in as much detail as possible, but at a minimum include the following three fields in columns Product Name, Product Price, Product Weight (in grams). If you can, also include the description, store part number or Stock Keeping Unit (SKU) and EAN code or Manufacturer's Part Number (MPN) if your products have them. Don't worry if you can't fill out every field for all of your products at this stage, it is better if you can but it is not essential.

You will need either an EAN or an MPN for all of the items that you want to list on Google Shopping.

My sample spreadsheet for the example store looks like this

	A	B	C	D	E	F
1	Name	Price	Description	Part Number	EAN Code	Weight (g)
2	Black Leather Western Style Saddle	299	Big black saddle made in the western style, comfortable and easy to fit, great for long distance riding	WES-BLK	123456789	1500
3	Brown Leather Western Style Saddle	299	Big Brown saddle made in the western style, comfortable and easy to fit, great for long distance riding	WES-BRN		1500
4	Cream Leather Western Style Saddle	299	Big Cream saddle made in the western style, comfortable and easy to fit, great for long distance riding	WES-CRM		1500
5	Black Leather English Style Saddle	349	Black saddle made in the English style for use in competition and English style riding	ENG-BLK		1200
6	Brown Leather English Style Saddle	349	Brown saddle made in the English style for use in competition and English style riding	ENG-BRN		1200
7	Cream Leather English Style Saddle	349	Cream saddle made in the English style for use in competition and English style riding	ENG-CRM		1200
8	Pack of young Horse food 50Kg	99		YHF-50		500
9	Pack of young Horse food 100Kg	189		YHF-100		1000
10	Pack of mature Horse food 50Kg	89		MHF-50		500
11	Pack of mature Horse food 100Kg	169		MHF-100		1000

2. Gather and edit your product images and videos if you have them

Read the section of the book on product photography before doing this, your store will look a lot better if you make your product images have the same aspect ratio, background etc but that's not compulsory it just makes the store look better. Take your images, edit them and get them together into a folder on your PC, if you have a lot of images it can help to organize them in sub-folders, taking and editing your images can be the most time consuming part of setting up your products - but it is really worth taking the time to get them right. If you have product videos ready at this stage then include them in the folder too.

3. Write your product descriptions

Read the chapter on product descriptions and think carefully about how you want to describe your products, make the format as consistent as possible. Your descriptions are sales pitches for your products, focus on benefits, not features. Having product descriptions is not compulsory, nor is it compulsory for them to be unique and helpful, but your store will perform better if they are. Include your descriptions in their own column of your product spreadsheet as shown above. Note that yours should be a lot longer than the ones in my example.

4. Decide on the product categories that you want to display on your web

site

This is a great time to decide on the product categories that you want to display on your web site and what items will be in which categories.

As a good rule of thumb try to split your products into no more than ten categories, five or six is ideal as more than that can lead to customers becoming confused when they try to browse your site.

For my example store the categories will be

Food,   Saddles,   Clothing,   Tools,   Horse Care

These will be the most important categories that will show in the main menu across the top of my store.

About product categories in Shopify

Shopify calls product categories 'Collections'. Products can be in one Collection, not in any collections or in multiple collections so the system is very flexible. You can use collections to create special groups for offers and promotions as well as to define product categories.

For now just define your product categories and write them out on a sheet of paper and check that all of your products fit into at least one category, we will come back to this later. Try to avoid setting up categories with names like 'Misc' and 'Other' - they simply never get any traffic.

Set up a single product - it's really easy

We will upload the products from your spreadsheet shortly, but before we do that I want to explain how to set up a product manually as I think that will help you to understand the process and how Shopify stores product details.

To start the process of setting up a product manually, go to the products choice of the main menu in your Shopify admin system, the icon for that is a stylized price tag.

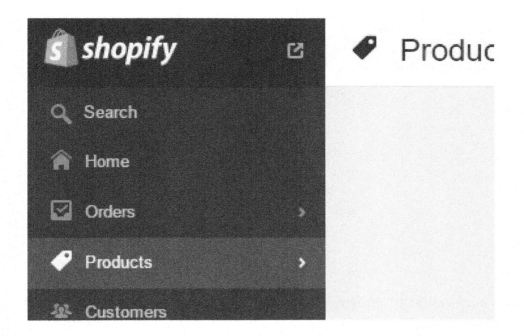

Select the 'Products' menu choice to bring up the 'Products' sub menu, which confusingly defaults to a sub menu choice called 'products' as well

To start adding a product manually, select either one of the blue 'Add product' buttons to bring up a form where you can enter all of the product details.

The form is quite long so I have split it into two parts, this is the top of the form

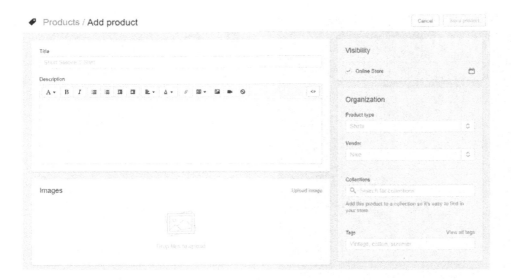

At the top is the section where you can type in the name of the product, which Shopify calls the 'Title', this will appear as the title of the item on it's product page and it will be used as a part of the URL for the product page so it's important that you make it accurate and complete. The name is really important for SEO - try to make sure that the name includes all of the terms that people who are interested in this item might search for on Google.

Under the Title you will find the product description editor, this is a really powerful editor that lets you set up detailed product descriptions with nice layouts, links embedded links, pictures and videos. It also lets you enter HTML directly if you know how to do that. You can switch the editor to 'HTML mode' by clicking the '<>' icon in the top right hand corner of the menu above the 'Description' box. Entering the description as HTML gives you a lot more flexibility on how the description is laid out, you can add tabs, complex tables and use extra fonts and effects - but laying out a product description is complex and time consuming so even if you know how to do it I recommend that you just use the regular editor for now.

Of course you can just type the product description into the box if you want - it works just like a regular text entry box and you can use the menu items above to layout the text in different ways and to add tables, images and video to the description - but this is not the right place to put your main product photos, they are added in the box below, they need to be separate so that they can be used on all the different pages where products are shown like the search results, category pages and home page.

Under the Description box is the Images section, to add an image simply click on the blue 'Upload image' link and choose the image that you want to add to your product from your computer. You can also add multiple images at the same time by selecting them together using the 'Shift' key to select several images that are next to each other in the same folder of by pressing 'Ctrl + Alt' to select several separate images. Alternatively, you can drag and drop images from a separate file explorer window if you prefer.

In the top right hand side of this section is the 'Visibility' box.

The box next to 'on-line Store' is ticked by default, this means that the product is shown on your on-line store, if you prefer to publish the item at a time in the future then you can click on the 'Calendar' icon

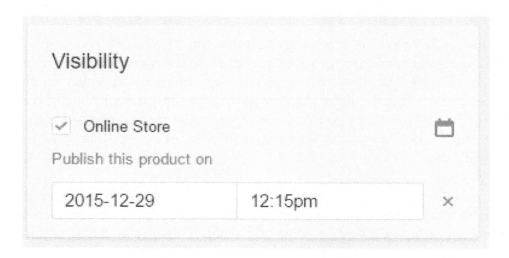

To set the exact date and time when the item will become available - this can be really helpful for product launches when you want the item to appear on the web site at a particular time as part of your marketing campaign for the product launch.

The 'Organization' box allows you to categorize products.

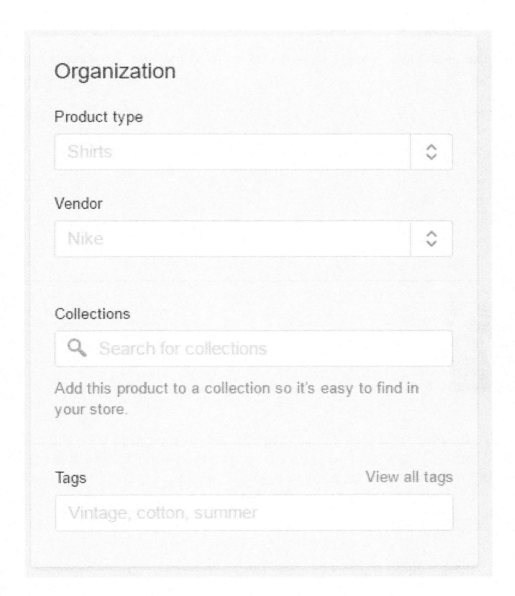

The 'Product type' and 'Vendor' boxes are effectively free text fields - you can enter anything you like into them or you can select from one of the values that you have already entered, both are optional fields.
The product type should be obvious to you and the vendor is the place that you buy the item from.

Ignore 'Collections' and 'Tags' for now, we will allocate products to collections later as you need to set them up first.

Here is how the page looks when I have set up my first product for the example store.

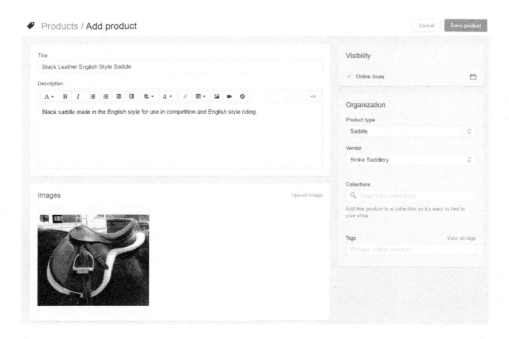

Once you have finished setting up the top part of the product page click the blue 'Save product' button, you should see a green confirmation band appear at the top of the page, but the rest of the page will remain unchanged.

Scroll down to fill out the bottom half of the page

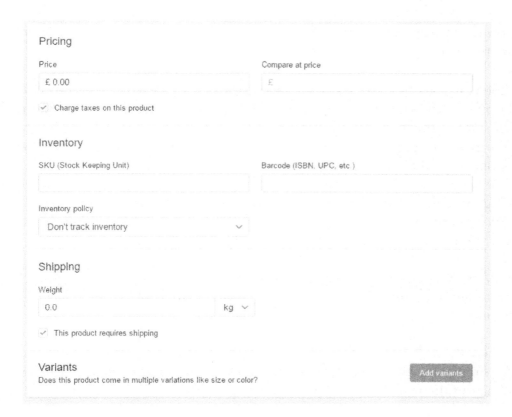

The 'Price' field is the selling price of the product, set in the currency that you chose in Settings > General

By default taxes (VAT, GST etc) are charged on all products, but if you sell some items that are not taxable you can un-tick the box for those items.

Ignore the 'Compare at price' field, we will not be using it.

The Stock Keeping Unit (SKU) is your own internal part number for the item, you can use the manufacturers part number or if you are the manufacturer you can allocate your own, this is used as part of the process of listing the item on Google shopping and it is search-able on the web site but it is not shown to customers.

The 'Barcode' field is where you enter the EAN code for your items, if you want to sell on Amazon or on eBay you will need each of your items to have an EAN code. ISBN codes for books and US UPC codes are both sub-types of EAN code. If you are buying your products in you can scan the barcode off the packaging using a barcode reader or you can get them from your supplier, if you are selling your own products you will need to be able to allocate EAN codes of your own, you can buy them at www.gs1.org

You can choose to have Shopify track the inventory in your store or not - but note that if Shopify is tracking inventory and the inventory reaches zero then the product will still be shown, but it will no longer be available for order through your store. If you make your own stock or if stock is freely available for the items that you sell it is safer to NOT track inventory.

The shipping weight of the item is used to calculate the cost of shipping to customers, it is set up by default in the weight units that you selected in Settings > General, but you can change that if you like and Shopify will convert for you.

If you sell 'Virtual' products like e-books or software downloads you can un-tick the 'This product requires shipping' box for these items and Shopify will not charge shipping on them at all.

We will discuss variants of products in the next section, but for now ignore that option and simply hit the blue 'Save' button in the top right when you have finished filling out the rest of the fields - my example product fields look like this.

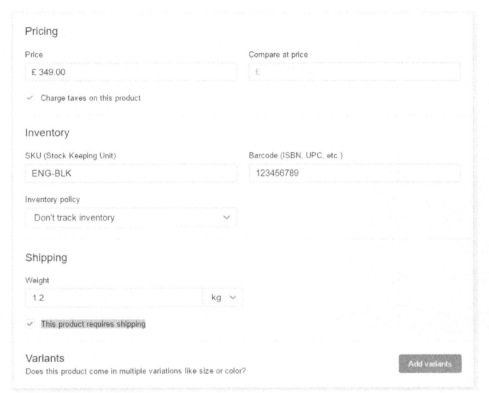

Once you have finished filling out your details it's a good idea to see how the product looks on your site, to do that click the 'View' button in the bar at the top of the screen, this will open up a new tab in your browser where you can see the product details that you have entered.

Don't worry too much about the page layout at this stage, we will be changing that in the section on 'Themes', but you can see now how the Title (Product Name), Description, Image and Price are shown on the product page.

Try editing the product to add more images and a longer description to see how the page changes.

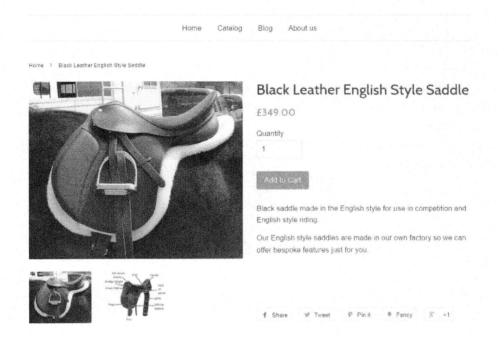

Right - now we are getting somewhere, it's time to add a larger group of products from your spreadsheet.

Chapter 43
Adding from a spreadsheet

How to add multiple products to your Shopify from a spreadsheet
Since we are paying Google for the Google Apps suite as well as our e-mail, it makes sense to use the Google Sheets application that is included in Google Apps to set up our product spreadsheet, to do that first log in to your Google account and go to your e-mail inbox.

At the top right hand side of the screen you should see an icon that looks like nine small squares stacked in a three by three box, click that icon.

This will pop up a list of commonly used Google Apps

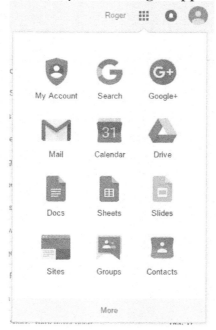

Select 'Sheets', then start a new 'Blank' spreadsheet by clicking the green '+'

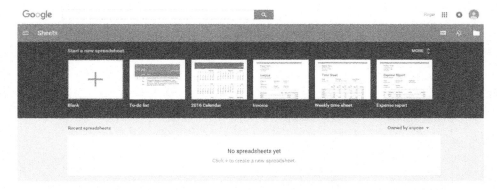

This will bring up a blank spreadsheet

Click on 'Untitled spreadsheet' to change the sheet name - I suggest 'Product List'

Set up the first six columns as 'Name', 'Price', 'Description', 'Part Number', 'EAN Code' and Weight

Now create your product list, one product per row, either by typing in the details or by using cut and paste to bring them over from other documents or systems

Here is my sample product list - note that the names and descriptions are truncated by the spreadsheet in this view, but the whole names and descriptions are in the cell.

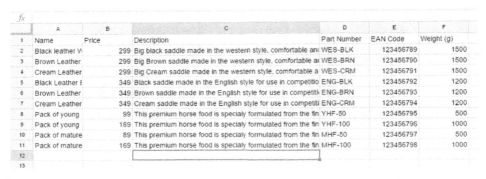

To upload these items into Shopify I first need to save the sheet as a '.csv' file on my PC.

To do this I select File > Download as from the menu in Google Sheets.

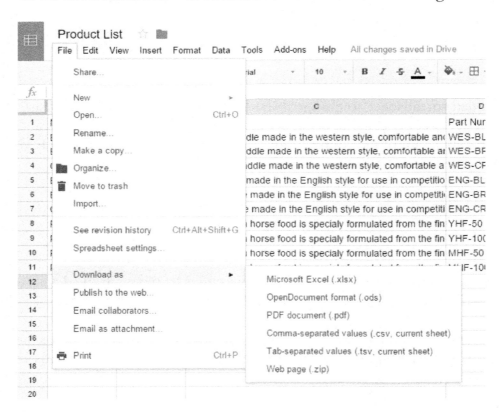

Then choose 'Comma-separated values (.csv, current sheet) from the final menu

Put the file in an easy to find location on your PC then switch back to your Shopify store admin in the Products > Products menu

Choose 'Import' from the top right hand corner of the screen and you will see the import file pop up

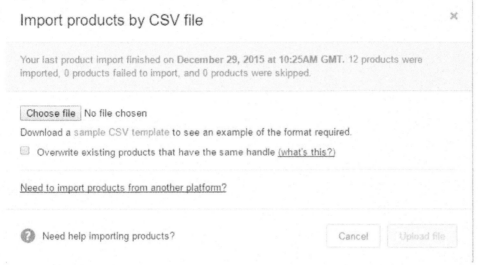

Select the 'Choose file' button and then pick the Product List.csv file that we just created from your hard disk, then press the 'Upload file' button.

NOTE - This will load the file into Shopify but it will NOT import the products into your store, you should see this pop up

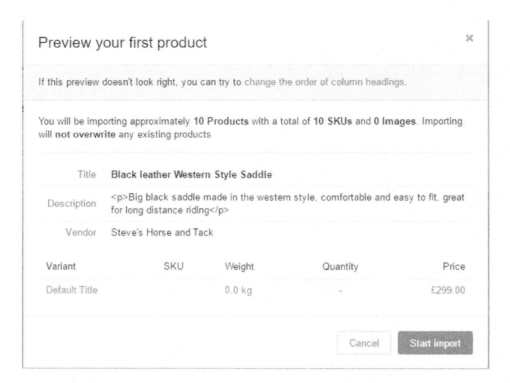

Click on the blue link 'change the order of column headings' and you will see a sheet where you can match the fields in your sheet to the fields in the Shopify product records

The first three columns should have been mapped automatically, but you need to select the correct fields to map the last three to the correct fields, scroll the window as far to the right as you can

Then select from the drop down menus at the top of the three columns that are set to 'Ignore this column'

'SKU' for the 'Part Number' field
'Barcode' for the 'EAN Code' field
'Weight in grams' for the 'Weight (g) field

Then click the blue 'Next' button

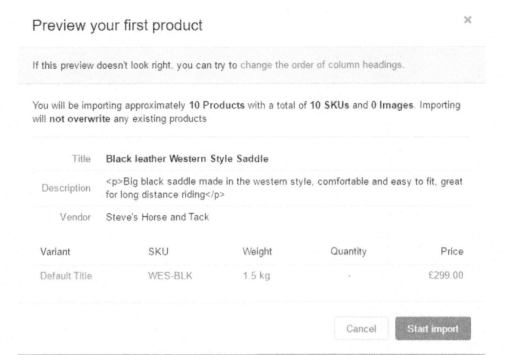

Check that the first test item looks correct and if it does press the blue 'Start import' button.

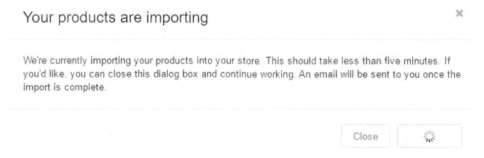

The products should then import and you will see them all on the Products > Products page

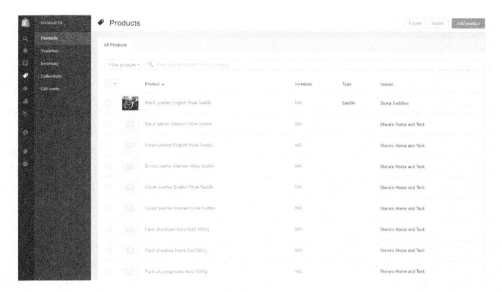

As you can see the item that we set up by hand has not been overwritten because we did not tell the importer to do so when we uploaded the file.

You will now need to edit each item in order to add the product images, to do that click on the name of the first product without an image to bring up the product editor and Add the images from your hard drive in the same way as we added the image on the product that we set up manually.

If you want to you can add the product types at the same time - alternatively you could upload them in the spreadsheet if you want to, you should be able to figure out how to do that for yourself now.

Once all the item images are added we will look at product variants and then you can move on to setting up collections.

Chapter 44
Product Variants

Shopify has a feature called 'Product variants' which allows you to display a single product page for a group of items that vary by color, size or other basic features. So for example you can use this feature to set up a single product page for a tee shirt with four colors and 3 different sizes which is actually 12 SKUs represented on one product page. Customers will be required to choose the color and size that they need when they add the product to their basket.

The problem with this system is that Google shopping will only list these items as one product rather than all 12 of the variants. Because of that I recommend that you only use this feature for items like clothing that vary in size, create different products for items in different colors so that people searching color specific items like 'Grey Tee Shirt' can find your products.

As an example in my Horse Tack store I will be offering jodhpurs (riding trousers), they come in three colors and 4 sizes. So I have set up 3 different products, one for each color and I will then create size variations for each one.

I have added the listings for the three new products to my product spreadsheet as shown below

11	Pack of mature Horse	169	This premium horse food is specialy formulated from the fin	MHF-100	123456798	100000
12	Cream Riding Jodhpurs	49	Cream riding trousers or jodhpurs, reinforced where they chafe dt	CRE-JOD	123456799	500
13	Black Riding Jodhpurs	49	Black riding trousers or jodhpurs, reinforced where they chafe dui	BLK-JOD	123456800	500
14	Green Riding Jodhpurs	49	Dark Green riding trousers or jodhpurs, reinforced where they cha	GRE-JOD	123456801	500
15						

And uploaded them to the web site and then selected the black version to complete the set up of that item.

First I added the picture, then scroll down to the bottom of the page

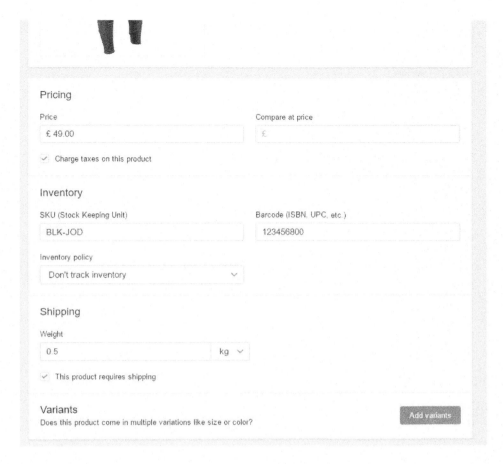

Press the blue 'Add variants' button and a new section will open up

Size is the default variation, I will leave that and then type into the 'Option value' box the list of sizes

When typing the variant names be careful to type exactly the names that you want your customers to see on the web site, I like to capitalize them as Small, Large,

Medium, X-Large. As I type the options change to green icons and below the list of variant parts is created.

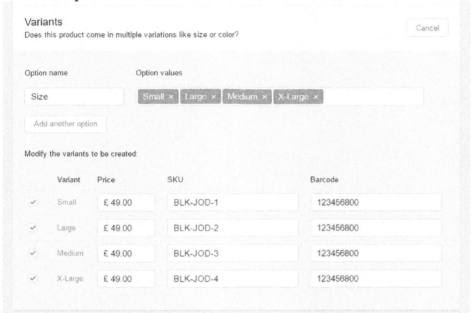

Here you can edit the SKUs and bar codes as well as the prices of the variants.

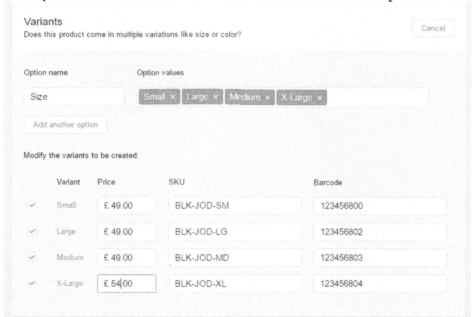

Then press the blue 'Save' button in the top right of the window.
Then you can click the 'View' button to see the product on the web site

You can see the drop down where customers can choose the size to buy - note that the first value that I entered is the default value on the product page, it's probably best to make this the most common choice.

Try setting up a multi variant product for your self, but remember that only the default item will appear in Google searches.

Chapter 45
Product Categories

Now that the products are set up on our web site we need to organize them into categories that make browsing the web site easier and list the categories on the menu at the top of the web site.

Shopify allows us to organize products into groups that it calls 'Collections'. Collections can be used as choices in the menu.

A product can be a member of any number of collections and you can set up as many collections as you like but as I suggested in the previous section I think that between five and seven main categories is the best number to have, any less than five is too few and any more than seven is hard to fit on the menu across the top of a web page.

You set up collections in the 'Products > Collections' menu and then you can manually allocate your products to collections or you can set up rules that automatically allocate products to collections based on rules that you define – this is very nice as it allows you to make sure that new items are allocated to the correct collections as they are set up in the future.

Before you start adding your own collections the 'Products > Collections' page looks like this

The one collection that is set up by default is called 'Home page' as you can probably guess that's the collection of items that appears on the home page of the web site - we will work with that later when we set up the theme for our site, but for now I want to set up new collections for my product categories so I press the blue 'Add collection' button

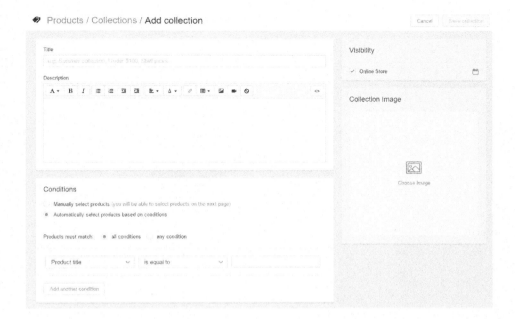

The first collection that I am going to set up in the example store is 'Saddles' and I am going to make it automatically populated with products that have the word 'Saddle' in their name. I will set the 'Title' of this collection to 'Saddles', add a short description of the products that will appear in this collection and choose a representative product image. The product Image will be used to represent this collection if I choose to add it to the home page.

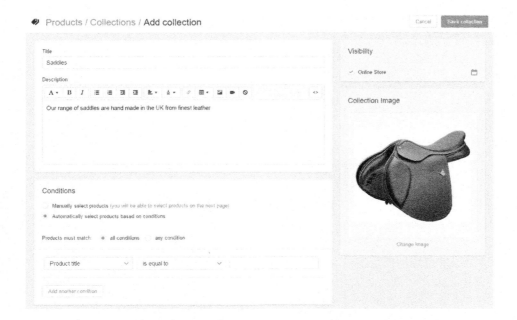

Now I need to set the conditions that will add a product to this category, I want any item that contains the words 'english saddle' or 'western saddle' in it's title to be automatically added to this collection so I make set the conditions up as below.

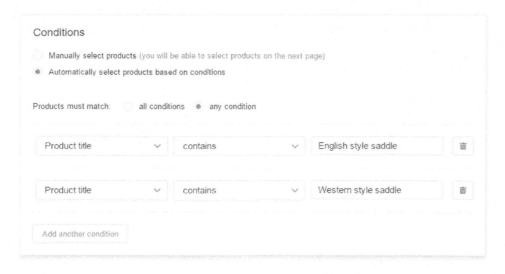

This will stop other items that may have 'Saddle' in the name being added by mistake. Once the details are set up I will press the blue 'Save collection' button on the top right of the screen and the items that match the required conditions will be added to the list under the conditions along with a drop down to choose how they will be sorted on the web site when the collection is displayed - I recommend that you set the sort method to 'By best selling'.

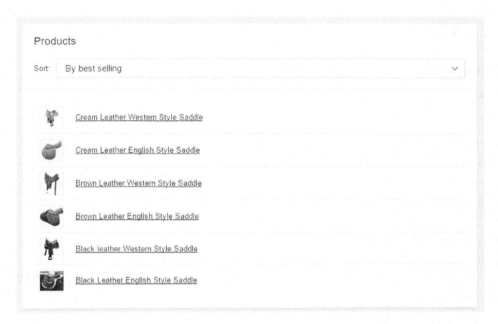

Finally - press the blue 'Save' button to save the collection and then go on to set up the rest of the collections that you need for your store, these are mine for the example store

Chapter 46
Choosing a Theme

Making your store look awesome with a Theme
The next step in the set up of your shop is to choose the theme for your Shopify store.

The Theme for your store defines the layout and design of the different pages that make up your site, the way that your store looks to customers is defined mainly by the theme, it can be modified a bit, and of course the images that you use have a huge impact but the theme sets the layout of the store.

Shopify has set your store up with a basic, default theme but of course you can change that if you want to for a more complex and detailed Theme. Some themes are free, but the best themes must be purchased for between $100 (£60) and $300 (£200).

To see the available Themes in your Shopify store admin system go to 'On-line Store > Themes'

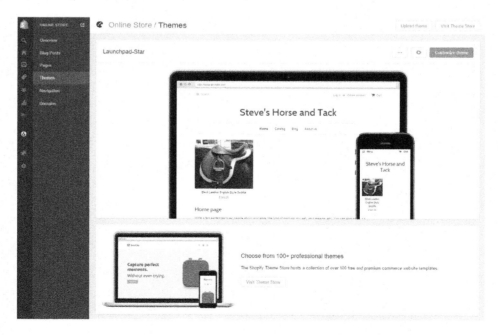

As you can see my example store is using a theme called 'Launchpad-Star' at the moment, this is a very basic theme so I will look for something else to make it a bit more interesting to look at.

To do this I click on one of the 'Visit Theme Store' buttons, to open up the Shopify Theme store in another tab of my browser.

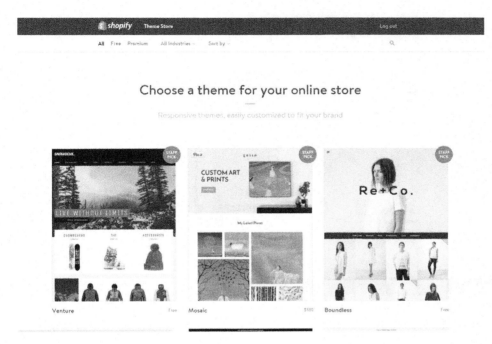

As you can see above there are a mix of free and chargeable themes, with lots of different features, you can filter to just see the free ones or the premium price ones or filter to just see themes that have been designed to work for particular types of shop.

Find a Theme that you like the look of and then click on it to see more details.

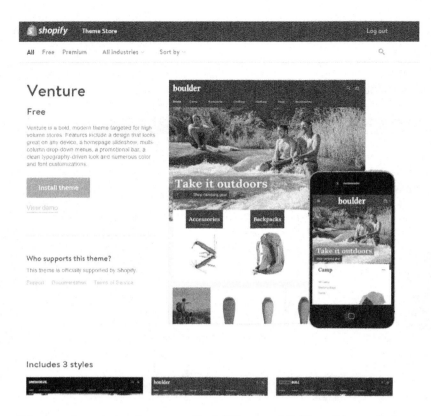

I have chosen a theme called 'Venture' I like this as it has a big header image and nice clean structure, it's also free !

So I click the green 'Install theme' button on the theme page.

This will copy the theme over, but it will not automatically publish it on my store, you can choose to have several themes installed at any one time - but you can only have one that is 'published' and active on your store.

Once the theme is downloaded Shopify gives me the choice to publish the theme or not with this message

I will choose to Publish this theme so I click the green 'Publish as my shop's theme' button

Shopify will take a few minutes to install the theme then show this message

Click on the big green 'Go to your Theme Manager' button to go back to the online Store > Themes page of your store admin system.

The store will now have been modified around the new theme, it will need modifying with banners and content to make it look good, but before I start doing that I want to look at how the store looks now so I click on the 'View store icon' that is the small box with an arrow pointing up and to the right next to the Shopify logo in the top left hand corner of the window.

This will open up a new tab with the store in it.

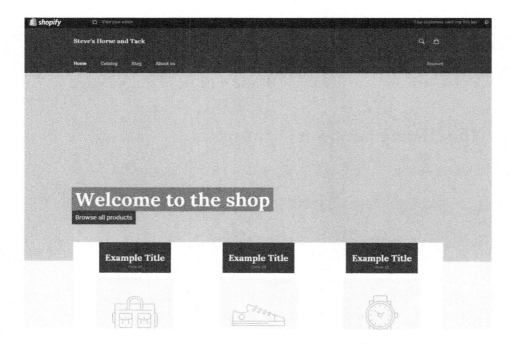

It looks pretty bland for now, but we can fix that.

Chapter 47
Modifying the Theme

Making your site look good is one of the really fun parts of setting up your store, to get started on it go to on-line Store > Themes and click on the blue 'Customize theme' button in the top right hand corner of the screen.

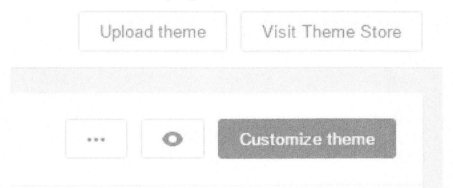

This will take you to the theme editor page where we will do most of the work to customize the site.

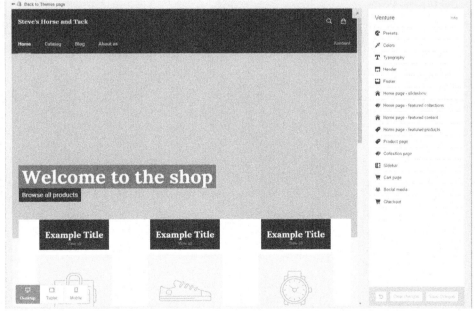

The theme editor has a menu down the right hand side of the screen that you can use to change most aspects of the look of your new store.

Each different theme will have a different set of options, many of the options are similar and they work in a similar way so I will go through each menu choice explaining how I plan to use it to set up the example store and why, this should help you understand enough to be able to make changes to the theme for your own store.

Chapter 48
Color and Text settings

The top three items in the menu (Presets, Colors & Typography) affect the whole site, they are used to control the color scheme of the site and the fonts used for text across the site.

The Colors menu is split into sections which correspond to sections of the website.

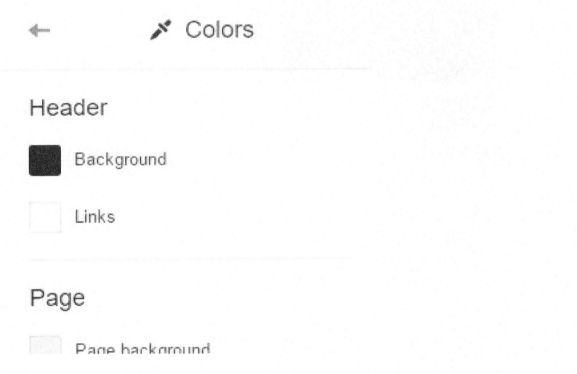

For example the top two items in the choice above set the background color for the header bar and the color for the links in the header.

I'm going to change the background color for the header from black to a dark blue, to do that I click on the color box next to the word 'Background' under 'Header', this brings up a color picker box.

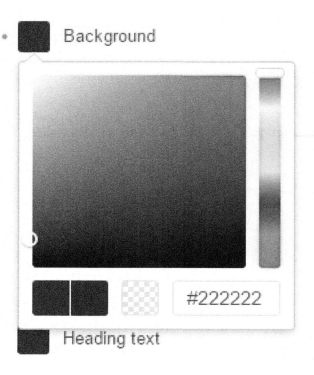

These boxes are used for every color selection in the theme settings, they are quite complex and can be used in a number of different ways.

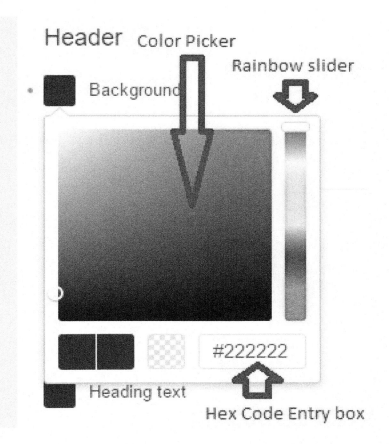

To the right of the window is the rainbow slider, by moving the selector along the slider you can change the available colors in the square color picker window and then by selecting a spot in the color picker box you select that exact color to be used on the site. Try it, it's very interesting, as you make the selection you will see the site image in the main window update in line with the color that you have selected.

But remember that you need to press he blue 'Save changes' button in order to make the update permanent.

You can also enter the hex code for the color that you want to use directly into the box at the bottom right if you prefer. There are lots of web sites that provide selections of colors that you might want to use with the corresponding hex codes, a great example is http://www.color-hex.com/, I used that site to find my blue, it is #00628b so I will paste that number into the hex code entry box and then I see the header background color update.

In this theme the background to the subheading text box that says 'Browse all products' also uses the header background color so that changes too.

I'm going to make a few other changes - here is my list of you want to follow me

Changing the page background to #f3f3f3 - that's a slightly darker grey that I prefer
Changing the Buttons, links and promotions bar, text background and links from the standard red to a vibrant blue #0000ff - I much prefer blue !
Changing the footer background to #00628b to match the header

Now the page looks like this

The Typography menu allows you to change the fonts used by the different parts of the site and to change the text size

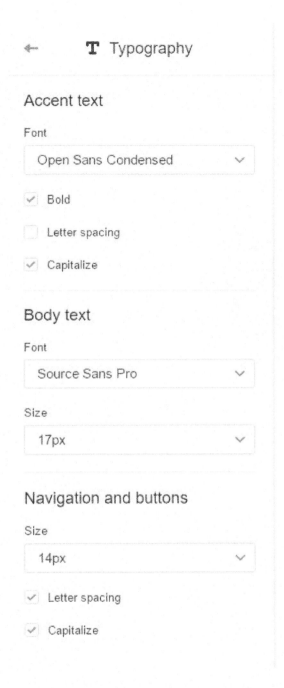

I want the Navigation menu at the top of the page to use bigger text so I am going to increase the size to 17px.

I like the fonts used by default in this theme so I will leave them as they are and

Save my change - the sample site will then update.

Now I am going to use the 'Presets' menu choice at the top of the menu - this allows me to save the choices that I made in the Typography menu and the colors menu as a pre-set group that I can come back to if I want to.

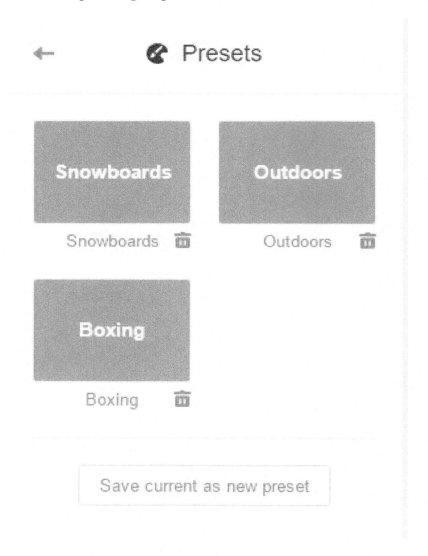

I simply press the 'Save current as new preset' button and give this setup a name

# Presets

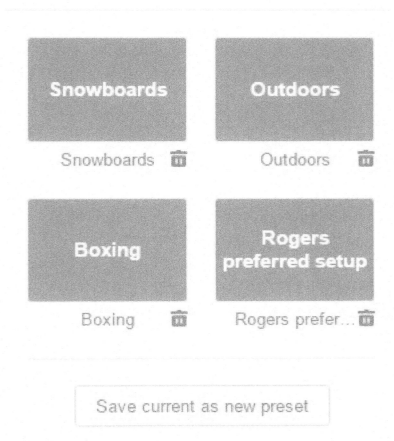

The 'saved preset' includes all 'tick box' options, font and color items on the following menus

Colors, Typography, Header, Product page, Collection page, Cart page, Checkout.

Chapter 49
Header and Logo

The header menu allows you to edit aspects of the header of the web page - that's the stripe across the top of every page

Get a logo for your store
The most important item in the header is the logo. Designing a new logo is one of

the really fun parts of setting up your store, there are lots of ways to go about it. You can try designing one yourself if you are comfortable using a graphics package like Corel Draw. If you prefer a DIY approach but you don't have the skills to do it from scratch, Designmantic is a great on-line service - http://www.designmantic.com/ you can use it to create a logo for free and then download a high res version for about $US50 (£35), it takes just a few minutes.

Alternatively you could use one of the logo design crowd sourcing sites like 99 designs http://99designs.co.uk/logo-design where a good logo in different sizes and formats can be designed for you by professional designers in a day or so for the same price.

A good logo for use in an on-line retail store should be about 4 times longer than it is tall as that works well at the top of a web page as part of the header bar. The best format to use is a '.jpg' If you make the high res version about 2,000 pixels long by 500 pixels tall that will work for print as well, the version to be used on the web can be scaled down to 400 x 100.

Here is one that I set up using Designmantic for the example store.

You will also need a favicon
A Favicon is the small logo that appears on the tab of a web browser page next to your name, like the ones from GoDaddy and MailChimp below

A Favicon is a square logo of 64 x 64 pixels which is not a lot of space to do anything complex, but as you can see from the two above you can make it quite nice all the same.

It's very easy to cut a square piece of your logo out to become a favicon using windows paint or similar, this is how I did it.

First open your full size logo in paint.

Then use the 'select' tool to select the portion that you want to use for the favicon.

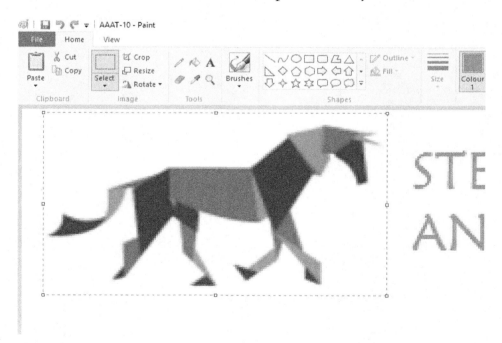

Don't worry that the part selected is not square, just select 'crop' to trim it down.

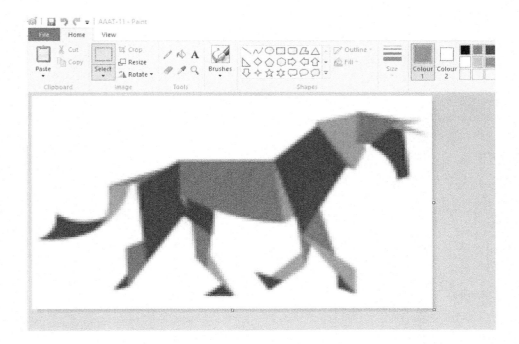

Then select 'Resize'

Un-tick the 'Maintain aspect ratio' box and then switch to define size by number of 'Pixels' rather than 'Percentage' of current size.

Set the size to 64 pixels horizontal and 64 pixels vertical. (Shopify says it should be 32 x 32 - but ignore that, 64 x 64 works better…).

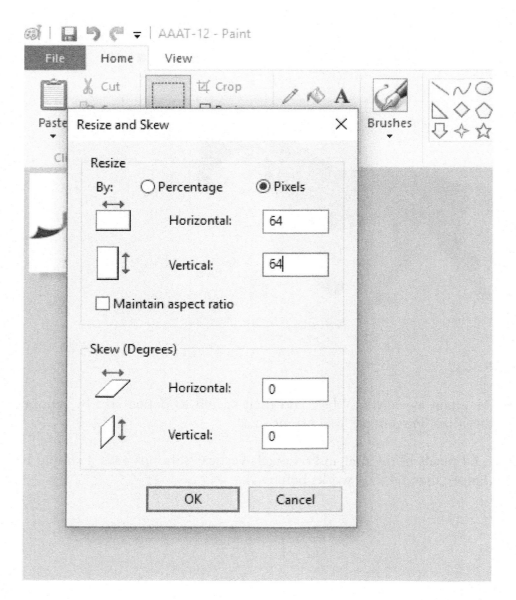

Then save the resulting image as 'favicon.png'

The aspect ratio has changed because we have forced the rectangular image into a square, but I think that it is eye catching and will look good on peoples browser tabs. You can always hit the 'Undo' key to go back and re-select a different part of the logo if you are not happy with your first attempt.

Uploading the logo and Favicon to your Store
To upload the logo and favicon go to the Header section of the Theme editor and then simply tick the 'Use custom logo' box, select the 'Choose file' button and select the logo file from your hard drive. My new logo is not a work of art - but it serves a purpose for now. (And when was the last time you bought something because you liked the store logo?)

Next I add my Favicon in the same way.

You can also set up a Promotion bar - I'm going to use this to try to get sign ups for my newsletter, so I add the text 'Sign up for our newsletter to get great deals' and then tick the 'Enable' box to turn the bar on.
Don't forget to hit 'Save changes'

Now my store header looks like this

Right now there is no link from the promotions bar - but we will add the link later after we have signed up for the MailChimp email marketing service.

Chapter 50
Organizing the Footer

The footer is the section of the web site at the very bottom of the page, as the name suggests.

Click on the 'Footer' menu choice in the 'Customize Theme' menu and scroll the preview so that you can see the footer of the preview alongside the menu.

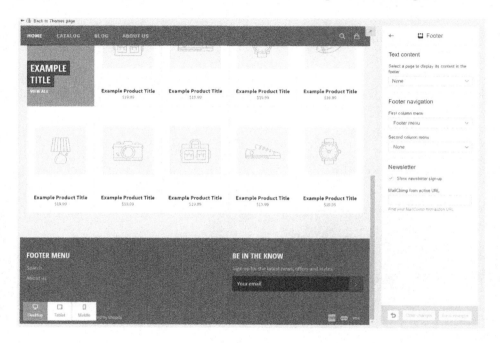

In this theme the footer is split into four sections, the first is a text space which we can define using a Shopify content 'Page', the next two are menus which we define using Shopify menus and the last part is the newsletter sign up box.

I want to have some contact details at the bottom of the homepage and then just one menu and the newsletter sign up box, so I need to set up a Shopify content 'Page' with our contact details.

To do that I open up a new tab in the admin pages of my store (you can do that in chrome by right clicking on your current tab header and then selecting 'Duplicate' from the drop down)

In the new window navigate to 'On-line Store > Pages'

Click the blue 'Add page' button

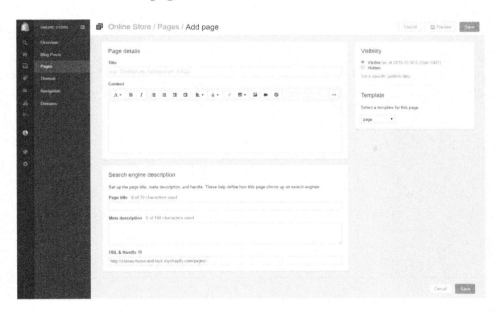

I'm going to make the title 'Contact Details' and then fill out the info that I want to show in the 'Content' section then I will press the blue 'Save' button to see the page below.

Don't worry about filling out the meta data for this page.

Now we can switch back to the original tab where we were editing the footer, click on the drop down under "Text content" and now the 'Contact Details' page that we just set up is available to select

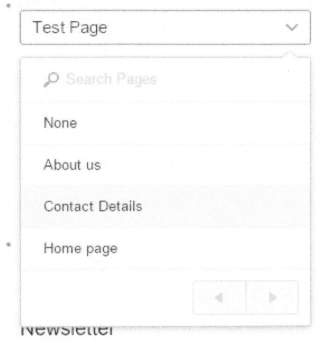

We select the Contact details page and see that in the preview window the text is now shown as a part of the footer.

I want to add another item to the Footer menu to point back to the home page and to change the text form 'FOOTER MENU' to 'LINKS' to do that I need to go back to the extra tab that we opened up earlier and navigate to on-line Store > Navigation, that's where we can set up and edit menus.

To edit the Footer menu we click on the blue link 'Edit menu' next to the title Footer menu

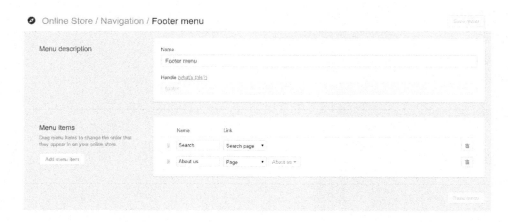

I want to change the title to Links, so I replace the text in the 'Name' box, I also want to add a new menu item so I press the 'Add menu item' button and then edit the new line that appears so that the name of that new link is Home and it links to the Home page, then press the blue 'Save menu' button

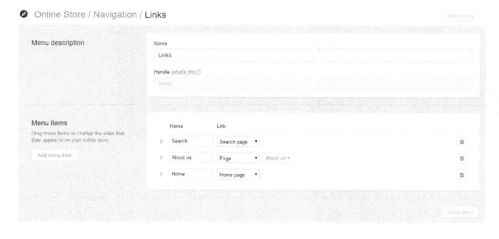

Now I want to move the Home link up to the top of the list, I can do that by

clicking on the small icon made up of eight dots to the left of the Name 'Home' I hold down the left mouse button and then I can drag the 'Home' menu item to the top of the list.

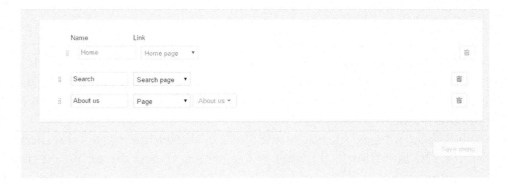

Let go of the mouse button and then click the blue 'Save menu' button and go back to the other window where we are editing the footer.
Refresh that window and you will see that the footer has been updated and looks a lot nicer

While we are here - just take a look at the three icons in the bottom left of the preview screen - they allow you to see what the site will look like on tablets and mobile phone screens as well as on a desktop PC.

We will add the link for the newsletter sign-up later after we have signed up for the MailChimp email marketing service so for now we are done with the footer.

Chapter 51
The Slideshow

The homepage 'Slideshow' is a series of large, high resolution adverts that appear at the top of your home page, in the theme that I have chosen there can be up to five different slide show photos. Each image is automatically overlaid with a message made up of a Heading and a Subheading that you can change really easily, and each banner can be linked to one of your products, categories or other pages so they make great adverts.

You set up the slideshow images, messages and links in the 'Home page - sideshow' menu choice of the On-line store > Themes > Customize theme menu. When you select that, you see this menu

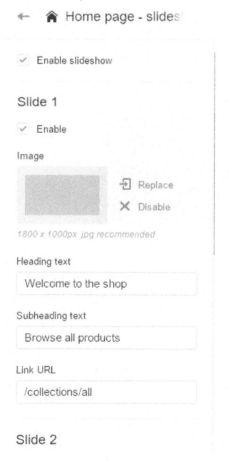

The tick box at the top allows you to turn off the slideshow altogether if you

prefer to do without it, simply un-tick the box and the slideshow will not be used at all. This does have some advantages as it pulls all of the featured products up the page to show on the main page, it also makes the page load faster which can be important to customers on slow connections and to SEO, but lots of people prefer to use the slideshow as it can make your web page look much more professional and up to date.

I recommend that you conduct some basic testing to find out if a slideshow helps your store, try running the store with a slideshow for a week or two and without for a week or two and see if there is any difference in your store performance as a result. Changing things up in this way can also help make your store more interesting to customers so even if you stick with the slideshow I recommend that you change the images every week or two in order to keep the site changing.

The best pictures to use for the banners are your own unique and original product shots, pictures of your products in use work really well as do detail shots showing special features of your items.

As you can see in the image above Shopify recommends that your images have a particular size, in this case it's 1800 pixels wide by 1000 pixels tall - try to get your images to this size - but don't panic if you can't get it exact, Shopify will cope with images that are a bit out and adjust them to fit - but they may not look so good. Don't upload really big images as they will slow your site's load time down to an unacceptable degree and of course low res images look awful.

If you can't get photos of your own then you can use stock images, there are quite a few sites that offer high res images for free, try https://unsplash.com/ and http://gratisography.com/ or just search for 'free images'. Try to make sure that the images that you use are free of copyright - it can cost a lot if you use a copyright image without permission.

If you can use Photoshop, Gimp or a similar graphics package then you can manipulate the images to the correct resolution using that, if not you can use paint which is free with windows.

Open the image in paint then use the Select > Rectangular selection function to highlight an area that is about the correct size (the size of the selected area is shown on the bottom bar in paint, see below)

You only need to get the image close to the required size, then you can use the 'Resize' function to make it exact.

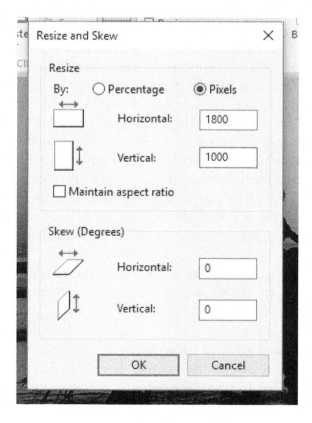

Un-check the 'Maintain aspect ratio' box and select resize by 'Pixels' then you can set the image to exactly the correct size, it will be changed a little by the process, but as long as you got the selection close to the required size or a multiple of the required size (like 3600 x 2000) to start with then the distortion should not be noticeable. Experiment with how much you can change the size of an image - you will be surprised how much you can change it without making it look too bad.

You can then 'Save As' to create a new image file that is separate from the original. Use the '.jpg' format for slideshow images

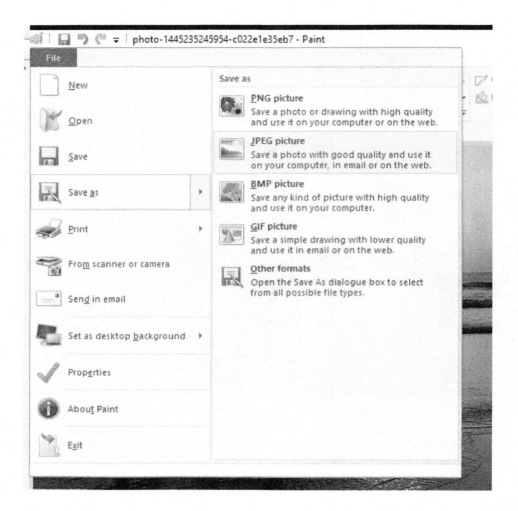

To upload your images as banners and set the Heading text you need to go back to the browser tab that is pointing at the 'Home page - sideshow' menu choice of the Shopify Admin pages on-line store > Themes > Customize theme.

Make sure that the slideshow is enabled and that slide 1 is also enabled, then click the 'Choose file' button or the 'Replace' link for Slide 1 and choose the banner image that you created and saved to your hard drive.

The image should load automatically and show in the preview pane - nice - right?

Now add a link from your new slideshow link to a collection page or a product page.

To get the right link you can simply open up your store in a new browser tab, find the page that you want and then select the URL for that page from the bar at the top of your browser and right click with your mouse to copy it.

then go back to the store admin page and right click on the 'link' box to paste it into the link box in your store admin.

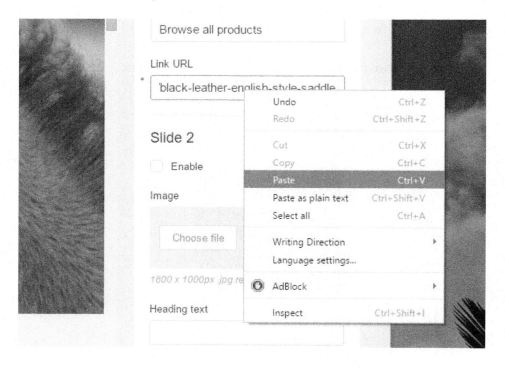

Then change the 'Heading text' and the 'Subheading text' to a more appropriate message

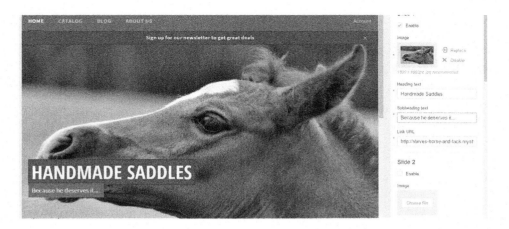

And don't forget to click the blue 'Save changes' button

Add 2 or three more slides, make sure that you enable them after setting them up or they will not show on the site.

The right images can really make your site look amazing - try a few different ones.

Chapter 52
Featured collections, content and products

The next three menu choices that we need to understand are the featured collections, content and products on the home page.

These three menu choices each control a section of the home page which can be turned on and populated or turned off through the menu, this gives you a lot of options to make your home page different and to change it from time to time.

The image below shows the site home page with all of these sections turned on and labeled.

Slideshow

Featured Collections

Featured Content

Featured Products

Footer

The featured content section displays the content of a specific page that you can set up in 'on-line Store > Pages'. The content can be text, images or video or a mix of all three, in the example I have just used a simple text message with an image.

The images used to represent each collection are the ones that you set up in Products > Collections and they can of course be edited in there as well, they are used for the Featured Collections page and for the image to the left of the product in the Featured Products section on the home page.

If you activate the Slideshow, Featured Collections, Featured Content, and Featured Products the page becomes very long and a bit jumbled - I recommend that you only activate 2 of the four sections at any one time, I like to have products shown directly on the front page so I am going to set up the example store with just the Slideshow and the Featured Products active.

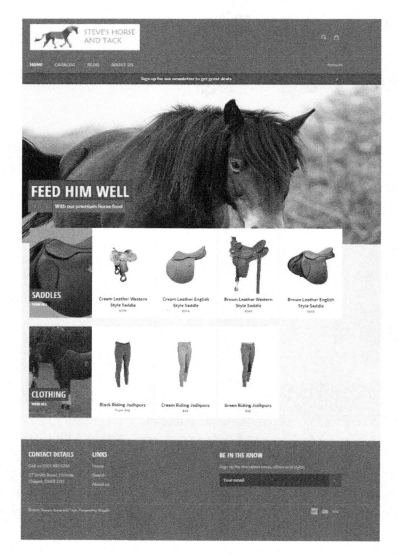

If you are following this through on the setup of your own store at this point I suggest that you try turning the sections of your home page on and off to see how it looks, try all the different options and change the images on your products and collections to get the 'look' that you like best.

Chapter 53
Product, Collection and Cart Options

There are a number of simple options that you can change in the menus for the Product page, Collection page and Cart page.

Product Page
The only option on the Product Page is to decide if the stock level will be shown on items with less than 10 items in stock. This can help sales in some circumstances, but as I have chosen not to track stock in my example store it is not relevant to Steve's Horse and Tack.

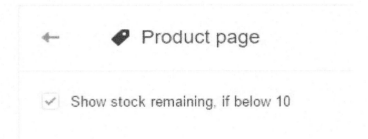

Collection page
The collection page is the page that you see when you click on a collection in a menu or when the 'Featured Collections' section is enabled on the web site home page, the example 'Saddles' collection page looks like this

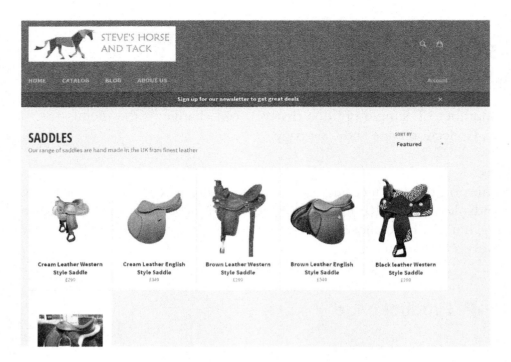

The options for the Collection page are

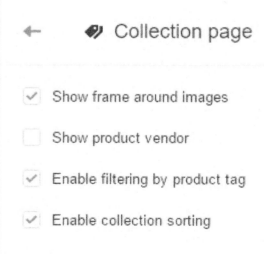

You can switch the preview pane in the editor to the collections page by clicking on one of the collection images in the Featured Collections section or in the Featured Products section, then you will see the effects of each of these options by turning them on and off.

I like to turn off frames around images but leave filtering by tag and collection sorting on. If you only have a few products in each category then you may prefer to turn sorting off.

Sidebar
Leave the sidebar turned off, it just looks awful, especially on mobile browsers.

Cart Page
There are two options that you can change on the cart page

They are very simple, but very important because they change the way that orders are placed on your site.

If you leave 'Enable order notes' ticked then this allows customers placing an order to pass you a message with the order - the upside of this is that is allows customer communication which is always helpful, but the downside is that customers tend to use this kind of opportunity to make requests that you may not be able to comply with, which can create customer service issues. I recommend that if you are selling small, low cost items then you turn this feature off, but if you are selling larger items with a higher average selling price you should leave it on to offer a higher standard of personalized service to your customers.

The second option is quite key - if you leave it ticked then when a customer adds an item to his or her cart the site will give a message telling them that it has been done, but the page will otherwise stay unchanged, the result can be that customers don't notice that the item has been added and try again, or worse abandon the cart and go elsewhere thinking that the site is broken. I recommend that you un-check this box so that when a customer adds an item to their cart the page changes to show the shopping cart page. The only exception to this would be if you expect customers to normally add a lot of separate products to their basket - but that is quite rare.

Don't forget to press the blue 'Save changes' button if you have made any changes.

Chapter 54
Integrating Social Media with your store

The Social media menu choice on the on-line Store > Themes > 'Customize theme' menu is where you enter the details for your social media accounts so that they can be integrated with your store, the menu is split into two sections, at the top there are a number of boxes where you can enter the URLs for your company pages on a number of different social media sites such as Facebook, twitter, Google plus and so on.

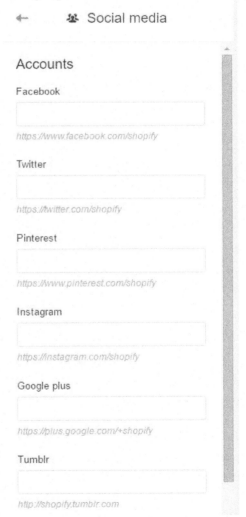

If you add a link to any of these boxes the logo of the network will be added to the footer of your web site, the logo will be linked to your page on the social media network.

You should link your store to your company page only - don't use personal pages for any of these.

Below these boxes you will find a number of 'tick boxes'

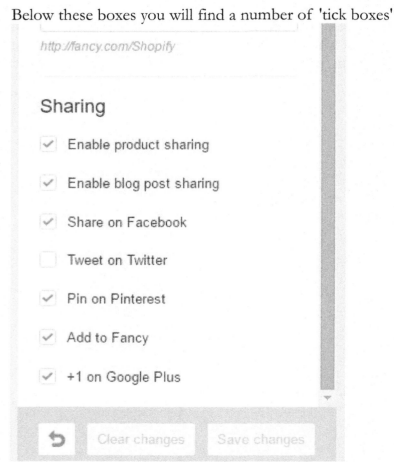

If you navigate the preview pane to a product page you will see the effect of removing the ticks on some of these integrations on the 'share' icons that are shown under the product description.

These settings are completely separate from the social media links above. They do not require any integration as they use the customers social media account so you can have Facebook sharing active without having a Facebook link set up for your store.

Note that trying to share in the preview pane does not work - you need to check this feature on the live site.

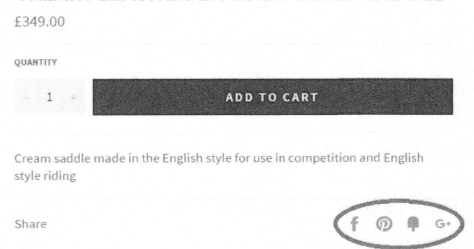

I recommend that you only have integrations with networks that you check regularly and understand, if you have to choose I recommend Facebook and Pintrest with Google+ if you want an extra option. So that is what I am setting up on the example store.

Chapter 55
Checkout Page options

The Venture theme has a lot of options that you can change on the checkout page - that's probably for the best as the checkout page is by far the most important page on your store because it's where the transactions happen.

Before starting to make any changes to the checkout page options you should navigate the preview pane to the checkout page so that you can see the effect of any changes that you make. To do that click on any item and add it to your cart and then click on the shopping bag icon in the top right hand corner of the screen to go to the cart page and once there press the 'CHECK OUT' button.

The screen should look something like this

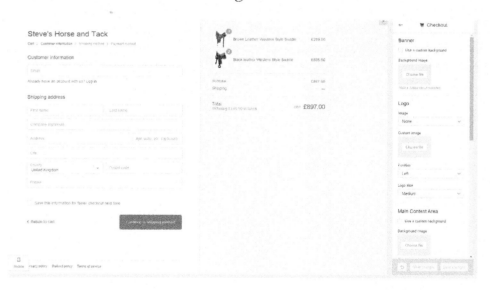

By default I find that really boring!

To improve the look of the checkout page do the following

Firstly add a custom background image, just like the banner images it helps if this is one of your own images of a product or a product in use, I found a nice image of a horse to use on a free image site. This process works just like adding a slideshow image but the image is thinner as it goes across the top of the screen.

Next you can add a special logo image or use the one from your store, I think it's better to use the one from the store for consistency - any changes at this stage could put customers off, select 'Storefront' from the dropdown under Logo, Image rather than using a custom image for the checkout.

Similarly I'd keep the logo on the left as that is where it appears on the main store, but I'd like to make it larger than standard so I will pick 'Large' from the Logo size dropdown.

The page is looking a lot nicer now

The next two sections allow you to set up background images for the Main

Page 233

Content Area and the Order summary area, these can look OK if they are well thought out, but I like the checkout page to be clean and uncluttered so I recommend that you do not use these options and I will not.

The last section lets you change the fonts and colors used on the checkout page.

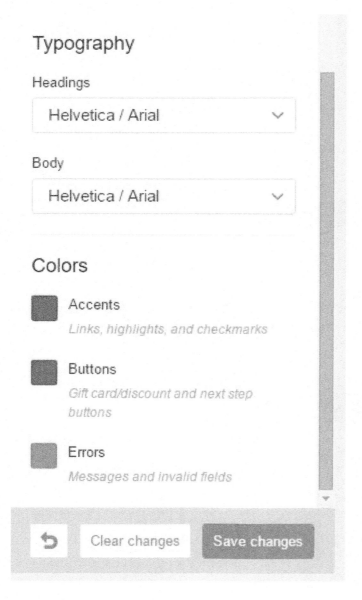

The default colors for Accents and Buttons are reds - which I find quite off putting, I think checkout pages should always use blue as it's a much more soothing and 'trust inducing' color, (I used hex code #2343d8) but the default fonts are OK and I will leave the Errors in the default orange color.

Colors are changed here in just the same way as the colors in the top menu option, refer to the Chapter on Color and Text settings for more details. Once they are done you can see the finished checkout page.

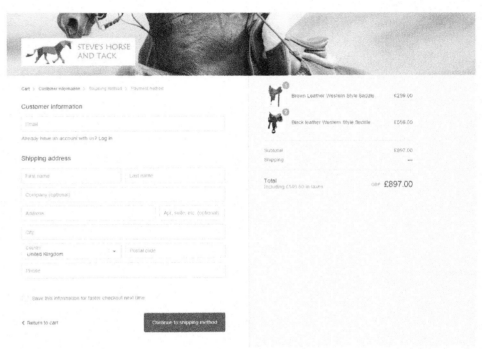

Nice isn't it? - The checkout page is really important so it's worth checking out how it looks on tablet and phone as well to be sure it's OK

Remember these icons in the bottom left of the preview screen?

They let us see how the checkout will look on other devices

On tablet

🛒 Show order summary ⌄   £897.00

Customer information

[Email]

Already have an account with us? Log in

Shipping address

[First name] [Last name]

[Company (optional)]

[Address] [Apt, suite, etc. (optiona]

[City]

[Country: United Kingdom ⌄] [Postal code]

[Phone]

☐ Save this information for faster checkout next time

‹ Return to cart   [Continue to shipping method]

Privacy policy   Refund policy   Terms of service

And mobile

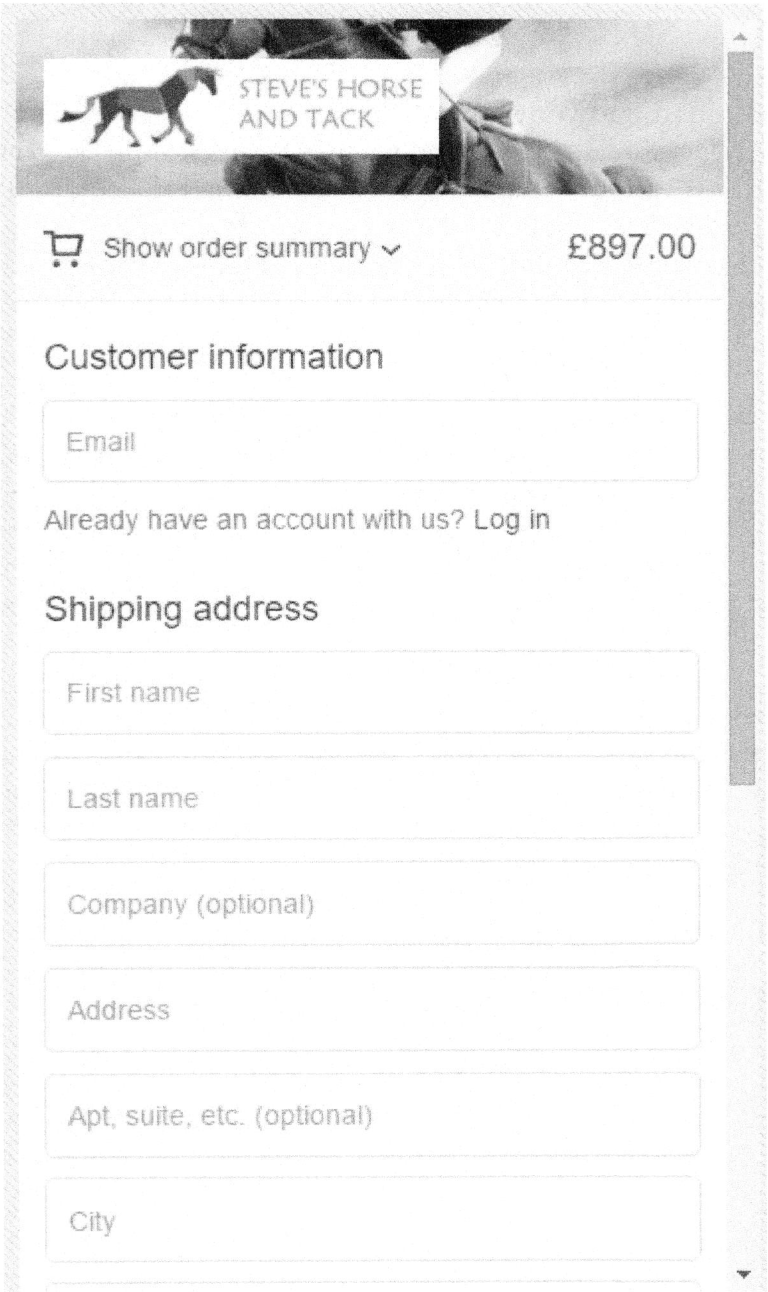

Thats all good…

Chapter 56
Domain Name

How to point your domain name at your Shopify store
As well as it's 'people friendly' domain name like 'www.steveshorseandtack.co.uk' your store will also have a 'Computer friendly' Internet address called it's IP address. An IP address looks like '192.168.201.64'
The Domain Name Service often referred to by the acronym DNS is a system that works like a directory, matching domain names to IP addresses so that web browsers looking for your web site can find the server that hosts the pages.

Your Domain Name Service is used to point both web traffic and email to the correct places, if you have followed the instructions in this book closely then your DNS is provided by GoDaddy as part of the domain registration. We set the DNS up to point your e-mail at the Google servers when we set up your Google account, now we need to tell the DNS to point your web URL to the Shopify servers, we also need to let the Shopify servers know what URL they should expect traffic from.

DNS for the web URL that we set up is controlled from GoDaddy, but before we change the DNS settings there we need to let Shopify know what the URL for our store will be, to do that we go to on-line Store > Domains in the Shopify admin section.

Then click the 'Add existing domain' button in the top right hand corner of the page to bring up a pop up window where you can enter your domain name

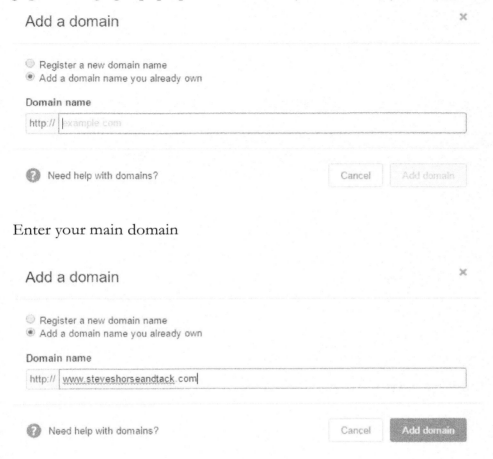

Enter your main domain

And then press the blue 'Add domain' button to bring up a pop up window telling you to set your CNAME for the url, the pop up has a 'Done' button, click that to dismiss the pop up and then open a new tab to login to your GoDaddy account.

Log in to your GoDaddy account.

Click on your login name in the top right o the screen and then select 'Manage My Domains' from the menu

Click on your domain name to bring up the 'DOMAIN DETAILS' page

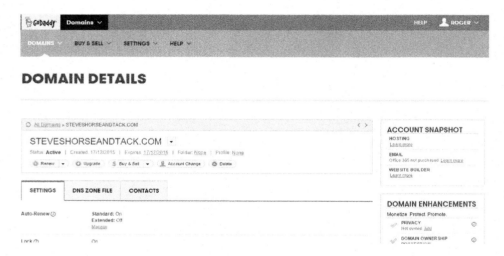

In the DOMAIN DETAILS section, click DNS ZONE FILE

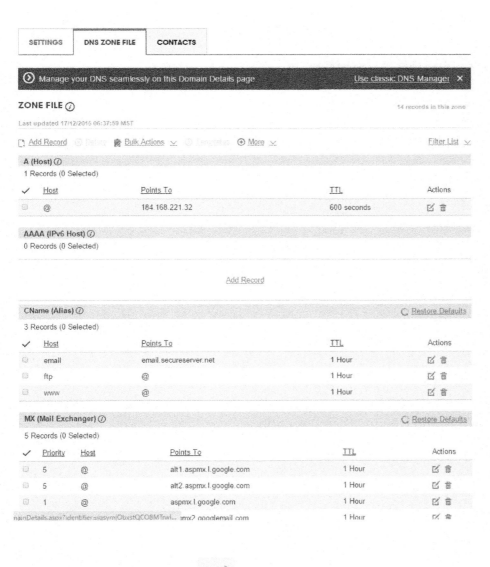

Click the Edit Record icon next to the '@' A (Host) record

A dialog window opens. Change the 'Points to: ' field to Shopify's IP address: 23.227.38.32

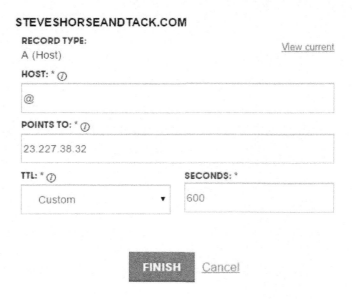

Click the green 'FINISH' button to go back to the 'DOMAIN DETAILS' page and scroll down to the CName (Alias) section.

Click the Edit Record icon on the line of the www host record, a dialog window will open. Change the Points to: field to point towards YourStoreName.myshopify.com (replace YourStoreName with your actual .myshopify.com store name - you made a note of it earlier when we set up the store in Setting up a Shopify Store). For my example store I have these settings.

Click the green 'FINISH' button to go back to the 'DOMAIN DETAILS' page and note the red bar at the top of the screen

Click 'Save Changes' in the action needed bar to complete the DNS set up and see the confirmation on the top right of the screen

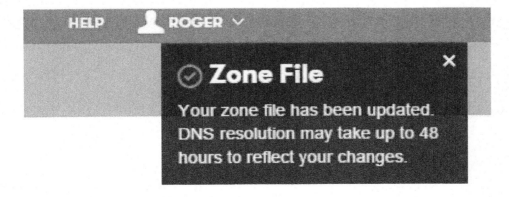

As the message says it can take a while for DNS to update, but you can check by simply pointing your web browser to your URL

Mine worked right away

If it takes more than 2 hours you probably made a mistake - re-check that the IP address and the name in the CNAME records are correct.

You can point extra domains over to your store by following the same process, but you can only have one 'master' domain, others will be re-directed to the master domain I will point the '.co.uk' domain that I bought to the '.com' domain in this way.

Then I will set the '.com' as the primary domain

In the on-line Store > Domains page of your admin system

Choose the 'Primary domain' drop down

And select the domain that you want to be the 'master domain', then select the 'Redirect all traffic to this domain' tick box

Then press the blue 'Save' Button and all traffic that comes to any other domain will be re-directed to the primary which helps with Google analytics etc.

Chapter 57
The Blog in Shopify

Your Shopify web store has a built in Blog that you can use to post updates and stories to your web site.

Blog entries can include text, video and images and they are visible to Google so they can be used to bring traffic to your web site through natural search or simply to post messages and updates to your regular customers.

Some themes have a space for a short excerpt from the latest blog post on the homepage or in the footer, all themes can include a link to blogs on any menu, and that is the normal way to link to them from your homepage or elsewhere on the web site. The difference between linking to a page and linking to a Blog is that the link to a page will always show the same information, while the link to a blog is dynamic - it will show the latest post in the blog and customers can click through to see all historic posts - which can be used to make a homepage change and look more dynamic as a result.

You can set up several different blogs if you like, so each member of staff could have their own blog feed, on the other hand if you don't want to use the Blog you can disable it or simply remove the link to it.

Many site owners make the mistake of writing long blog articles with lots of opinions, chat and humor but before you do that just think - does anyone care? And even if they do, will it help your store to sell?

The time that you would have to spend on a blog may be better spent on product descriptions, videos and photos which will have a more direct impact on sales. The best use of a blog is to simply provide news updates for your customers, let them know about store opening times, new product launches and last shipping dates before the holidays etc.

If you do keep the blog active then you should try to make sure that there is a new entry each month at the very least add it to your regular diary tasks.

Using the Shopify Blog
The Shopify blog is found in the on-line Store main menu, to see the menu go to

on-line Store > Blog posts

You can create as many blogs as you like in Shopify and each blog can have as many posts listed under it as you can write.

When you first look at the page you will see that there is a single blog set up called 'News' with a single post called 'First post'

If you do not plan to use the blog on your public site then you can just ignore this and not link to the blog from your main site, however if you plan to use the blog, then the first step is to change the default post to something more appropriate. To do that first click on the blog post name 'First post' shown in blue as a link. You will then go to the 'Edit Post' page where you can turn the default first post into your own first post.

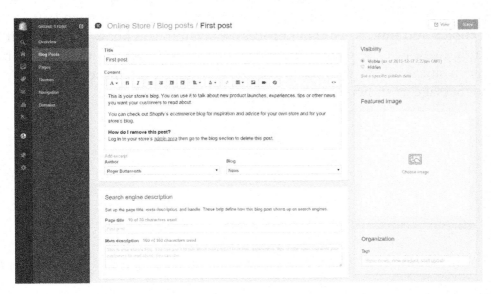

If you have set up some product pages you will see that the blog editor is very similar to the product page editor, it also shares some features with the product record editor - the Blog content section is exactly the same as the product description editor.

At the top of the page you will see the blog 'Title', currently set to 'First post', Try changing that to a title like 'Welcome to the new {your store name} store'

Under the Title you will find the main editor for the blog post, it is just like the editor on the product page and the one on the 'Pages' editor this is a really powerful tool that lets you set up blog posts with embedded links, pictures and videos included. It also gives you the option to enter HTML directly if you know how to do that you can switch the editor to 'HTML mode' by clicking the '<>' icon.

Setting up a blog post using HTML gives you a lot more flexibility on how the content is laid out, you can add tabs, complex tables and use extra fonts and effects - but it is a complex and time consuming process so even if you know how to do it I recommend that you just use the regular editor for blogs. If you do that for your first post you can simply delete the blog text in the content and replace it with your own welcome message as shown in the example from my store below.

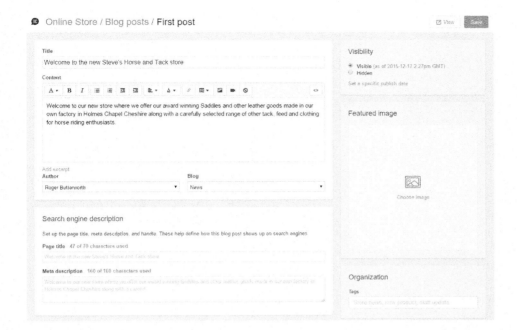

You can see above that the title that I have added and the first 160 characters of my new text in the 'Content' section is mirrored in the 'Search engine description' section - the text there will be used to set the keywords that will bring your blog post up in Google, if you want your blog post to be found easily on Google then you should change the text here to reflect the keywords that you think your customers will use to search.

You can also add a 'Featured image' to your blog - this is used as a icon for the blog in some (but not all) themes. You can add any image that you have on your hard drive by simply clicking on the 'Choose image' link. My finished blog post looks like this

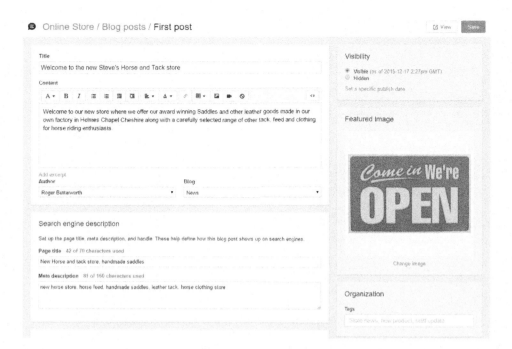

Before I Save the post there is one last thing to check, look at the 'Visibility' box in the top right hand corner of the page

The default post is set to Visible already here, but if you set up a new post from scratch it will be set to 'Hidden' until you switch it over to 'Visible' manually or set a specific publish date by clicking the link and set the date and time that you want the post to go live.

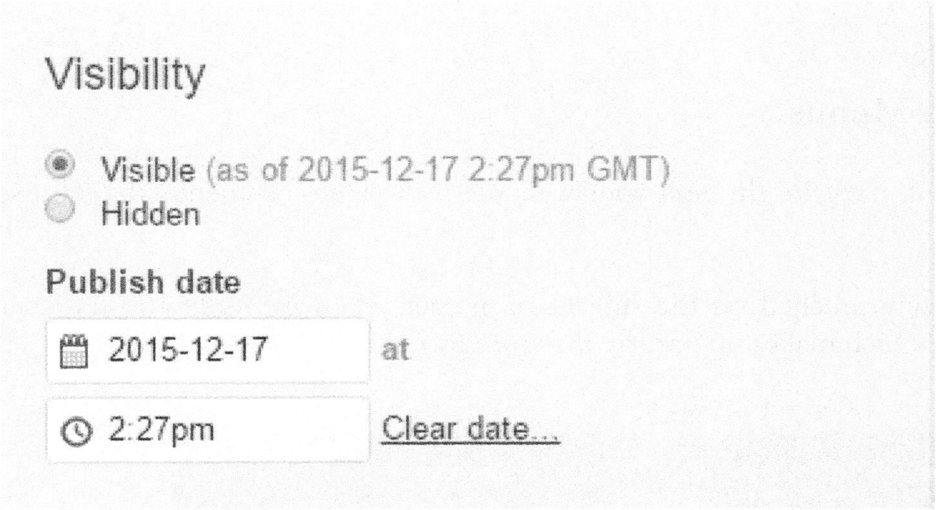

Visibility

○ Visible (as of 2015-12-17 2:27pm GMT)
○ Hidden

Publish date

📅 2015-12-17   at

🕐 2:27pm   Clear date...

This is really good for blog posts about product launches or special offers that you want to tie together with other activity to make a big splash and support an event.

You can now hit the blue 'Save' button to save your post, but there is one last part of the blog that I want to explain. At the bottom of the page you will see this box

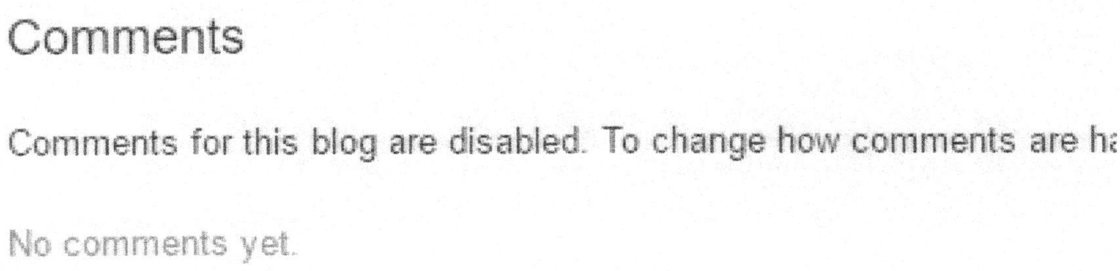

Comments

Comments for this blog are disabled. To change how comments are ha

No comments yet.

As I mentioned above you can have several blogs running each with it's own posts - you can have a 'comments' section for each blog where web site users can post comments about your blog entries. Unless you are going to monitor these every day I would recommend that you leave this feature turned off, the posts that you will get could be from anyone and as well as the good natured and helpful comments of customers you will also get comments that are negative, mischievous or even malicious.

Chapter 58
Setting up Menus

Customers will navigate through your web site using a set of menus that you set up.

We have already touched on the subject of menus when we looked at the small 'Links' menu which makes up part of the store footer

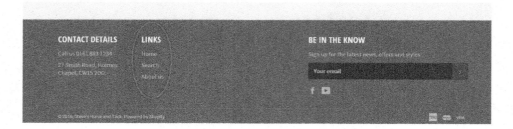

There is also a menu built into the header at the top of every web page

In most themes, including the one that I am using for the example store this is called the 'Main Menu', as you can see at the moment it is a bit sparse.

To edit menus you click on 'On-line Store > Navigation' from the main admin system menu.

When you click on those options from the main menus you will see a page like the one above for my example store where I have two menus set up, the 'Links' menu that I set up in the chapter on Organizing the Footer and the main menu which you can see in the picture above, it currently has 4 options 'Home', 'Catalog', 'Blog' and 'About us' which you can see in both illustrations.

I want to change the main menu to include category links for my main items and to remove the blog link which I will switch to the footer menu and call 'News', this is how I do that.

First I click on the 'Edit menu' link in the top right hand corner of the box where the 'Main menu' is shown

This is the page that you can use to edit the menu options and change where they take the user when he or she clicks on them.

The boxes under 'Name' in the 'Menu items' boxes define the text that is shown in the menu, you can simply edit them by clicking in the box and typing, be careful of typing menu choices that are too long, Shopify will try to make them fit but they

Page 253

may look ugly. The best menu names are less than 8 letters in total.

Next to each Name is a drop down menu which you can use to choose the type of link that the menu choice will activate.

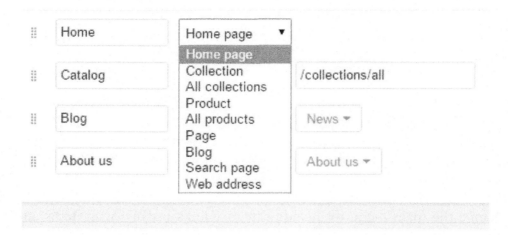

Depending on the choice that you make in this menu a third box may open up to allow you to complete the definition of the menu item, this gives you a lot of flexibility in where you point the menus, you can more or less point them to anything anywhere on your site of through the 'web address' choice anywhere else on the Internet

The choices and the best way to use them are are;

Home Page
This one is pretty obvious, it has no extra info required and it just points to the home page of your Shopify store

Collection
When you choose to point a menu item at a Collection you get an extra box with a drop-down menu where you can choose which one of your store collections to point the menu option to.
A collection is just a group of products that can be defined manually of automatically based on the products names or tags - You can set up collections in Products > Collections from the admin page - for more details see the chapter Product Categories

I will use this option to set up links to 'Saddles' 'Clothing' and 'Feed' on my example store.

All Collections

This option has no sub-choice required, it points the menu item to a page showing all of your product collections with a sample of the best sellers in each category. This is helpful if you have a lot of items in your store and want to show the range in a logical way. The 'Collection Image' is shown at the far left of each section as you can see in the example below.

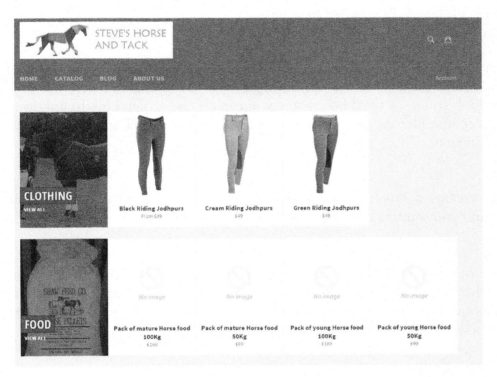

Product

As the name suggests, this option points your menu choice to a specific product, when you choose this you get a new box where you can choose the item that you want to link to.

All Products

This option has no sub-choice required, it points the menu item to a page showing all of your products in all of your collections.
This is quite helpful if you only have a few items in your store and want to just link to a page showing them all.

Page
This is another obvious one, it links the menu choice to one of your custom pages set up in the on-line Store > Pages section of your store admin. It produces a third box with a drop-down list of your current pages. See chapter 'Static Content Pages' for details on how to set up custom pages.
You can use this option to set up links to pages with any kind of static content for example the 'About us' page, competition pages, Terms & Conditions pages or pages with your physical store location details etc.

Blog
This option creates a link to one of your blogs (see the chapter 'The Blog in Shopify' for details on how to set up a blog) as you may imagine when you pick this type of Link you get a third box where you can choose which blog to link to.
Blog content is just like the content of a page, but it should change more often and be more current

Search page
This option creates a link to your search page, very useful if you have a big product set and you want to encourage users to search your site often.

Web address
This option opens up a new box where you can enter any web URL that you want to link to, either a part of your own site or any other site on the Internet. Linking to sites off your own web site is a good way to lose customers - so try not to do that unless you have to.

I'm going to change the main menu of my example store to;

Home, Saddles, Feed, Clothing, Categories, About Us
To make that work I'm going to start by deleting the two existing menu options that I do not need, to do that I simply select the rubbish bin icon next to the options that I don't need. Then to add the new options I press the 'Add menu item' button

This just adds a new menu choice to the list, when I have six choices set up the menu looks a bit dull.

I will change the names first

And then set up the links

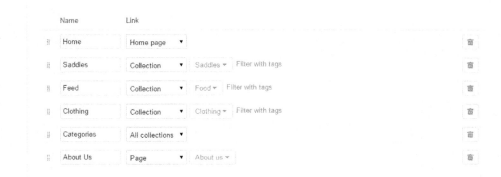

Before pressing the blue 'Save' button

And now you can see that the home page has updated.

If you are following these instructions through it's worth testing each menu item on your live site - just to be sure that they work the way that you expect, just click on each link in turn.

Chapter 59
Static Content Pages

Setting up extra Pages of static content

Every Shopify store needs a few pages of static content to provide things like an 'About Us' page, Terms and Conditions (Ts&Cs) page and a Contact Details page.

When I call these pages 'static content' I don't mean that the content can never change, just that you have to change it manually as opposed to the 'dynamic content' found on category pages that change as new items are added, removed or in line with the popularity of individual items.

Just like product description and blog entries static pages are easy to edit and can be created as simple text messages or they can include images and video, they can be created from scratch as HTML pages with complex content.

The static content pages that you set up in Shopify can be used as pages on their own or, in some themes, they can be used as part of the home page or as a part of category pages.

To edit pages you need to go to 'On-line Store > Pages' from the main admin system

Here you can see a list of the pages that have already been set up, some as part of the work I have already done on the web site and some as part of the default set up provided by Shopify.

As a minimum your site will need an about us page, a contact details page and a terms and conditions page, you might also want to set up a privacy policy page and a returns policy page in addition to the basic terms set up by Shopify as standard with the store. There are some samples that you can use on my web site - feel free to cut and paste from them as you see fit!

About Us page
The About us page is set up as a default part of the store, but it needs editing, to edit it you go to On-line Store > Pages from the main admin system and then click on the page name link 'About us' colored in blue, this will bring up the Page details.

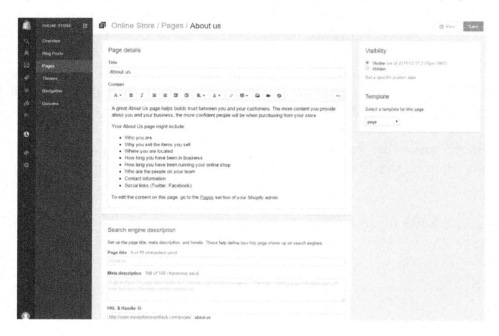

Shopify puts some suggestions in the Content window for this default page - I recommend that you work with them and create an About Us page that you like for your store.

Here is the one that I have set up for the example store.

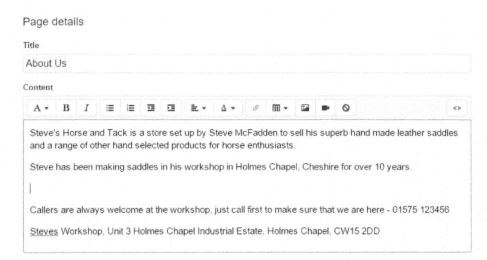

Now I want to add an image of the workshop to the 'About us' page in the middle where the cursor is shown in the image above.

To do that I click on the 'Image' button in the editor menu to bring up the 'Insert image' window

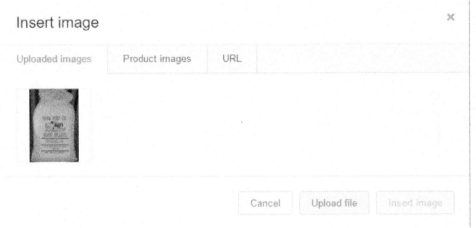

The same window is used to add images to blog posts and product descriptions as well as static content Pages

The three tabs at the top (Uploaded images, Product images and URL) represent three different ways to add images.

You will find all of the product images that you have already uploaded in the 'Product images' tab.

I have the image that I want on my hard drive so I will click the 'Upload file' button, find the item on my hard drive and then upload it. Once it is uploaded I will see it in the same window

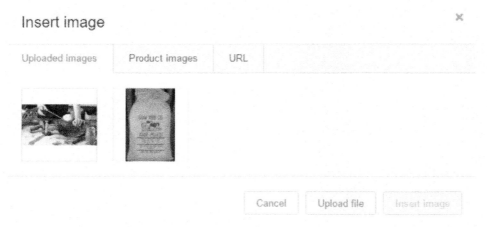

Now it can be used in any section of the site without uploading it again.

I select it and a section below opens out

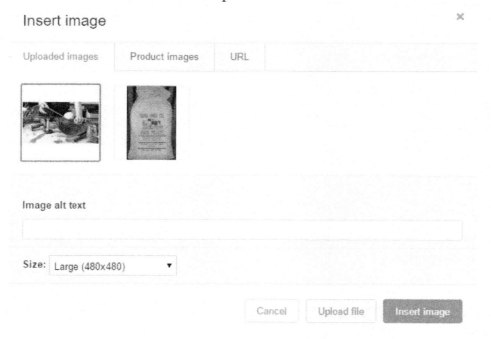

Fill out the Image alt text box with a description of the image, using key words, then define the product size that you want to use and then choose 'Insert image'.

If you are not sure what size to use, don't worry, choose 'Original' or choose 600 x 600, then if it does not look right just remove the image and re-insert it using a size up or down from there.

If you want to see what the page will look like, first you need to press the blue 'Save' button and then press the 'View' button in the top right of the screen. This will open up a new tab in your browser showing the page as it will appear to your customers.

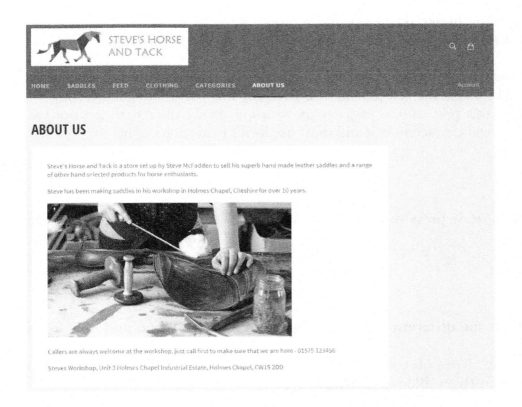

The last stage of setting up the page is to take care of the search engine optimization (SEO) for the page, this is done at the bottom of the page in three different sections

Search engine description

Set up the page title, meta description, and handle. These help define how this page shows up on search engines.

Page title 27 of 70 characters used

About Steves Horse and Tack

Meta description 96 of 160 characters used

Steve's Horse and Tack, Steve McFadden, handmade saddles, horse food, horse tack, horse clothing

URL & Handle

http://www.steveshorseandtack.com/pages/ about-steves-horse-and-tack

☑ Also create a URL redirect for about-us → about-steves-horse-and-tack

The page title should be obvious, but don't leave it as 'About us', the meta description should include the same key phrases as the home page.

The last, and perhaps most important piece of SEO work is to choose the 'Handle' for the URL, this is the last part of the URL for this page, Google gives a lot of emphasis to this part of the page so try to use a strong phrase. It can not have spaces or special characters in it and must use lower case letters only.

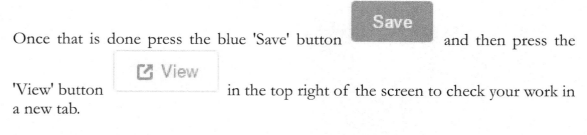

Once that is done press the blue 'Save' button and then press the 'View' button in the top right of the screen to check your work in a new tab.

Notes about the different kinds of content in Shopify, when and how to use them

There are four types of content that you can set up in Shopify, they are Product Pages, Content Pages, Blogs and Menus

Products

Obviously products are a special type of content - they can be purchased by your customers so the need information like price, weight and EAN code, but your product pages are still the most important part of the content on your web site. Try to keep product pages consistent, make your product images and videos as consistent as possible, keep your images square if possible and use the same layout for specifications, videos and text in the descriptions.

Content Pages
Static content pages are best used for pages like 'contact us' details, terms and conditions pages or other content of the same type that will only change rarely.

Blogs
Blogs are the best place to make announcements or post news pieces that will be interesting for a few days and then be archived, but you need to both post regularly on your Blog and try never to post irrelevant puff pieces - it's hard to strike that balance correctly.

Menus
Menus are a form of content as well especially the ones that are shown on the top of your web page header and the footer of your page - make them consistent and choose the names listed there carefully.

Chapter 60
Testing your store

Once you have completed the setup of your on-line store it is really important that you spend some time testing it to make sure that all the pages look good and that the checkout works as you would expect.

Your PC and web browser will have stored images and data while you were working on the site in a process called 'caching' so you may not see the site as a user would from the PC that you set it up on. If you have access to a separate PC from the one that you set the site up on it is helpful to use that for testing, but if not try clearing the cache on your browser (search on Google for 'clear chrome cache' to learn how) and access the site with a clean browser.

Use Google Chrome, Microsoft Edge, Mozilla Firefox, Apple Safari and Internet Explorer to view the site - you should see some subtle differences in the way that it looks due to the way that the different browsers render web pages, but the main thing is to make sure that the checkout works in all the browsers, place trial orders using credit cards and bank transfer to make sure that everything works as it should. It's a good idea to set up a low cost item to order on the tests, but beware that you don't place too many orders on the same card, I have had my credit card blocked by my banks fraud screening team a number of times because I was using it for testing and the activity looked suspicious to them!

Test your site from an iPad and from a phone, browse and place test orders.

You should test the site every week or so, I recommend making the home page one of the 'home' startup pages on your web browser so that you see it load whenever you turn on your web browser - encourage family and friends to do the same thing and let you know if anything looks wrong.

You should go through a testing routine after any major change to the site, especially if you have changed the payment settings or the checkout in any way.

I'd recommend that you get into the habit of placing a test order first thing in the morning every day just to make sure that the checkout works so I have included that in the list of regular checks in the chapter On-Going tasks

Chapter 61
Communications

Communicating with your customers is a big and important part of running an on-line store. Your reputation, some of your larger sales and your ability to handle problems will all be affected by the effectiveness of your communications with your customers.

When you first set up, very few of your potential customers will know who you are so they may call or e-mail simply to check that you are really there, it is of course very important that you answer those calls or e-mails quickly. Larger customers who want to order in bulk will often e-mail before placing their orders either to get a discount price or to check availability of a larger batch of items.

Today there are a lot of ways to set up easy to use communications channels that allow your customers to interact with you without it becoming a major drain on your time, the main options are e-mail, Phone, On-line Chat, Twitter and Facebook messaging.

I recommend that you offer your customers as many methods to talk to you as you can, you must at least have an e-mail address available and I would recommend that you have a phone line that customers can use to call you as well. If you have the extra resource available then you should offer on-line chat and if you are selling on Facebook or using it as part of your marketing plan then you should use Facebook messenger as well.

I recommend avoiding Twitter completely as it is just not suited for business use, but if you disagree then you can use that as well.

Chapter 62
Voice Over IP (VOIP)

Using a Voice Over IP (VOIP) service is a great way to get a standard land line phone number for your store that you can answer from more or less anywhere at a low cost.

A VOIP service provides you with a standard land line number and connects callers who dial that number with you through a soft phone, to a Voice over IP handset connected to your Internet router or to your mobile phone. A VOIP service is great for a new startup web store with limited staff resources.
(A soft phone is an application running on an Internet connected PC)

I recommend that you use Voipfone (http://www.voipfone.co.uk/) to set up your VOIP service, they can provide you with a phone number and a Virtual PBX service that allows you to activate Voicemail (sent to you as an e-mail attachment) and the ability to route calls to different users anywhere in the world if you want to use overseas staff to help with your customer service.

Just go to the Voipfone web site and click 'Signup' to try the service for free, after that the cost of a single line is less than £10 ($15) per month and there is no long term commitment to worry about.

Chapter 63
Customer Service eMail

Tame the Customer Service eMail monster with Helpscout
It helps you to look bigger than you are and 'punch above your weight' if you have multiple e-mail addresses for your sales inquiries, returns requests, technical support and financial queries.

You can run your different e-mail addresses through your Google apps account using Google groups, but even with separate folders for each address it gets difficult to manage everything through a single email account after a while. Then when you need to add an extra user who can also access the same folders it gets really difficult.

Helpscout is an email management system that allows multiple users to access the same e-mail folders. It allows you to manage your customer e-mails quickly and consistently through a system of customized stored responses and a flexible auto responder. Before systems like Helpscout became available to manage e-mail it was common for on-line retailers to use help desk systems, these are expensive, complex and not very customer friendly, Helpscout is much more useful.

Helpscout can also be easily integrated with MailChimp and the Chatra chat system so that you can see all of the text based interactions that you or any of your staff have had with each customer through mailers, e-mail or chat in one place.

The system for creating a set of pre-written responses to common customer inquiries is particularly helpful, it allows you to write carefully worded responses which the system will personalize and send to your customers, or when you type a long reply to a customer enquiry, you can save it so that it can be re-used when another customer asks you the same question.
As a result every customer gets the same e-mail no matter who sends it, which is really good for your consistency and can help to re-enforce your chosen brand image.

When you use Helpscout every reply to your customers e-mail will come back to them from the address that they sent the mail to - so e-mails sent to 'sales@steveshorseandtack.co.uk' get a reply from that address and e-mails sent to 'returns@steveshorseandtack.co.uk' get a reply from that address - regardless of who is typing the reply.

Helpscout is Free for first 3 users sharing a single mailbox and then $US15 (£10) per month per user for the full system, which is excellent value.

Helpscout works through your Google mail account, Google mail is used to accept, sort and forward your inbound e-mail to Helpscout where you can process your replies.

To help you to decide if you want to use Helpscout the first step is to list out the e-mail addresses that you would like to publish on your site

If you choose to use Helpscout from the start of your business the first thing that you need to do is to decide what e-mail addresses you want to publish for your customers, it can be really helpful to have 2 or 3 addresses to sort your inbound e-mail into categories for prioritization or for different people to deal with

I suggest that you use a minimum of two

sales@ - for pre-sales inquiries
help@ - for post sales inquiries and returns requests

But then if you prefer you can also add extra addresses like

purchasing@ - to filter off emails from suppliers and potential suppliers
finance@ - for payment related e-mails

For my example store I am just going to set up sales@ and help@ - this is how to do it

Chapter 64
External e-mail addresses

Set up Google groups for your external e-mail addresses

Firstly I will create these e-mail addresses as 'Google groups' in my Google mail set up.

Log into your g-mail account and then click on the 'settings' menu icon in the top right of the screen and then choose 'Manage this domain' from the drop down menu that appears, that should take you to the admin console for your Google account.

Groups is found in the 'MORE CONTROLS' section at the bottom of the screen, just click on 'MORE CONTROLS' to pop up the extra options,

Then click on 'Groups' to open up the Groups control window

Click on 'Create a group'

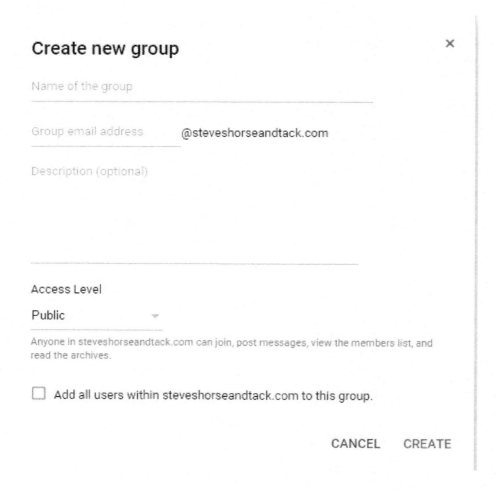

The first group that I will set up is the 'sales@' group - here are my settings

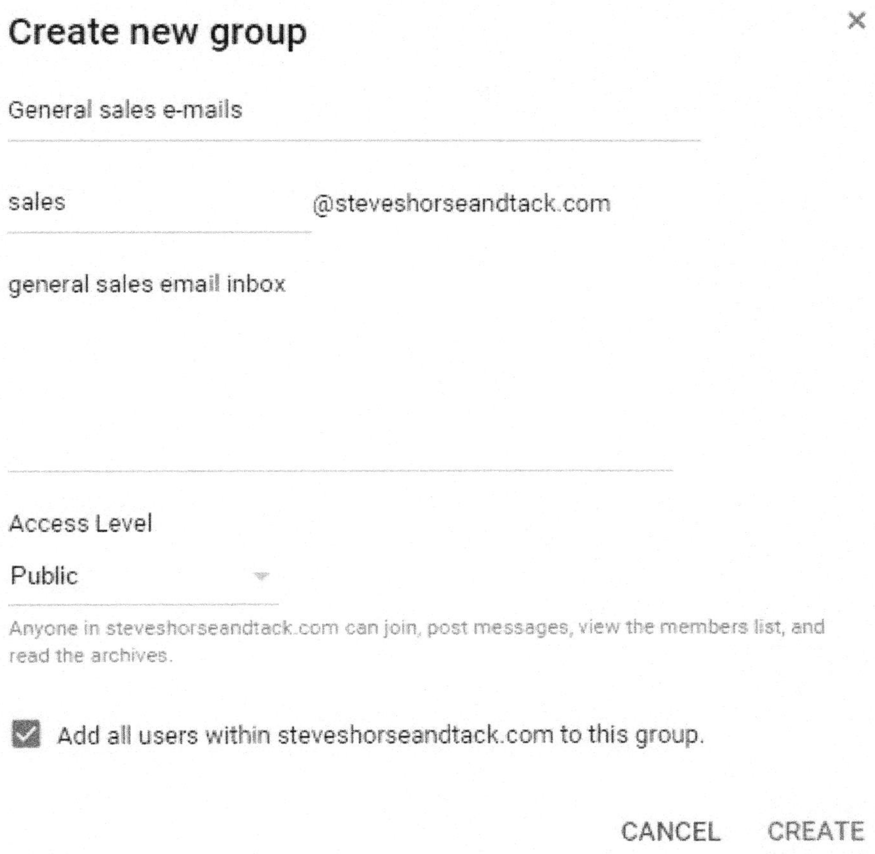

Create new group ✕

General sales e-mails

sales   @steveshorseandtack.com

general sales email inbox

Access Level

Public ▼

Anyone in steveshorseandtack.com can join, post messages, view the members list, and read the archives.

☑ Add all users within steveshorseandtack.com to this group.

CANCEL   CREATE

Then I hit 'CREATE' to set up the group.
When the group is first created it can not receive e-mails from outside the company as the group is set up as an internal company group by default, we need to change that next.

From the group page shown below, click 'Access Settings'

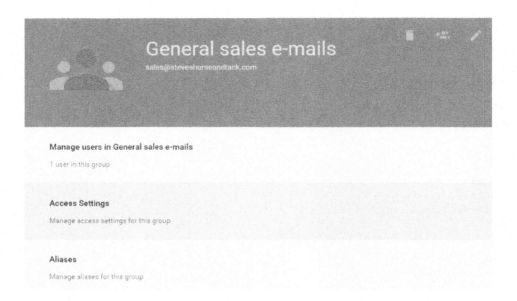

This will bring up the group settings page in a new tab

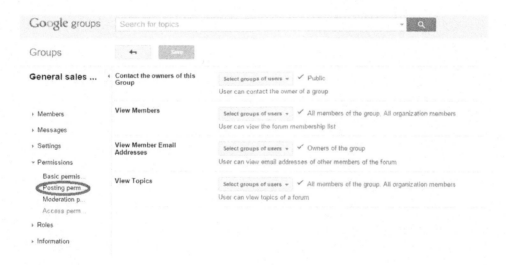

Select 'Posting permissions' under the 'Permissions' menu

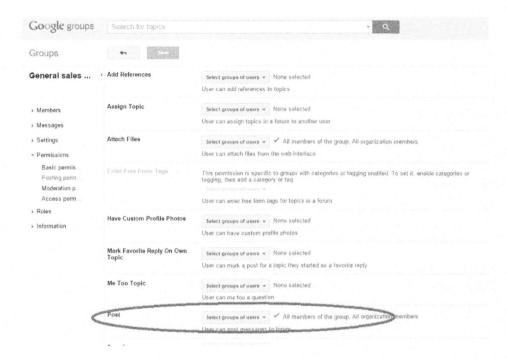

Select the drop down next to 'Post' which is set to 'Select groups of users'

Then choose 'Public' to add a tick next to this option and hence allow anybody in the world to send e-mails into this new Google group

Post	Select groups of users ▼	Public
	✓ Owners of the group	
	✓ Managers of the group	
Post Announcements	✓ All members of the group	ect
	✓ All organization members	ım
Post As The Group	✓ Public	ect

Then click the blue 'Save' button at the top of the screen to complete the change

Now any e-mail sent to sales@steveshorseandtack.com will be accepted into the group and will appear in your e-mail inbox where it can be sorted and passed on to Helpscout, the next stage is to set up your account with Helpscout.

Chapter 65
Helpscout e-mail Forwarding

Forward your inbound e-mails to Helpscout

Back in your Google mail account choose the settings drop down menu again, but this time select 'Settings' from the drop down.

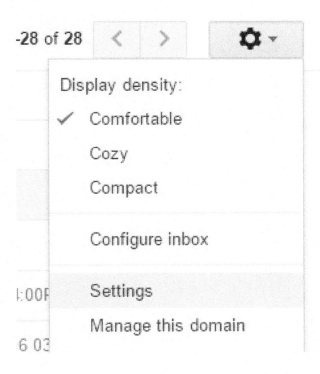

The settings system is a big system with lots of different options

The blue text across the top of this page are a row of ten tabs each with different options.
Select the option called 'Forwarding and POP/IMAP'

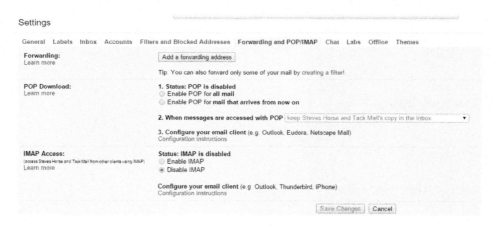

We want to set up a filter to move e-mails coming into your mailbox addressed to 'sales@steveshorseandtack.com' over to Helpscout, to do this we first need to add an authorized forwarding address to your account by clicking on the big 'Add a forwarding address' button at the top of the tab.

When you click on the button a window will pop up

Page 278

Go back to the Helpscout tab that we left a little earlier

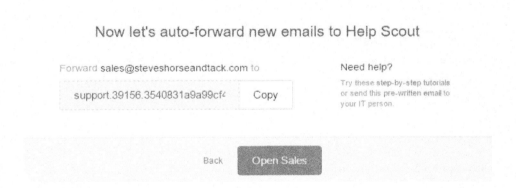

Press the 'Copy' button in the window and the Helpscout email address will be copied to your clipboard, go back to the g-mail settings window and select the text box under 'Please enter a new forwarding email address' then press 'Ctrl+V' to paste the address into the box, then press the grey 'Next' button. A confirmation box will appear

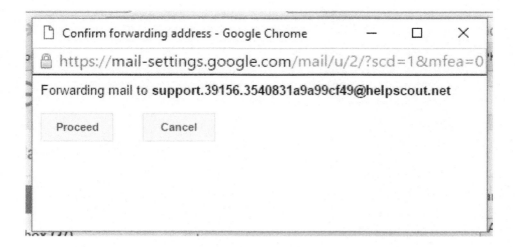

Click 'Proceed' and a confirmation code will be sent to your helpscout inbox to confirm that you are allowed to forward to that box.

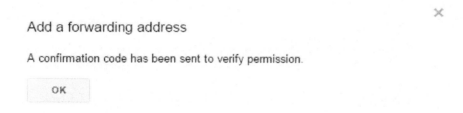

Click OK, and you will see the forwarding address has been added, but you need to input the confirmation code that Google has sent over to your Helpscout account to activate the address.

To get the code go back to the Helpscout browser tab

And press the blue 'Open Sales' button, this will open up the Helpscout inbox that you have created

In my example the confirmation code is in the spam box, click on 'Spam' in the left hand menu and then click on the e-mail to open it

Select the confirmation code and copy it (Ctrl+C) then move back to the Gmail tab of your browser

Select the box next to the new forwarding address where it says 'confirmation code'

Select the box and paste (Ctrl+V) the code into it, then press the 'Verify' button

This will confirm the address

We only want to forward mail that is sent to the 'Sales@steveshorseandtack.com' over to the helpscout box, we do that by creating a filter, to do that press on the blue 'creating a filter' link

This will bring up a box where you can define rules for the kind of mail that gets sorted and sent over to your Helpscout account

We want any item that is sent to 'sales@' to be forwarded regardless of what it says or who it is from so just fill out your sales email address in the 'To' box and then select the blue link 'Create filter with this search >>' in the bottom right hand corner of the box

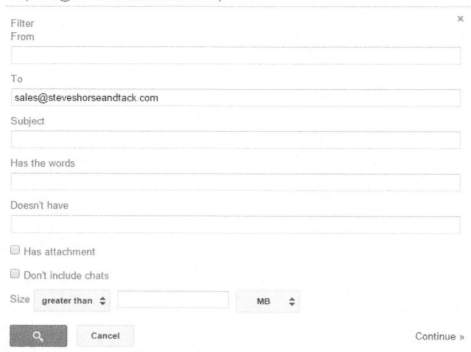

Another window will appear where you can decide what happens to these mails

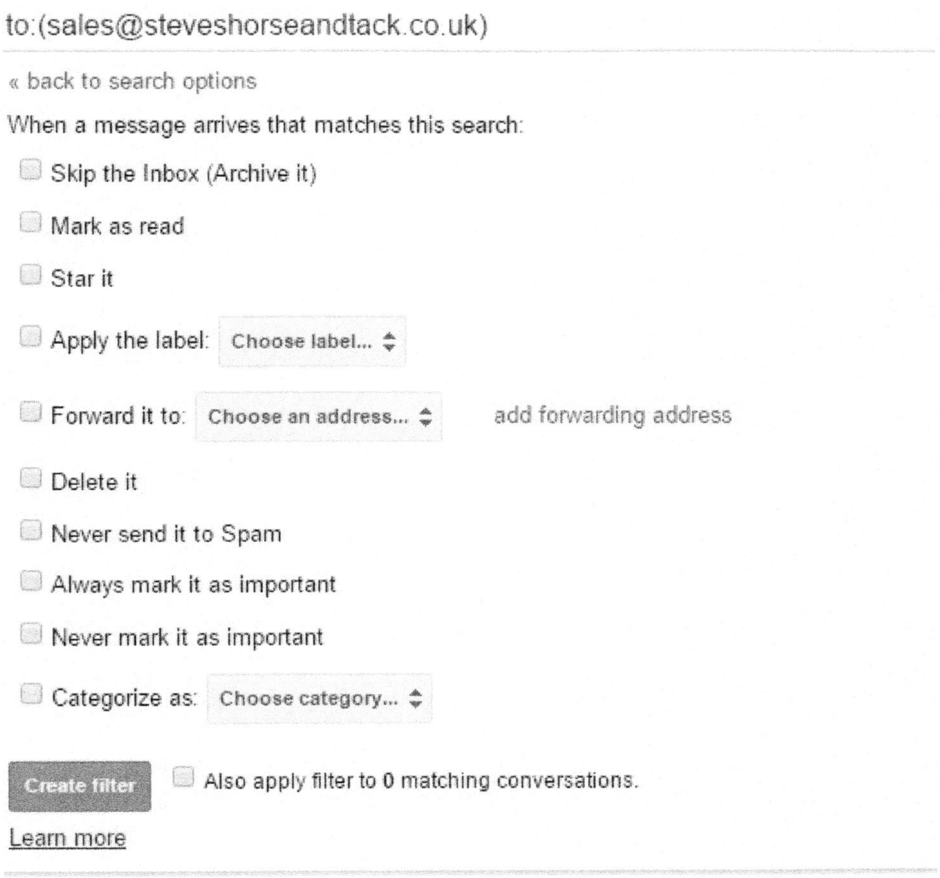

to:(sales@steveshorseandtack.co.uk)

« back to search options

When a message arrives that matches this search:

☐ Skip the Inbox (Archive it)

☐ Mark as read

☐ Star it

☐ Apply the label: [Choose label... ▾]

☐ Forward it to: [Choose an address... ▾]   add forwarding address

☐ Delete it

☐ Never send it to Spam

☐ Always mark it as important

☐ Never mark it as important

☐ Categorize as: [Choose category... ▾]

[Create filter]   ☐ Also apply filter to 0 matching conversations.

Learn more

Tick the 'Skip the Inbox (Archive it) button, this will remove mails sent to 'sales@' from your inbox once they have been forwarded to Helpscout

Then Click the 'Forward it to:' box and select the Helpscout inbox address from the drop down.

Then tick 'Never send it to Spam' because you want all the mail to get over to Helpscout

Click 'Also apply filter to _ matching conversations.'

The box will then look like this:

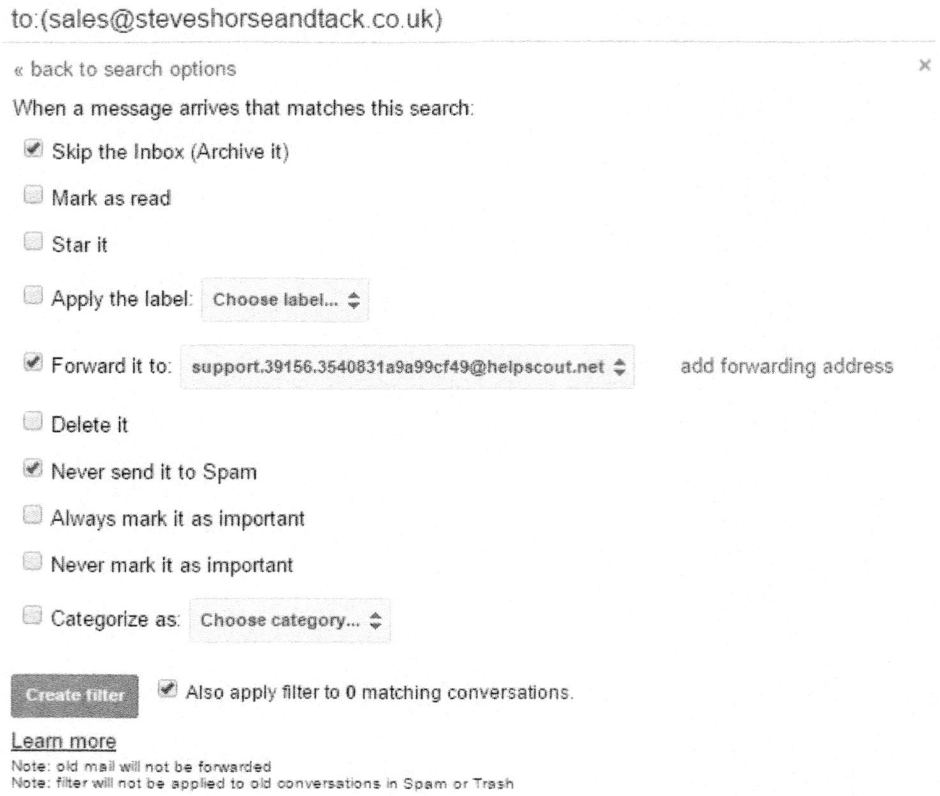

to:(sales@steveshorseandtack.co.uk)

« back to search options

When a message arrives that matches this search:

☑ Skip the Inbox (Archive it)

☐ Mark as read

☐ Star it

☐ Apply the label: Choose label... ▼

☑ Forward it to: support.39156.3540831a9a99cf49@helpscout.net ▼   add forwarding address

☐ Delete it

☑ Never send it to Spam

☐ Always mark it as important

☐ Never mark it as important

☐ Categorize as: Choose category... ▼

[Create filter]   ☑ Also apply filter to 0 matching conversations.

Learn more

Note: old mail will not be forwarded
Note: filter will not be applied to old conversations in Spam or Trash

Click the blue 'Create filter' button and confirm in the pop up

Go back to your e-mail account and send a test e-mail to your 'sales@' email account, within 5 minutes you should see it appear in your Helpscout inbox

While waiting for the test mail to come through, go back to your Shopify Admin and go to 'Settings > General' and change the Customer email address to 'Sales@'

![Customer email field showing sales@steveshorseandtack.com]

Then press the blue 'Save' button in the top right corner of the screen.

You can then repeat the process to set up the next mailbox for 'help@' the new mailbox in Helpscout will have it's own e-mail address for forwarding, be careful to choose the correct one when you set up the filter, it may be handy to make a note of which Helpscout address is for which mailbox that you can refer to when you need it.

Once you have set up all of the mailboxes you need, and you have set up forwarding for them you can let your customers know that they are there by adding them to your 'About Us' and 'Contact Us' pages on the web site. Go to 'on-line Store > Pages' in your Shopify admin and editing the pages accordingly.

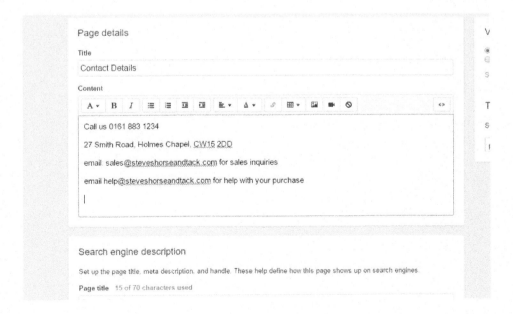

Page 287

One last thing - it is really helpful to have copies of all of your order confirmation e-mails in Helpscout so that you can see them in the chain of mails from and to your customer, to make sure that this happens you can add your 'sales@' email to the list of addresses that are copied on your order confirmation e-mails. Go back to your Shopify Admin and navigate to Settings > Notifications and scroll down to the 'Order notifications' section

Click on the 'Add an order notification' button and type the address that you would like to be copied into the box that comes up

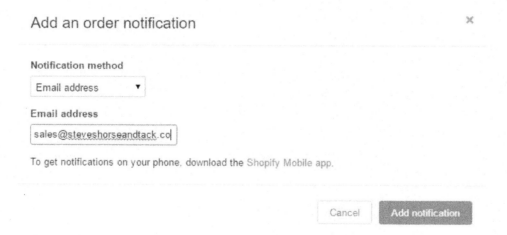

Then press the blue 'Add notification' button.

Chapter 66
Saved Replies in Helpscout

To get started on saved replies go to the mailbox that you want to add them to (Helpscout saved replies are mailbox specific) and select the icon for the settings

drop down menu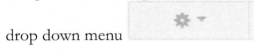

Then pick 'Saved Replies'.

This will bring up the Saved Replies list, but as it's the first time you have gone in here there will not be any to see yet

Press the big blue 'New Saved Reply' button to get started on your first saved reply

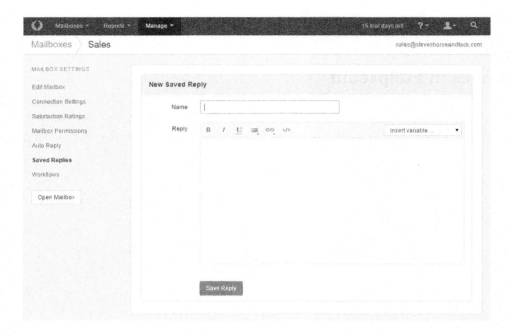

There are a few suggestions for saved reply e-mail's on my website - have a look through them and see if there are any that you want to use.

I'm going to set up a standard one for the example store to be sent to customers who have ordered something that takes a couple of weeks to make.

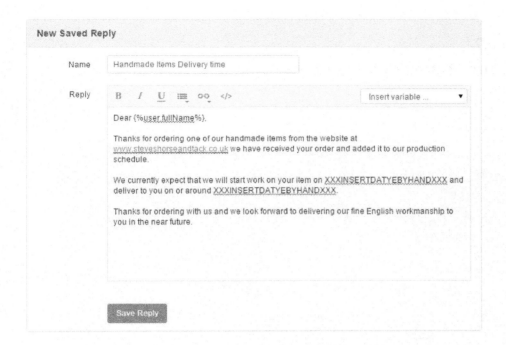

As you can see I have used the 'Insert variable' dropdown to personalize the mail to my customer and I have put markers into the text where I will need to insert dates on a customer by customer basis - but that's still a lot faster than typing the mail each time.

You can also save a reply that you originally created for a specific customer, this happens a lot when you are typing up a reply to a customer question and you think that it could be a question that may be asked again - to do that you simply press the saved replies icon in the e-mail editor and then select 'Save This Reply' from the dropdown menu.

Chapter 67
Set up your Helpscout Account

To start the set up of your Helpscout account go to http://www.helpscout.net/

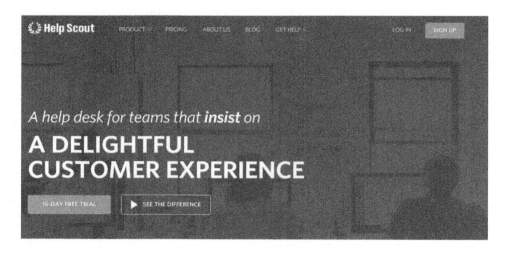

Click the blue 'SIGN UP' button

This will bring up the form to sign up for a free 15 day trial which you can fill out as below

Then click the blue 'Create My Account' button and go on to set your industry, preferred Timezone and Time format

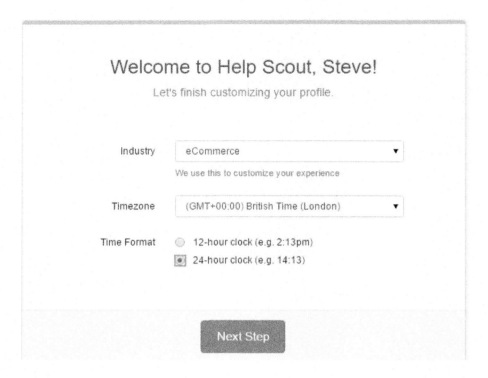

Next you get the chance to install Docs - skip that for now, just click 'Next step'

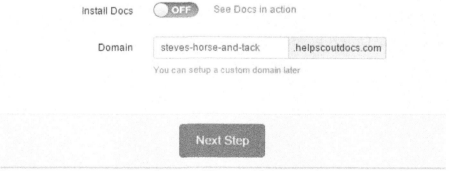

Lastly you set up your first mailbox address and name

Then press the blue 'Next Step' button

You will only have one user to start with so on the next screen, just press 'Next Step'

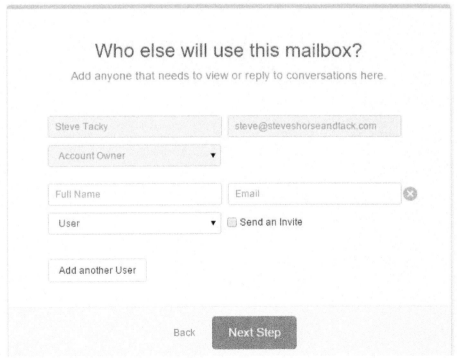

Finally you will see a page like this

    Showing the address that we need to forward your sales emails to in order to have them appear in Helpscout, don't worry that you can't read it, we can still copy it into our G-Mail setup. Just leave this tab open and move over to another tab of your web browser to set up the forwarding from your g-mail account.

Chapter 68
Automated responses

One of the best features of Helpscout is it's auto responder, this works a bit like an out of office reply on a regular e-mail system. It's a pre-written message that is sent as a reply to every address that e-mails your e-mail inbox. This is really helpful if you can't get to your e-mail box every hour but still want customers to get a fast reply.

Like saved replies, automated responses are specific to a mailbox, if you set up a automated response in one mailbox it will not be triggered by mails that come into a different mailbox so before you set up your first automated response you need to open the mailbox where you want it to operate.

To set up your first automated response log in to your Helpscout account and open the mailbox that you want to work on, here is my example store's sales inbox

On the left hand side you can see the settings menu icon  click on that to open up the settings menu.

Page 297

Select 'Auto Reply' to open up the auto reply function for this mailbox

Switch the auto responder on and a box will open with a basic automatic response already set up

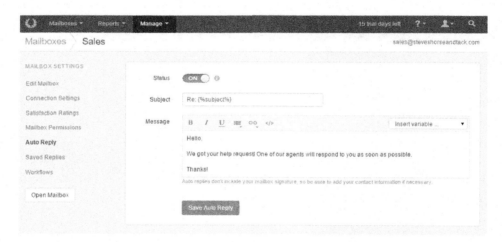

Both the auto responders and the saved responses in Helpscout use codes enclosed in curly brackets like this {} to show where variable data will be inserted in the mail.

The code '{%subject%}' in the subject line shows that the subject line of the email sent in by the customer will be used for the reply, but with Re: inserted at the start.

If you want to personalize the mail you can insert the users name or other variables using the Insert variable drop down menu.

Edit the main body as you see fit and then click 'Save Auto Reply' here is mine for the test store.

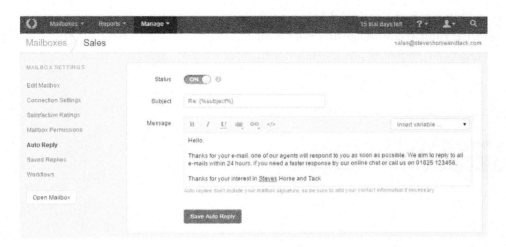

Now a copy of that mail will be sent to anyone who mails into that mailbox.

It's a good idea to have one for each mailbox that you have active.

Using automated responses to meet requirements for communication when selling on Amazon and eBay

You can use Helpscout automated responses to make sure that anyone e-mailing you through the messaging services on eBay and Amazon gets a fast response, re-direct your amazon and eBay emails to separate mailboxes in Helpscout and set up auto-reply e-mails with a set of helpful information about your products, returns policies etc. You can then reply in more detail later if needed.

Chapter 69
Helpscout notes

Some basic notes on how to use Helpscout
Helpscout is an e-mail management system so most of it's functions are the same as you would expect to find in any e-mail client, it is easy to use and most functions are obvious.

You can add signatures and aliases in Settings > Edit Mailbox

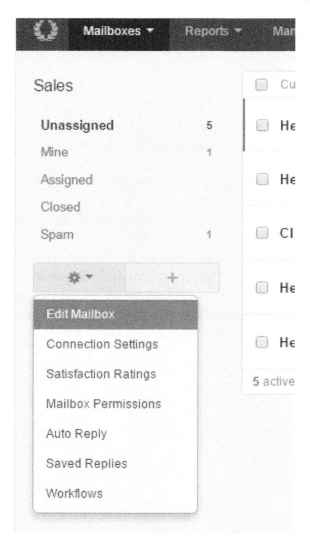

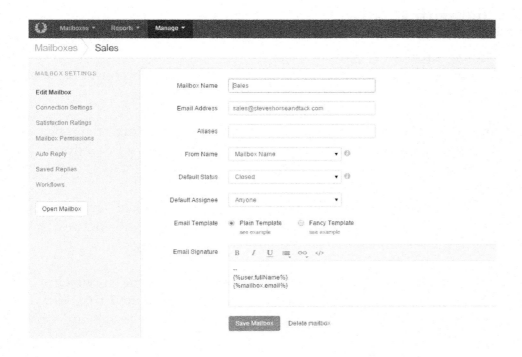

If you have multiple users you can use Helpscout to assign particular conversations to users who are best placed to reply to them.

The Help system in Helpscout is accessed through the help icon in the top right it has lots of extra functions that you can explore.

Chapter 70
On-line Chat with Chatra

Delight your customers with on-line Chat
on-line chat is a great way to interact with your customers at their convenience but at a low cost to you.

You can use saved replies to make the process faster and more consistent and you can chat with multiple customers at the same time so chat has a lot of advantages over using the phone.

Chat is not essential, but if you add it to your web site and make sure that chat inquiries are answered quickly, professionally and correctly it will increase your sales and hence improve your conversion rate, so it is worth doing.

After trying a number of different chat systems for Shopify, some of which were too complex and others which simply did not work I recommend that you use Chatra as your chat system for your Shopify store, it is easy to install and works well in my experience.

At the time of writing in January 2016 Chatra has a free option but it has a limited feature set, they charge $9 (£6) per month, per user for the paid version with a much more comprehensive feature set so I recommend the paid version. The Chatra system is simple to use, but fully featured and it has an integration with Helpscout as well as Shopify so it can form a part of your complete integrated system. The Helpscout integration is only available in the paid version so that's another reason to use the paid version.
See the Chatra plan details here https://chatra.io/plans/

Add Chatra to your Shopify Store
Integrating Chatra into your Shopify site is really simple, you can install it directly from the Shopify App store - here are instructions on how to do it;

To begin log go to the Shopify admin system and choose 'Apps' from the main menu.

Then click the blue 'Visit the App Store' button to open the Shopify app store.

Type 'chatra' into search box, you will see the possible matches appear below the box and refine as you type.

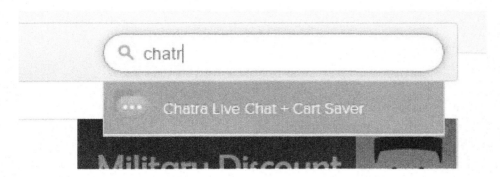

Select the Chatra Live Chat + Cart Saver app from the drop down menu

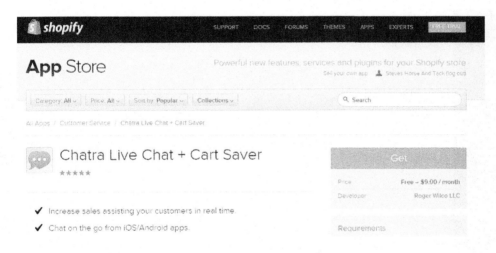

Click the green 'Get' button to install the App on your store

Chatra Live Chat + Cart Saver

Steve's Horse and Tack

You're about to install Chatra Live Chat + Cart Saver

This application will be able to access and modify your store data.

This application will be able to:

Read **Customer** details and customer groups
Modify **Script Tags** in your store's theme template files

Install App

Click the blue 'Install App' button and you should see a screen like this

The Chat application is now installed, you can see on your web page, just open up a new window and you will see it in the bottom right hand corner

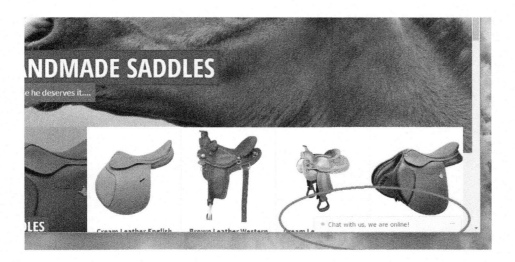

Try testing it to see what happens.

You can use Chatra through your web browser if you like, just keep this browser tab open, you will hear an audible notification when you receive a chat and go to the 'My queue' menu choice to select the chat and reply to it.

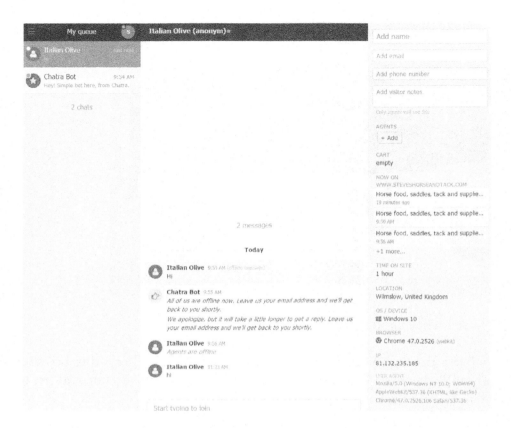

To get back to the Chatra page just go to the Apps menu in Shopify and click on the Chatra logo

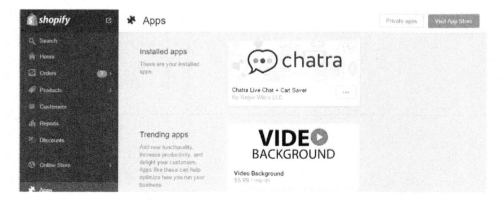

There are a couple of things that you can do to customize your Chatra system.

Click on the 'Set up & customize' menu choice in the Chatra browser tab

You will see a list of things that you can change if you wish

Scroll down the right hand side and you can change the language, the location that the chat window pops up, the sound for the new chat notification and the color

scheme of the pop up as well as the e-mail address for offline chat messages.

For the example store I have chosen a blue color scheme and updated the e-mail address for offline messages to my 'Sales@' address so they go into Helpscout.

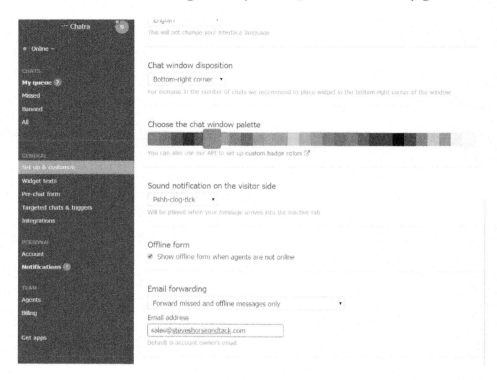

You can also create some custom triggers to pro-actively initiate chats on certain pages, to do that choose 'Targeted chats & triggers' from the main menu

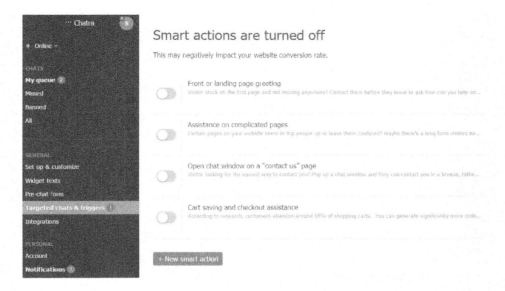

Turn any of these features on and then click on the name to change the settings, specify the pages that they are triggered by etc.

You can also set up extra users if you choose to do so by clicking on the 'Agents' link.

Lastly if you want to commit to using Chatra all the time you can install their client apps on your desktop PC and/or your phone, to do that click the 'Get apps' menu choice

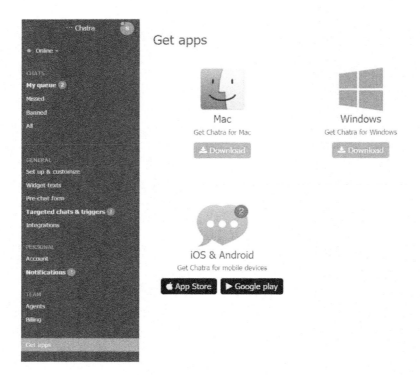

Once you have installed the app you will need to log in to it, your Shopify store login e-mail is the address that you will use to login - after first installing the app you will not have a password, just click the 'Lost password?' link to get an e-mail sent over with a password reset link and set one up.

You will then have your chat set up in a desktop application which can be a lot more convenient than using a web browser for chatting with customers.

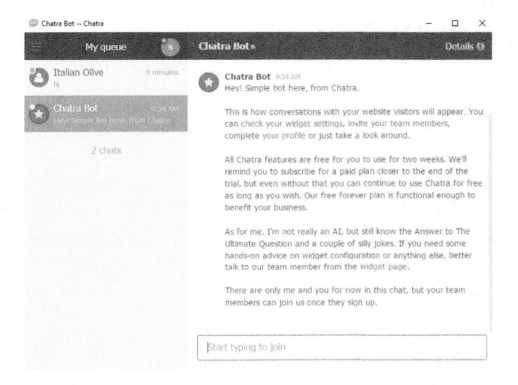

Chapter 71
MailChimp eMail Marketing

Shopify does not have a built in e-Mail marketing tool, I recommend that you use MailChimp to provide this function.

To use MailChimp as a part of your Shopify web store you first need to sign up for a MailChimp account

Go to https://login.MailChimp.com/signup fill out your e-mail address (use the one that you set up for the business) and use that as your user name.

Then set your password - MailChimp requires a complex password. The requirements for the password are shown under the box and they 'grey out' as your password meets them

MailChimp will send a confirmation e-mail to the address that you specified, open it and click on the confirmation button to go back to the MailChimp site and confirm that you are not a robot and complete the sign up.

You then need to let MailChimp know who you are, fill out your details and set the industry and the correct time zone for your customers. I also recommend that you subscribe to the MailChimp 'getting started e-mails' they have some great information and ideas in them.

Now your account is set up you can start the process of integrating MailChimp into Shopify, firstly open a new browser window and log into your Shopify store admin, you need to be logged into MailChimp and Shopify at the same time to make this process work smoothly.

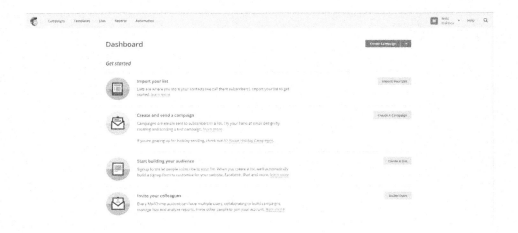

Now in MailChimp we need to create a customer list to integrate with Shopify. A list is just a group of e-mail addresses that you can send to as a group. MailChimp lets you sub divide your contacts into lots of lists, but for our purposes we only need one to get started so click 'Create A List' from the MailChimp dashboard, or click the 'Lists' menu

Click the 'Create List' button highlighted, this will bring up a form for you to complete to tell MailChimp who will be sending mails to your customers.

Call the list something like 'Main Newsletter List', use your business e-mail address for the 'from' e-mail and use your company name as the 'From Name' that way customers will get your marketing mails from your business name with your business e-mail as the reply address.
For the sign up reminder type 'You signed up for this list through our web site' then save the list.

All of that information will be used to populate the legally required part of your marketing e-mails

Next we need to create the link between MailChimp and Shopify, select your name next to the down pointing arrow in the top right of the screen in the example my name is 'Maki'

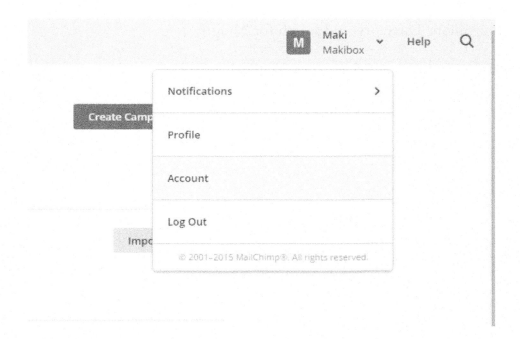

And from the drop down select 'Account'

Then from the sub menu select 'Integrations' to see the screen shown below

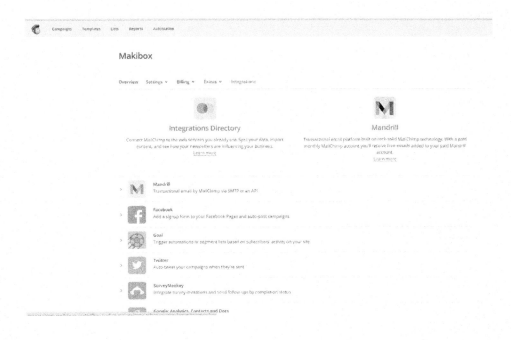

Select the 'Integrations Directory' and search for 'Shopify'

As you can see there are loads of integrations for MailChimp and Shopify, this is the one that you want, the free one developed by MailChimp

Click on 'learn more' which will take you through to the integration details page, click the 'learn more button' again and follow the instructions to activate the integration, you will then see this screen where you can add your Shopify store to the MailChimp end of the integration.

Click 'Add Store' and you will see this page

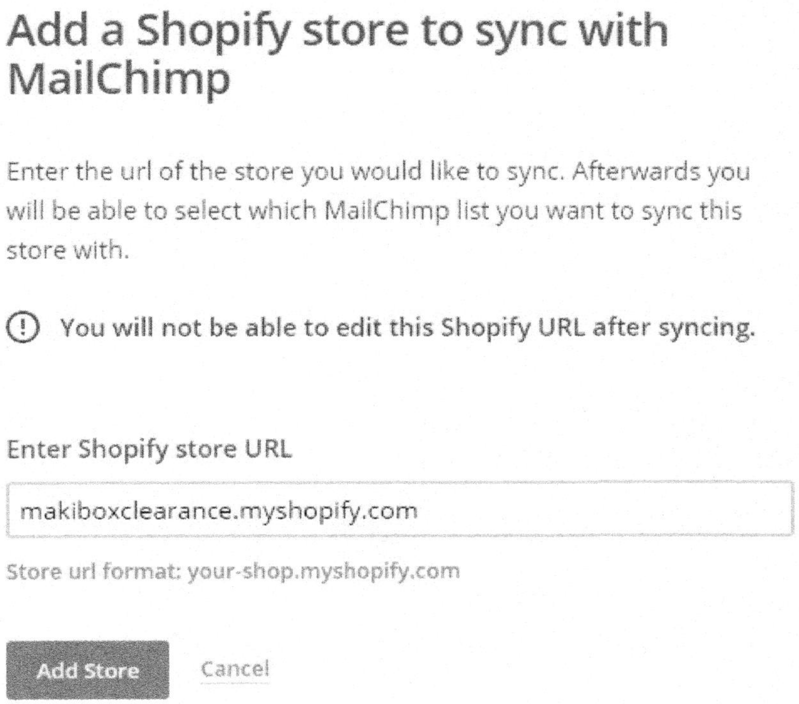

Add a Shopify store to sync with MailChimp

Enter the url of the store you would like to sync. Afterwards you will be able to select which MailChimp list you want to sync this store with.

① You will not be able to edit this Shopify URL after syncing.

Enter Shopify store URL

`makiboxclearance.myshopify.com`

Store url format: your-shop.myshopify.com

[Add Store]   Cancel

Enter your Shopify store maintenance URL (that's the one that ends with '.myshopify.com' rather than the customer visible URL) and click 'Add Store'

As long as you are still logged into both sites you will now be redirected to Shopify and you will see this page where you can authorize the Shopify end of the integration and you can see the list of changes that will be made in your Shopify system as a result of the integration.

Click the blue 'Install App' button to install the Shopify 'end' of the connection and go back to finish the set up in MailChimp.

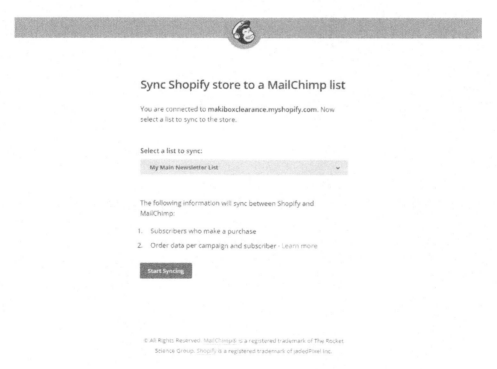

Make sure that your list is named as the list to sync and then click 'Start Syncing'.

Now when customers sign up for your mailing list through Shopify they will automatically be added to your MailChimp list.

You can also create a specific page in your Shopify store where interested people can sign up for your mailing list, try this.

Go to the MailChimp home page (you can get there by clicking on the monkey's head in the top left of the screen) then select 'Lists' from the main menu and 'Signup forms' from the secondary menu that appears lower down the screen.

Press the 'Select' button next to 'Embedded forms' to bring up the page where you can generate the code of your sign up form.

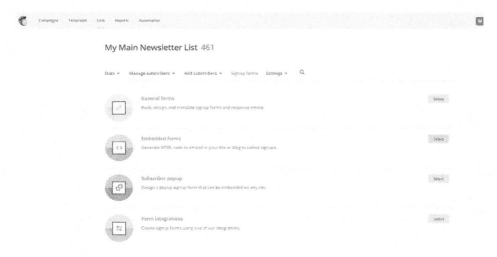

I prefer the slim form so pick 'Super Slim' from the top menu, then click just once on the text in the box headed 'Copy/paste onto your site' this will select all the code in the window.

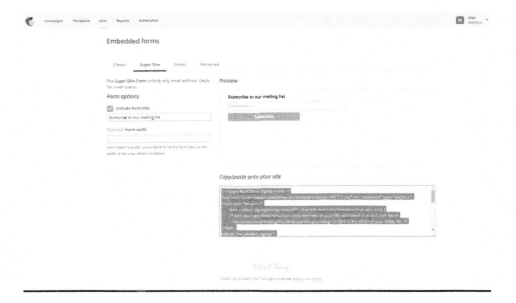

Press 'ctrl C' to copy the code out of the box into your computers clipboard and then switch back to the Shopify window where you navigate to 'on-line Store' and 'pages'

Select the blue 'Add page' button in the top right

Set the name of the page to 'sign up page' and change the editor to the HTML editor by clicking the '<>' button at the top right of the content window

Click into the HTML editor window and press 'ctrl v' to paste the MailChimp code from the clipboard into the window.

Then press save, you will see the page as it will appear on the site in the window and a green pop up will offer you the option to add the page to your store's navigation

Click 'add to your Stores Navigation'

I think that the best place to add it is the Footer so click 'Edit Link list' in the 'Footer' window

Click the 'Add another link' button and another line will appear in the links, set the Link Name on the new line to 'Newsletter Signup' and change the 'links To' dropdown to 'Page' then select the page that you just created as the target page.

Press one of the blue 'Save' buttons and you are done

Go back to your web site and you will see the newsletter sign up link on the footer of the site, try it !

You can now integrate your MailChimp account into the e-mail sign up box on the web site footer, in your Shopify admin go to on-line store > Themes and click on the blue 'Customize theme' button, then choose the 'Footer' menu
At the bottom of the 'Footer' section you will see this section

Click on the 'Find your MailChimp form action URL' and follow the instructions there to complete the integration.

We can also now connect the Promotion bar that we set up earlier to the newsletter sign up page, go to the 'Header' menu and look at the Promotion bar section at the

bottom

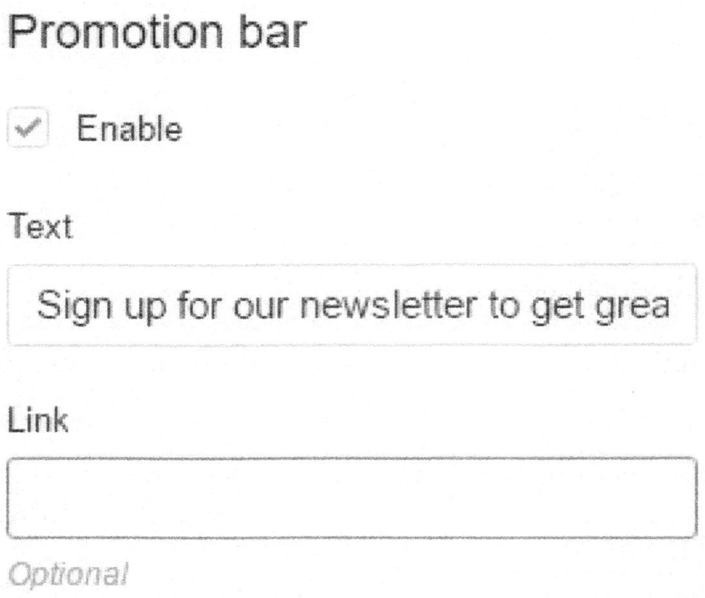

Promotion bar

☑ Enable

Text

[Sign up for our newsletter to get grea]

Link

[   ]

Optional

Paste the URL for your newsletter sign up page into the 'Link' box here and save the changes.

Chapter 72
Cross-Over Integrations

Now that you have accounts set up with Shopify, Helpscout, MailChimp and Chatra that are all integrated to some extent you need to complete the fully connected system by adding cross over integrations between the different Apps.

Integrate Chatra with Helpscout

Integrating Chatra with Helpscout will show your chats in Helpscout histories which can be really helpful and it's easy to do.

First go to 'Integrations' in your Chatra admin page.

Remember to get back to the Chatra page just go to the Apps menu in Shopify and click on the Chatra logo.

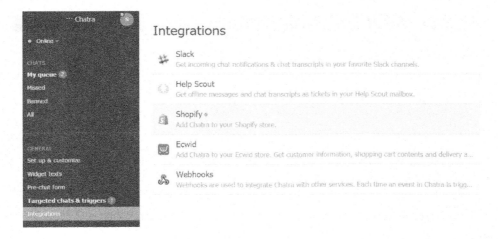

Click on the Help Scout listing to bring up the Help Scout integration page

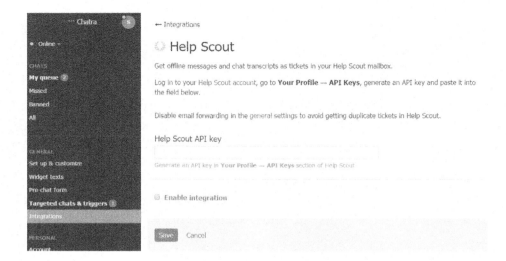

Now open up a new web browser tab and point it to helpscout. Once there log in to your Helpscout account.

Click on the icon of a head and shoulders in the top right to bring up a drop down

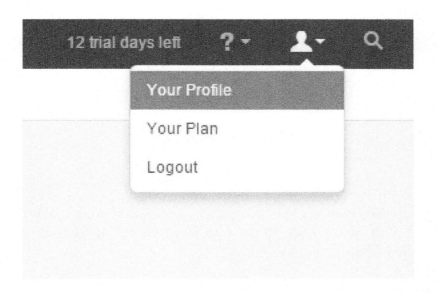

And select 'Your Profile'

Then pick 'API Keys' from the left hand menu

Press the blue 'Generate an API Key' button

Click on the 'Add a label' button and change the name to 'Chatra' and click the blue tick to save the name

The last step is to copy the API Key, select it and then press Ctrl+C to copy to your clipboard then switch back to the Chatra window and paste the key into the box there labeled 'Help Scout API key'.

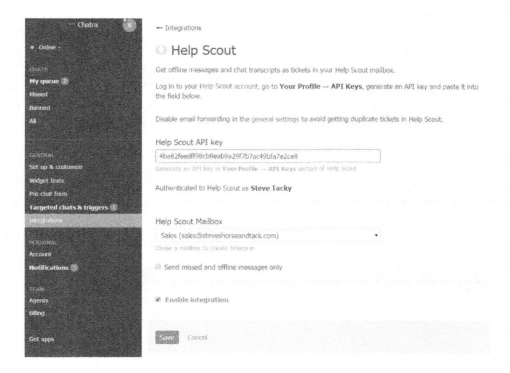

Make sure that the tick box next to the green text 'Enable Integration' is checked and then press the blue 'Save' button.

The integration will then be enabled and you will see a green spot next to 'Help Scout' in the Integrations list as shown below.

Note that you need to sign up for the premium service with Chatra to keep the system active after the free trial as it is not a feature of the free system.

Integrate Helpscout with Shopify

Next we want to integrate Helpscout with Shopify directly, by doing this we make Helpscout import customer contact information from Shopify and pull over key metrics such as lifetime value and average order value to display next to customer messages in Helpscout, it will also display up to 10 of the customer's most recent orders next to their messages.

Completing the integration is quite easy, open up the browser tab that you used to login to Helpscout or open up a a new browser tab and login to Helpscout.

Then go to the 'Manage' menu and select 'Apps'

Scroll down until you find the 'Shopify' logo

Click on it

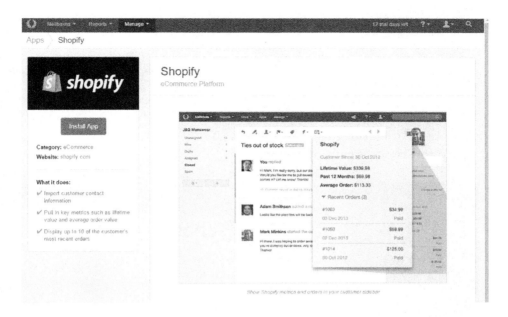

Then press the blue 'Install App' button to bring up the integration page

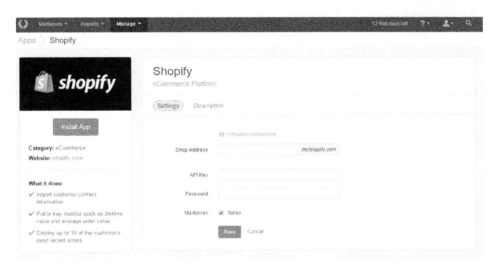

Next you need to go back to the admin section of your Shopify account to get your shop address, API Key and API password (not your store password).

Your shop address is the text before '.myshopify.com' in your browser address bar. In the example below, our shop address is 'steves-horse-and-tack'.

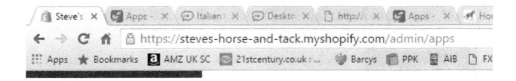

Next you need to generate an API key and Password in Shopify. Click on the Apps option from the main Admin menu and then click on the Private Apps button in the top right corner of the page.

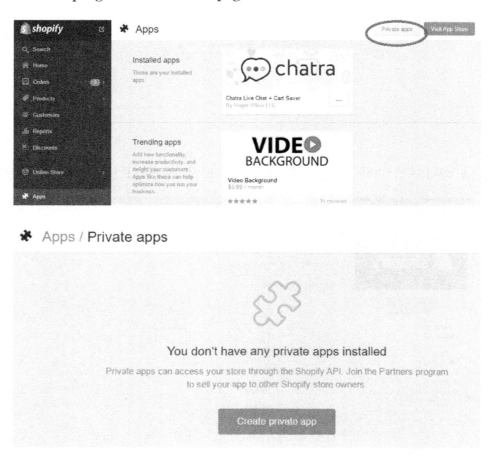

Click on the blue 'Create private app' button.

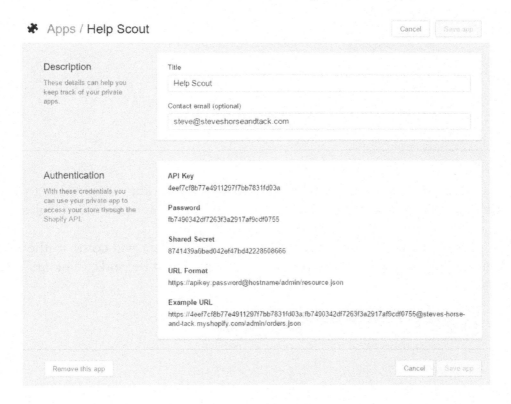

Then type "Help Scout" in the Title field and click either of the two blue 'Save' buttons, this will generate the API Key and password

Now copy and paste the API Key and Password from this tab to the boxes on the Help Scout page and press the blue 'Save' button to complete the integration.

Shopify
eCommerce Platform

Settings   Description

                        ⓘ Activation instructions

Shop Address | steves-horse-and-tack | .myshopify.com

API Key | 4eef7cf8b77e4911297f7bb7831fd03a |

Password | •••••••••••••••••••••••••••••• |

Mailboxes   ☑ Sales

Save   Cancel

Don't forget to select which mailboxes you'd like to connect to Shopify before you hit the Save button. In the example I only have one called 'Sales'.

The confirmation that the integration is complete will come in the form of a green box at the top of the screen, it only stays a few seconds, blink and you will miss it...

Now Helpscout will import customer contact information from Shopify and pull over key metrics such as lifetime value and average order value to display next to customer messages, it will also display up to 10 of the customer's most recent orders next to their messages.

Integrate MailChimp with Helpscout

It helps to integrate MailChimp with Helpscout, this allows us to see all of the mails sent to customers through MailChimp in Helpscout conversation records and it allows us to subscribe customers for our newsletter through Helpscout.

In Helpscout go back to Manage > Apps menu

And find the 'MailChimp' Logo

Then click on it

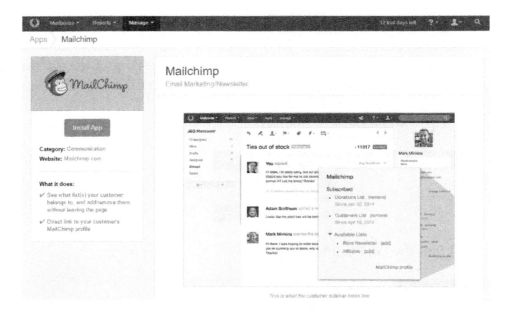

And then press the blue 'Install App' button

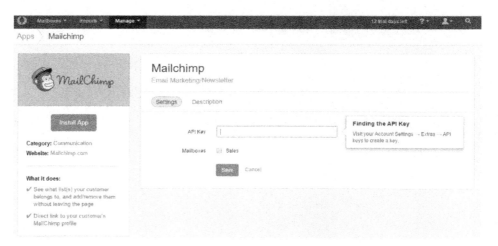

To complete the integration we need to get an API key from MailChimp, you should know the drill by now, but here are the details.

Open up a new tab and go to MailChimp then log into your account.

Press the arrow pointing down next to your user name in the top right of the screen

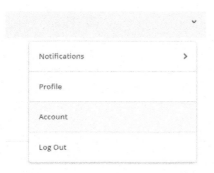

And select 'Account'

Select 'Extras' from the new menu in the middle of the screen and then 'API keys' from the drop down menu.

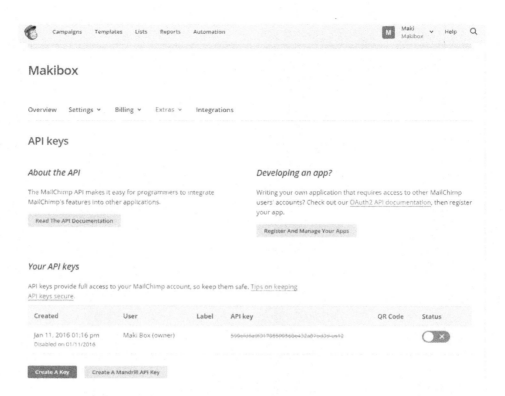

Click on the grey 'Create A Key' button to generate a key

Copy and paste the key from the MailChimp tab over to the Helpscout tab.

Check the box to show which mailboxes you want to integrate and then press the blue 'Save' button to see the 'Settings saved successfully' message

You can see that the apps are installed in Helpscout on the Manage > Apps page - installed Apps have green ticks in their top left corner.

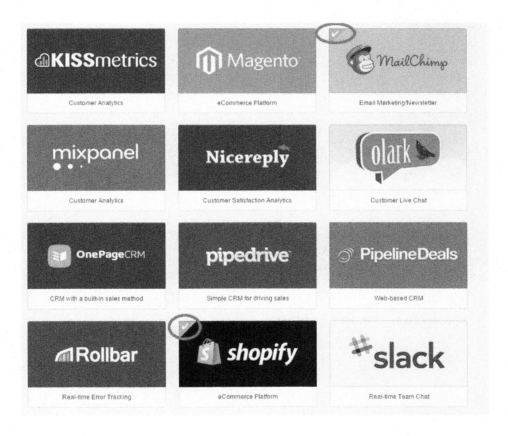

Integrate MailChimp with Shopify

The last cross over integration is the integration of MailChimp with Shopify

This one is really easy, first of all make sure that you have a browser tab open that is logged into MailChimp.

Then go back to the Shopify Admin system in another tab and point it to the Apps menu choice of the main menu of the Shopify store admin

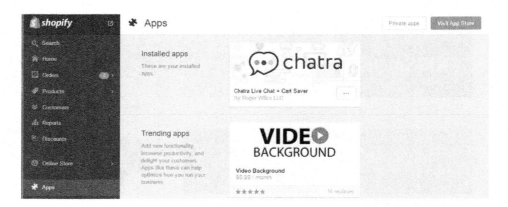

Then select the blue 'Visit App Store' button.

Type 'MailChimp' into the search box and then select the 'MailChimp for Shopify' app from the drop down list.

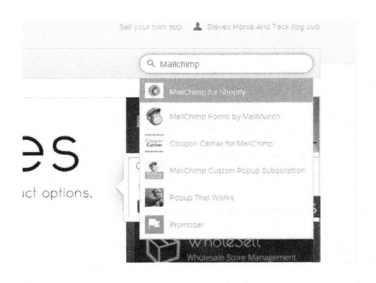

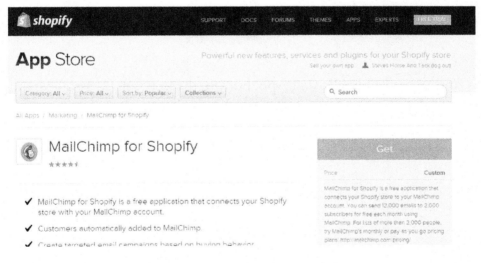

Click the green 'Get' button.

MailChimp for Shopify   Steve's Horse and Tack

You're about to install MailChimp for Shopify

This application will be able to access and modify your store data.
Once installed, links will be added to your Shopify admin.

This application will be able to:

Read Store content like articles, blogs, comments, pages, and redirects
Read Products, variants and collections
Modify Customer details and customer groups
Read Orders, transactions and fulfillments

- Add a link labeled **Email using MailChimp** to the product details page
- Add a link labeled **Email using MailChimp** to the custom_collection details page
- Add a link labeled **Email using MailChimp** to the page details page
- Add a link labeled **Email using MailChimp** to the blog details page
- Add a link labeled **Email using MailChimp** to the products action drop down page
- Add a link labeled **Email using MailChimp** to the smart_collection details page

[Install App]

And then the blue 'Install App' button, the app will be installed and you will see this screen

Sync Shopify store to a MailChimp list

You are connected to **steves-horse-and-tack.myshopify.com**. Now select a list to sync to the store.

Select a list to sync:

My Main Newsletter List

The following information will sync between Shopify and MailChimp:

1. Subscribers who make a purchase
2. Order data per campaign and subscriber · Learn more

Start Syncing

Choose the list to sync and then press the grey 'Start Syncing' button.

Your subscribers and order data will now sync between Shopify and MailChimp.

Chapter 73
Other Shopify Apps

As you will have already seen if you are following through the book as you build your own store Shopify is open to the addition of 'Apps' which add on extra features and capabilities to your on-line store, we have already added on the Chatra chat system and the integrations with MailChimp and HelpScout to your store, in the next section we will also add the Google Shopping App. If you explore the App store in Shopify which you can find in the Admin section under the 'Apps' menu you will find over 1,000 Apps available.

I encourage you to look through the App store and look at what is available, the drop down menus 'Category', 'Price', 'Sort by' and 'Collections' shown in the image below can be used to filter the Apps to find different Apps that you might find useful to develop your store.

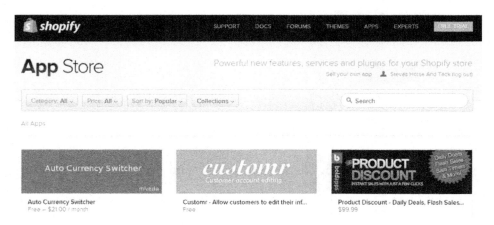

But before you go crazy and add a huge range of Apps to your store I would recommend that you run the store with the Apps that we have recommended for a few weeks or even a couple of months, just so you fully understand the Shopify system, it's user interface and how it works, and bear the following points in mind.

Shopify is complex, not all Apps work with every Theme and some Apps clash with each other
When you install a new App you need to test the functionality of your store and all of the Apps that you rely on carefully. Shopify has a testing process for new Apps but bugs sometimes get through and with more than 1,000 Apps and hundreds of

Themes it's just not possible to cross check every combination of Theme and already installed Apps for clashes - you need to double check everything after you install a new App.

'Free' is not always Free

There are a lot of Apps that offer limited functionality for free or free trial periods which then charge quite a lot of money for full functionality or charge per transaction fees, make sure that you read the small print and be sure what you are getting into. I have even seen Apps that charge 10% of your advertising spend on Facebook or AdWords to 'manage' it for you - if you install one of those you are nuts!

Just because someone built an App for it does not mean that you need it

Some Apps, even really popular ones are just a waste of time, there are a range of loyalty program Apps and marketing Apps that go a long way to proving that point, I recommend a healthy dose of skepticism when you look at Apps, especially in the marketing category.

Recommended Apps

Here are a few Apps that I have used and found to be useful

Aftership

Aftership automatically pulls data from your shipping partners tracking system and e-mails updates to your customers as their parcels make their way to them, this saves a lot of customer service calls and e-mails and helps make you look professional and bigger than you actually are.

It's very helpful if you ship over long distances or internationally, but less useful if you ship on a next day basis in a smaller country where delivery is usually next day anyway.

AfterShip
From $0.00 / month

★★★★★ 750 reviews

Aftership is free to install, but you need to buy credits to send the tracking e-mails, they are very cheap at about 1c of a US$ per credit, but if you ship a lot of orders it can add up.

Shopify Facebook Store
The Shopify Facebook store App makes all of your products available to buy directly from your Facebook page, it is built by Shopify and works well. It does require all images to be Square to look good on the page but it's quick to install and very helpful if you are marketing on Facebook and best of all it is included in your payments to Shopify.

Facebook Store
Free

Made by Shopify

★★★★☆ 219 reviews

Shippo

Shippo allows you to create shipping labels and access discounted shipping rates directly from Shopify. It's very US centric, but the discounts are quite good for small volume shippers and it is easy to use.

Shippo charges $US0.05 per label plus I assume they make a margin on the shipping costs.

If you are starting to ship international parcels or if you only ship a small number of items this is a great App and a useful service.

Shippo
From $0.00 / month

   189 reviews

Auto Currency Switcher

It can be really helpful to offer your international customers the option to see your prices in their own currency, that's what this App does.

But remember the customers will still be charged in your store currency and the conversion rate that their credit card company use may not be the same as the one that you used on your web site which can lead to customer service issues, also the automation uses the customers IP address to decide where they are located - which is not always perfect.

Auto Currency Switcher
Free – $21.00 / month

★★★★★   158 reviews

Parcel2Go

Parcel2Go (https://www.parcel2go.com/) is a UK based service that allows you to compare prices for shipping from a number of different couriers, it integrates with Shopify through a private App which copies over address details so you can avoid re-typing or copy - paste addresses for every order that you ship, sign up for an account at https://www.parcel2go.com/ and follow the instructions to integrate with Shopify.

Part Three: Running your store

Chapter 74
Sales & Marketing

Now that your store is set up, it's time for us to talk about the things that you can do to make it work. The job of your store is to make a profit, to make that happen it needs to sell products to customers, In the next few chapters we will look at ways to make that happen, to start the process of making your store sell we need to decide how to get some customers to look at your store and then buy from it.

In essence, a web site marketing strategy is the way that you have decided to get people to look at your web site and then buy from it. Many marketing strategies focus on the first part of the process to the detriment of the last part, don't fall into that trap with your new store, remember that web site visits are not your goal, orders are your goal. A site that takes 50 orders a day from 1,000 visitors is a much better store than one that takes 50 orders a day from 10,000 visitors.

To effectively market your web store you need to have both a marketing strategy and a marketing plan.

These two terms are often used interchangeably by people who don't really understand the difference, but as I intend to use them in this book each is a very different concept.

Marketing Plan
A marketing plan is a list of things that you will do to achieve your goal. A plan deals with how, when, where, who, and what will be done. You need to have a marketing plan, it is vital to the success of almost any business. However developing a plan should not be the first step to marketing your business, before you can start your marketing plan you need a marketing strategy.

Marketing Strategy
Your marketing strategy is bigger than the marketing plan, it deals with the question of long term objectives, why you want to achieve them and how. A strategy looks at all the influencing factors and the possible routes to get to the goal, then decides on the best options - which become the marketing plan.

You need a marketing strategy before you can come up with an effective marketing plan. Whatever you do, don't try to fit a strategy around existing plans it is much better to develop your marketing strategy and then create the marketing plan from the strategy.

Chapter 75
Marketing Strategy

Developing a marketing strategy is important for any business and vital for a start up in On-Line retail. If you don't have a well thought through marketing strategy, your efforts to attract customers are likely to be a mess and worse they are likely to cost you a lot of money.

Before you can define your marketing strategy you need to be really clear on what you want your business to do and how you want it to be perceived by customers.

Start off your marketing strategy by deciding what the two main things that you want your company to be known for in the market are.
Be realistic, you can not be known for the lowest prices AND the best customer service, that's just not the way the world works, cheap stores can not afford to offer the BEST customer service. Thinking about how you want the world to see your business is a great way to make sure that your products and services meet customer needs.
Once you understand how you want to be perceived by the market you can focus your strategy around developing profitable relationships with customers.

SWOT Analysis
If you don't know how you want to be seen by the market a SWOT (Strengths, Weaknesses, Opportunities and Threats) analysis can help you to consider your options, get a piece of paper and divide it into four sections, write Strengths, Weaknesses, Opportunities and Threats, one at the top of each sections and then thinking about your business compile a list of 3 or 4 points for each. If you have existing customers try to conduct some market research on your existing customers, it will help you to build a more honest picture of your reputation in the marketplace.

Strengths like;

Unique or special product and service
Special features or benefits that your product offers
Specialist knowledge or skills that you and your team have

Weaknesses like;

Limited financial resources
Nobody knows who you are
Limited personnel resources

Opportunities like;

Lower costs than your competitors
Your new on-line store allows you to reach new markets
Your smaller size makes you more flexible and responsive to changes in the market

Threats like;

Incumbents discounting to fight you off as a new competitor
New legislation increasing your costs
Bigger competitors getting cheaper prices from your suppliers

Having done your analysis, you can then think about the potential effects each element may have on your marketing strategy. Your strategy should take account of how your business' strengths and weaknesses will affect your marketing.

Customer Segmentation
Next think about your potential customers, split them up into groups or segments, characterized by their "needs". Identifying these groups and their needs, then addressing them more successfully than your competitors, is the heart of a successful marketing strategy. As a start up you will only be able to address a small number of customer groups so think about which are the largest and most profitable groups that you can address. If you can afford some market research then that can be helpful, if not try calling a few potential customers yourself, or contact them through Facebook, linked-in or even by approaching them in the street, every bit of information you can gather will he helpful.

Define your Strategy
You can then create a marketing strategy that makes the most of your strengths and matches them to the needs of the customers you want to target. For example, if you identify a group of customers that is looking for service first and foremost, then any marketing activity aimed at them should draw attention to the high quality

service you can provide rather than highlighting price.

Once this has been completed, decide on the best marketing activity that will ensure your target market know about the products or services you offer, and why they meet their needs. Limit your activities to methods that offer the best return on investment for your limited budget, avoiding spreading your budget too thinly on lots of different messages or marketing activities.

Chapter 76
Marketing Plan

A strategy is all well and good, but actions come about as a result of a detailed plan so the next step is to draw up a detailed marketing plan that sets out the specific actions to put that strategy into practice.

Get yourself a Plan
Your marketing plan should set out the aims, actions, dates, costs and other resources that you will use to market the business. It will;

Recognize your budget for marketing
Explain which group of customers you are targeting and how they can be recognized
Explain the message that you want to communicate to the potential customers about your business
Specify what you are going to do over a short term period to communicate your message to customers
Explain how you will know if you succeeded or if you failed and when you will know - most marketing has a very short term effect.

Approach a third party for feedback about your plan - they may be able to spot any gaps or weaknesses that you can't see.

Review the plan regularly
Measure the effectiveness of what you do. Be prepared to change things that aren't working, you will need to create a flexible plan so that you can monitor it's effectiveness and make any adjustments required to maintain it's success this control element not only helps you see how the strategy is performing in practice, it can also help inform your future marketing strategy.
Ask each new customer how they heard about your business.

Other Recommendations
Google Shopping is indispensable for an on-line retail business, you must use that at least as part of your plan. If that's all you can afford, just do that.

More money is wasted on marketing than any other aspect of business, approach every opportunity with a huge dose of skepticism, the following activities almost never work for an on-line store, do not do them!

- Banner advertising
- Bulk mail shots
- SPAM
- Price comparison engines

All advertising rates are highly negotiable, if you want to advertise offline in a specialist magazine or newspaper that can work, but the price that you pay should be 25% of the rate card value or less, haggle hard and measure the results carefully to make sure that you are getting value for your spend.

The next few chapters will go through some of the marketing activities that you should consider making a part of your plan.

Chapter 77
Google AdWords

It is pretty fair to say that right now in February 2016 if anyone is in control of the Internet it is Google. Google runs 'The Internet' because what most people are really referring to when they say 'The Internet' are the pages that they find when they search for something on Google.

As Google has become more and more important as a search engine it has also become the primary method for advertising an shop on-line. If you want to pay to advertise your on-line store you should start by advertising on Google.

Even though there are lots of search engines about including Yahoo (remember them?), Ask, Bing from Microsoft as well as the mighty Google, in the USA when people search on-line they use Google 80% of the time, In the UK and Europe it's more like 90%. The only places that Google does not dominate on-line search are Russia, China and South Korea. Russia uses a search engine called Yandex, China has Baidu and South Korea has Naver.

When you make a search on Google you will see two kinds of results. On the one hand you will see the 'natural search' results, here you will see that Google tends to return sites which carry information rather than selling things at the top of the page, Google does this on purpose as they prefer people who are selling things to pay them for the privilege of getting traffic from Google.
The other results at the very top and to the right hand side of the results are paid adverts, make some Google searches for the type of products that you are selling and compare the results with the ones shown below.

When I search for 'PLA Filament' using my laptop I get these results

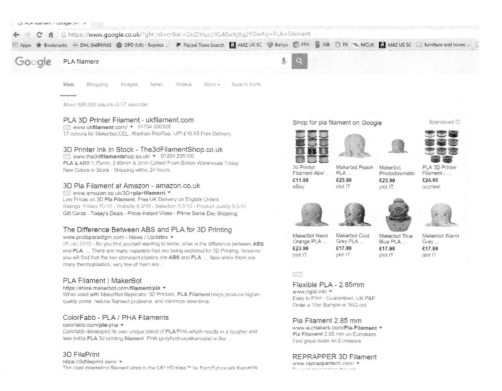

There are 18 listings on this page. 4 of them are 'natural search' and the other 14 are paid adverts, there are actually two different kinds of advert here. The image below shows the difference. The adverts in the top left box are AdWords adverts that bid the most, they are 'Top ranking' AdWords adverts, those in the bottom right are more AdWords adverts that rank lower than those in the top left, they continue if you scroll down and onto the following pages.

The box at the top right contains 8 adverts placed through a different part of the AdWords system called 'Google shopping' these adverts have pictures and prices, they are much more effective than the regular AdWords adverts.

It's worth noting that the four natural search listings are not directly selling things, although the bottom three are from shops that do offer filament the pages that are shown are information pages, not product sales pages - Google is not one of the most profitable companies in the world by accident. If you want to sell through Google, you pay Google to do it.

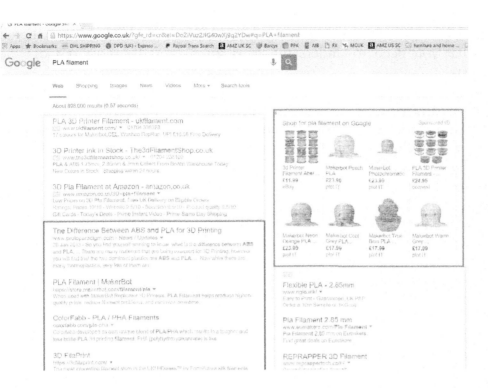

To make sales from your on-line shop you need to have your pages listed as high up on Google as possible. The difference between the sales that you will get as one of the retailers listed in the picture above and the sales that you will get as one of the people listed on the bottom half of page one, the bit that you can't see in the picture above, the ones that I would have to scroll down to see, is as much as ten times.

So the big question is how do you get your pages and products listed here?

The process of getting your pages listed as high as possible in the natural search section on Google is called 'Search Engine Optimization' sometimes shortened to the acronym 'SEO'. SEO is sometimes seen as a low cost way of getting traffic to your website, but as you can see above the amount of space that Google allows for natural search results is very small, it also discriminates against stores in natural search and since there are thousands of stores all aiming to get listed at the top of those results SEO is not really a great way to promote your small store, if you want to get sales through Google you need to put your hand in your pocket and pay for them.

Google AdWords and Google Shopping

Google makes it really easy to set up and run a campaign on AdWords but there is quite a lot that you need to understand in order to get the most out of your Google adverts.

To run Ads of any type of Google you need to have an account set up with Google AdWords. From your AdWords account you can run the 2 different kinds of Adverts on the Google search engine that are shown above, ('Text' ads and 'Shopping' ads) as well as Banner Ads on a huge range of web sites outside Google and Video Ads on YouTube.

You set these different types of Advert up in Google as separate 'Campaigns', each campaign is split up into one or more sections called 'Ad groups'. Within each Ad group you can define a number of Adverts and define when Google will show your Ads to people who are searching on Google or browsing the web.

It helps if you split up your activities on Google into logical sections, my recommendation is that you plan out what you want to advertise using a chart like the one below - this is what I am going to show you how to set up.

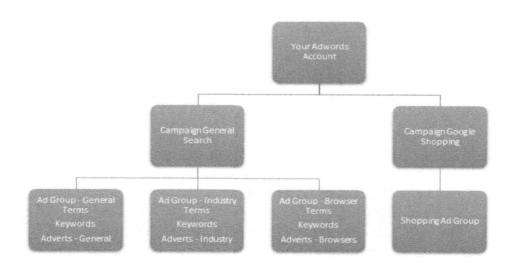

I'm not going to show you how to set up Video Ads or Banner Ads - my experience has been that they do not have a great return on investment for a small store, but you can experiment with them as well once your Shopping and Ad Words campaigns are set up and you are familiar with the interface.

This is how you set up a new Google AdWords account;

Use Chrome
I'm sure that it comes as no surprise to you that all Google services work better if you use the Google Chrome web browser, some parts of the AdWords service ONLY work in Chrome so it's important that you use Chrome as your web browser when accessing AdWords.

Log in to your Google Account
To use any of the services offered by Google you need to log in using your 'Google Account', If you followed my recommendation about using Google Apps for your business e-mail then you already have a Google account and you can just log into that, if not then you need to set up a new Google account to access Google services, you can do that here. https://accounts.Google.com/SignUp?.

You can use an existing e-mail address with a service other than G-Mail as your AdWords login if you want to or sign in with your personal Gmail account, but think carefully before you use a personal Gmail address as the login for your business Google AdWords account - I'd recommend setting a new dedicated account instead to keep your business separate even if you don't use Google Apps for your company mail.

Set up an AdWords Account
Once you are logged into your Google Account you can go ahead and add AdWords to the Google Services that your account can access, go to https://AdWords.Google.com/ to set up your AdWords account.
Google uses a simple form to have you enter all the details needed to set up your AdWords account - but of course Google is a business and the form is set up with defaults that are intended to maximize your spend with Google, I'll show you how to set up your account to get the best ROI

On the first page of the setup Google will auto populate your email address if you are logged in to your Gmail account and ask you to enter the domain name for your store, do that and press 'Continue'.

The next step is to create the settings for your first campaign on AdWords using the form shown below.

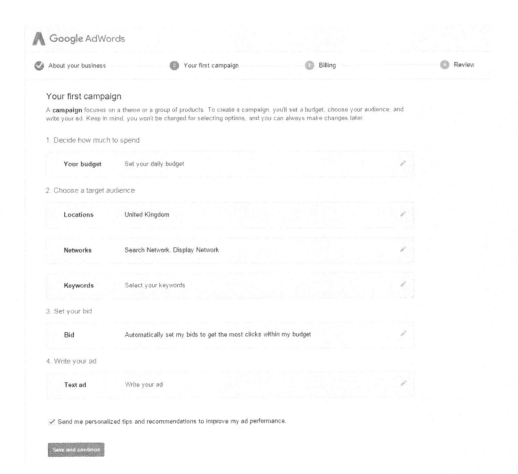

This is a quick form intended to get you set up quickly, we will use it to set up the General Search Campaign part of our Google AdWords Campaign

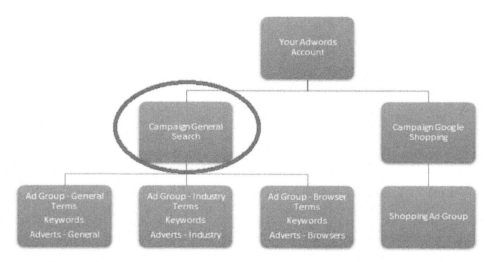

Start by setting your budget, click on the 'Your Budget' box at the top to open it out.

When you set your budget you will also set the billing currency for your account - the budget can be altered later so set the budget low to start with and increase later. I suggest £10 or US$15 per day to start with - that's still over £3,000 (US$5,000) per year.

The currency that you will use to pay for advertising on Google is fixed for ever when you set the account up, I recommend that you choose the currency of the credit card that you will use to pay your bills to avoid paying currency conversion fees.

The location will have been set from your account details, you can change it if you like, but I will leave it set to 'United Kingdom' to cover the whole UK, if you are shipping large of bulky items you can use this section to exclude areas like offshore islands or remote areas that you can not ship to easily. If you can't ship to an area why pay for your ads to be shown to people who live there?

You can exclude regions by post code or name, just start typing and options will appear for you to select from a drop down menu. If you don't see the area that you want try phrasing the name differently, Google's naming can be a bit awkward. The whole campaign will be targeted at the physical location or group of locations that you build in this section you can add and subtract areas using the 'Add' link to include a region or the 'Exclude' link to exclude a region. You can target countries, towns or areas made up of complex combinations of all three like 'France except Paris and the Pas de Calais'. If you are not sure where to target just target your first campaign at the whole of your home country, you can change it later if you like.

Next you can choose where your AdWords run, by selecting the 'Networks' section

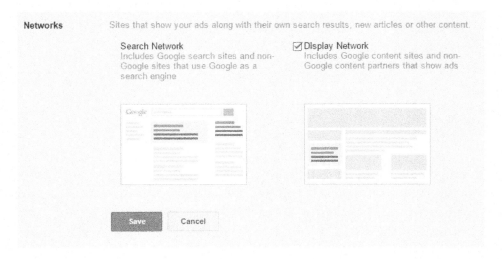

You can choose which 'networks' your ads run on - I strongly recommend that you restrict your ads to run on Google ONLY. If you don't restrict them then your Google ads will run on a wide range of sites outside of Google, these sites are

members of the 'Google Display Network'. Sites outside Google that run Google ads get a big share of the money that you pay Google for displaying the adverts, in my experience there are lots of scammers using these adverts to generate revenue through clicks by people who have no intention of buying anything so avoid them by setting up your campaigns to run on Google only by un-ticking the 'Display Network' box.

Next you need to set up the first Keywords for your ads, these are the phrases that will trigger your Ads when they are used in Google Search, open up the 'Keywords' section of the form

Keyword	Search popularity
horse tack	60500
saddles	40500
western saddles	14800
horse supplies	27100
horse saddles	12100
saddles for sale	12100
western saddle	33100
horse saddle	22200
english saddle	14800
western tack	4400

Google will go and collect product data from your web site and suggest a group of words that you could use, next to each you will see a green line and a number that gives you some idea of the popularity of each phrase. If you just hit the 'Add' button at the bottom of the window all of the suggested keywords will be added to your campaign. If you click the grey 'X' to the right of any of them they will be removed from the list and if you hover over any one you will see a button appear marked 'More like this' which you can use to add extra phrases that are similar to the one you highlighted.

At this stage you want to manipulate the list to show 10-20 key words that you think will be helpful in bringing buyers to your site, you can use the suggestions or just type extras into the box at the bottom of the list separated by commas.

When choosing keywords now and in the future remember that you want buyers, not browsers, so make the phrases as specific as possible, general phrases like 'Horse Tack' for my example store are best avoided as they will bring in a lot of general traffic, but not buyers, 'Black English Saddle' is a much better phrase for the example store. When you have a list that you are happy with press the blue 'Save' button and you will see your list of keywords in the window.

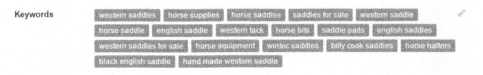

Leave the list for now, we will modify it a lot later.

The kind of advert that you are setting up on Google is called a 'Pay Per Click' advert, you pay Google for each time that a user clicks on the advert to be connected to your web site, the next part of the set up is to set the 'default' bid for your campaign or to let Google automatically set the bid for you.

Honestly Google offer to decide for you how much you should pay them - if you are crazy and rich then let Google do that for you.

If not then open out the window, change the setting to 'I'll set my bids manually' and set a low bid to start with like 10c or 10p (set as $0.1 or £0.1), you can always raise it later and you don't want to waste too much while you are still getting to understand the system.

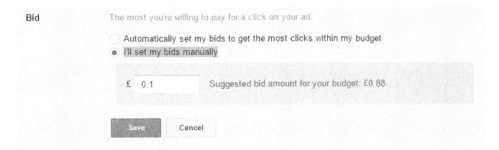

Once that's done click the blue 'Save' button and move on to the bottom section to write your first Ad, like the keyword set up section this part of the form is just there to get you started with a single Ad and help you understand how they work, but you will be able to modify the Ad or set up lots more later so there is no need to spend too much time on it.

Page 371

Opening out the section shows this editor

The 5 boxes on the left allow you to create the Ad and the image on the right shows you what it will look like when it is shown to customers.

Before you start to fill out the form open up a new tab and do a Google search for some of your key phrases - look at the AdWords that appear from your competitors and think about how you want your Ad to fit in.

Here are the search results for my example store

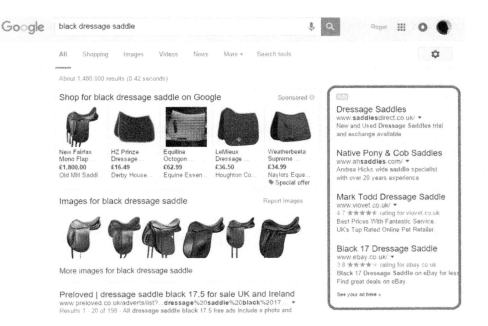

The AdWords text ads are highlighted in red

This is a great time to remember all of the work that you did on your Marketing Strategy. Make your Ad up using the key selling points that you want to highlight with potential customers.

As you type you will see tips popping up, you will also see a counter in the far left of the box telling you how many characters you can still use in this section and the sample Ad will appear over to the right as it will look to your customers.

When you are done click 'Save' to go to the payment details page.

First choose your Country, where you are based - by doing this you change the options that Google offers for payment method etc.

Country: United Kingdom

Tax information
Tax status
Business
This service can only be used for business or commercial reasons. You are responsible for assessing and reporting VAT.

VAT ID (Optional)
GB -

If you are based in the EU Google will offer you the option to enter your European VAT registration number into your account, by doing this you become eligible for billing of Google AdWords charges excluding VAT. This is possible because Google bills you from Luxembourg. You are supposed to report this VAT free billing from an EU state on your VAT Returns and pay over the VAT separately, however I understand that some people tend to forget to do that…

The next step is to complete your company details and payment method. I recommend that you pay for your AdWords by allowing Google to make automatic charges to your credit card to start with. Google also offers to collect cash by direct debit direct from your bank, but a credit card gives you more control over the spend and it will have a built in limit to stop the spend getting out of control.

Lastly you need to set the time zone for your account - this is really important, the time zone that you set should be the time zone of the target customers for your Ads - this time will be used to set the time that your Ads run and to decide when each day starts and ends for reporting purposes.

From time to time Google send out vouchers for free advertising through AdWords, they do deals with registrars like GoDaddy and sometimes with Shopify, look around and you may be able to find a voucher for £75 (US$100) of free AdWords. It's worth looking.

Press the blue 'Save and continue' button and you will be taken to a final page where you review your information and accept the Google Terms and conditions, once you have done that you can click the blue 'Finish and create campaign' button, this will take you to a confirmation page like this

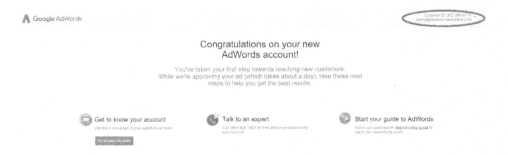

Congratulations, you now have a Google AdWords account set up and ready to go. Your AdWords Customer ID is shown in the top right hand corner of the page, circled in red in the top right hand corner of the screen, It's worth making a note of this number now as you will need it later.

Once you have noted the Customer ID click on the blue 'Go to your account' button to open the normal AdWords interface for your account, Google will give you a quick tour showing you where all the key features are, then you will see the standard AdWords interface with the one Campaign and Ad group that you set up already.

Page 375

Before you start using your new AdWords account you need to understand a bit more about how AdWords works.

Account Structure
As we explained above your Google AdWords account is split up into one or more Campaigns, each Campaign is set up to run a single type of Ad and contains a number of Ad groups each running adverts against a group of Keywords.

So far we have set up a Campaign that runs one Text Ad on Google and the Google Search network based on a short list of Keywords that we have selected to customers in a specific geographic region.

It makes good sense to split up your campaigns into as many ad groups as you can - because Google will show your ads more and at a lower cost if they think that they are more directly relevant to the things that customers are searching for.
OK - Of course 'Google' does not 'think' - 'Google' is basically just a big computer program, it calculates based on historic data rather than thinking.

The AdWords system is designed to favor Ads that get more clicks over those that get less by showing them higher up in the search results and showing them more often. It does this because clicks on your Ads mean revenue for Google, and it also favor's Ads that customers like better - because Google does better when people think that the results that they get on Google are more relevant than those on Bing, Yahoo and the other search engines. Google will show you how it rates your Adverts and keywords using a numerical value called 'Quality Score', the better your Quality Score the more often your Ads will be shown and the lower the cost they will have.

Quality Score

Quality Score is Google's rating of the quality and relevance of your keywords, landing pages, and PPC campaigns.

By splitting your campaigns into many Ad Groups each with it's own Ads and Keywords linked to specific landing pages you will improve your Quality Score for those keywords.

Quality Score is important to how high up the search results your ad will appear - but the amount that you are prepared to bid for a click is also important, it's the combination of the two that will get you to the top of the results.

The AdWords Interface

The Google AdWords interface is best viewed through Google Chrome, when you look at it you will see that it is based on the hierarchy that you see in the diagram above, when looking at the account you see a list of campaigns and then when you click on an individual campaign you see the list of Ad groups under that Campaign, within each Ad group you can edit the keywords and ads that are associated with that group as well as changing the bid that you are prepared to pay for clicks on each ad presented against that Keyword.

You can get help from Google to set up and operate your AdWords system, for basic help with the AdWords interface click on the settings icon in the top right hand corner of the screen and then select 'Help' from the drop down menu.

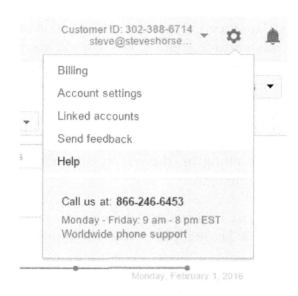

Click on Help to bring up a 'Help' window where you can browse articles written by Google as well as the user forums, you can also call or e-mail Google staff who will be able to help you with specific problems

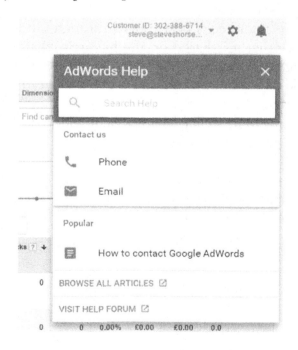

You can search for help articles using the box at the top of the menu.

The AdWords interface can be heavily customized, you can use it in many different

ways to analyze your Account performance and to change the way that your Ads appear, explaining everything that you can do with AdWords is beyond the scope of this book, however I will help you get started and avoid expensive mistakes at the start.

Understanding Keywords

When a prospective customer goes looking for a purchase using Google to find a retailer they will make a search, typing a word or phrase into Google and hitting the search button.

The name 'Keywords' is a bit misleading, what you set up in AdWords are actually phrases, they can be up to 80 characters long including spaces.

The Keywords that you set up in your Ad groups are the link between these searches and your Ad. You can choose to show your ad against any search that is similar to your keyword, to any search that contains your search or only against searches that exactly match your keyword these choices are called 'Match Types'

Match Types

There are three basic types of match between Google searches and your keywords, they are Broad match, Phrase match and Exact match.
To get a bit more control over where your Ads appear you can change the way that the Broad match type works by using modifiers and you can add negative keywords to campaigns and to Ad Groups to stop your ads showing where they are irrelevant.
Google has a really good help article that tells you in detail how the different match types work with examples I recommend that you look at that before adding keywords to your campaigns, but of course Google want you to spend as much money as possible with them, bear that in mind when reading all their help text.

In short the different types of Match work like this

Broad match
Broad match will show your advert against any search that is even remotely similar to the keyword that you choose, for example if you are selling horse tack and equipment and you choose to use the broad match keyword 'horse' your ad will show against any search with the word horse in it, or even searches that contain

words like 'equine' or 'mule' as Google considers these to be similes for 'horse'. Most of these searches will not be relevant to your store.

Phrase match
Phrase match keywords have to appear in the search exactly as they are typed, using the same example as above you might use a Phrase match of 'buy horse tack' - this is a much more tightly defined keyword, it will show a lot less, but anyone searching for 'where can I buy horse tack' or 'buy horse tack in Shropshire' will still see the Ad - and those people are the people that you want to get to your site - right?

Exact match
For your ad to show against an Exact match keyword the user has to search for EXACTLY the same thing that you entered as the keyword, that's the most closely targeted type of keyword.

Be aware that Google does actually stretch these definitions a bit - it will show Ads that have a singular keyword against searches for the plural in some circumstances and it will also cross over keywords to words that it considers to be misspellings.

How to get best value from keywords
From the point of view of someone setting up an AdWords account for an on-line retail business the key to running an AdWords account is to get value for money, that means that you only want people to click on your Ads who are going to buy something. With this in mind you will see that using Broad match is stupid, and lazy. Don't use Broad match.
Google makes Broad match the default for new keywords for a reason - it makes them a ton of money! Using broad match even with modifiers and negative keywords will produce lots of clicks but no orders.
I recommend using only Phrase match and Exact match keywords for all on-line retail adverts, in that way you can control the searches that your Ads appear against much more carefully - remember that you are trying to get orders NOT traffic.

When we set up the keywords on our first Ad group they were created as 'Broad Match' keywords - I want to fix that - here is how we do it.

Firstly, in the AdWords interface make sure that you are looking at the correct Campaign, you can do this by selecting it from the list on the left hand side of the screen.

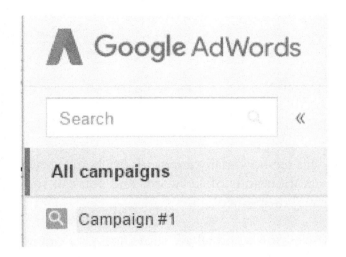

Then click on the 'Keywords' Tab to see all keywords in the currently selected Campaign

This will show you a long list of the keywords that are set up in the currently selected Campaign (if you select 'All campaigns' in the top left then it will show you all keywords in All campaigns)

If you look at the bottom of the list

In the bottom right hand corner you will see how many keywords are being shown, some campaigns have hundreds or even thousands of keywords and you can show up to 500 in the list using the 'Show rows' dropdown.

Here we are just looking at a list of 18 keywords and all are showing so we can just select them all by clicking on the select all box at the top of the list on the left.

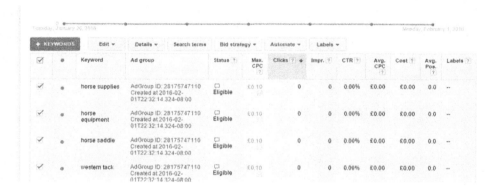

Then select the 'Edit' menu and select 'Change match types'

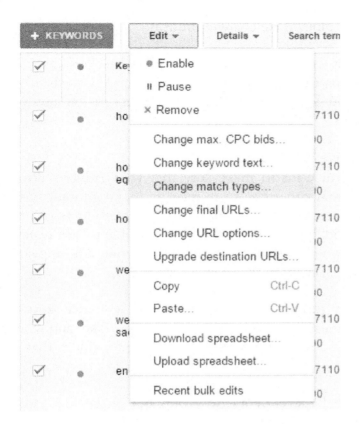

This will bring up the 'Change match type' window

You can see at the top how many keywords you have selected, which is a good guide, then below that you will see the type to change from and the type to change to, only keywords that are selected AND have the type of match set in the top part will be affected by the change, so select 'Broad match' at the top and 'Exact Match'

at the bottom and then press the blue 'Make changes' button

You will see that your keywords are now enclosed in square brackets [like this] Thats how Google shows you that they are set up as exact match keywords, if you choose to add new keywords you can add them directly as exact match keywords by typing them in square brackets.

Next we will add some Negative Keywords
There are always times when you want to make sure that your Adverts do not show in particular searches that may otherwise seem relevant to a computer system like Google, for example if you are selling Scandinavian Timber products you may use the keyword 'Norwegian wood' but if so you would be sensible to add negative keywords for "Beatles" and "song" and "Lyrics" to avoid your ads appearing alongside searches by fans of the song with that name.

Similarly if you sell top quality jewelry you will use a phrase match keyword 'Diamond Ring', but you should also use negative keywords like 'fake' and 'cheap' to make sure that bargain hunters don't cost you money looking for things that you do not sell.

Keywords can only be applied at the level of an Ad group, but Negative keywords can be used at either Ad group or Campaign level - applying a few negative keywords at Campaign level can help to save a lot of wasted clicks.

You always want to avoid showing your Ads in irrelevant searches as there is a chance that they will be clicked on by accident or by someone who misunderstands what they are doing, these clicks cost a lot of money and don't sell anything. Do that by choosing keywords carefully and using lots of negative keywords.

To add negative keywords in the 'Keywords' tab select 'Negative keywords' from the menu just below the tabs

You can add negative keywords at the Ad group or Campaign level, try to do both. For the example store I am going to add campaign level negative keywords for 'cheap', 'DIY', 'home made' and 'plans' by removing searches that contain this kind of phrase I think I will avoid clicks from people who are not interested in buying - they are still welcome on my site, but I just don't want to pay to get them there.

Once your Ads are running you can check which phrases have triggered your Ads by clicking on the Keywords tab, selecting some keywords and then selecting the 'Search Terms' button. Look through the list and find negative keywords that way.

Add some more Ad groups to your campaign
You should add some more Ad groups to your campaign, just 3 or 4 - set them up

in the same campaign so that they inherit the same settings, it will help you understand how the system works.

Understanding Ads
In each Ad group you can set up as many Google AdWords Ads as you like, each one is made up of a headline of up to 25 characters, a URL and two additional lines of text of 35 characters each, if your Ad appears on the right hand side it looks like this

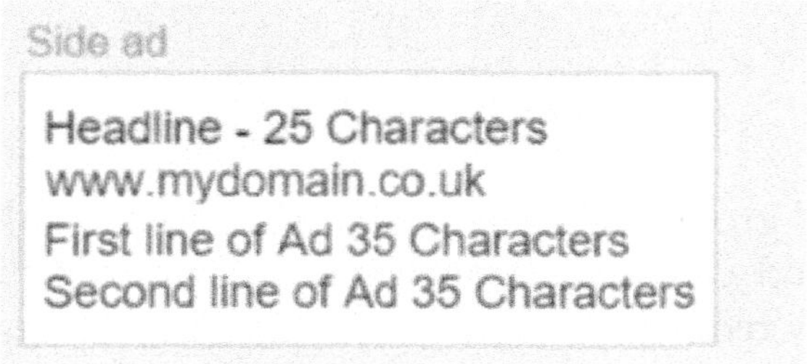

```
Side ad
Headline - 25 Characters
www.mydomain.co.uk
First line of Ad 35 Characters
Second line of Ad 35 Characters
```

If it appears at the top of the search results it looks like this

```
Top ad
Headline - 25 Characters
www.mydomain.co.uk
First line of Ad 35 Characters Second line of Ad 35 Characters
```

Writing an eye catching, informative and compelling advert in just 95 characters is an art in it own right.

You can set up as many Ads as you like in each Ad group, but you can not decide which ones get shown - Google will do that for you, so to get the top performance out of your AdWords campaign you need to keep checking back on the performance of your Ads and tweaking your Ads to improve the messaging.

To begin with just think of the main reasons why people should buy from your store and use them to create your Ad, make the headline the BEST thing about your store and the next two lines the things that make people buy from you.

Set up some more Ads
I recommend that for each of your first Ad groups set up at least 3 Ads using different messages and text.

Conversion tracking

It is really important that you track how many orders you get from your Google AdWords advertising, by doing that you can track what return you are getting from your AdWords Advertising and hence adjust your spend to make sure that you make money from your advertising.

To set up conversion tracking on a Shopify site is quite easy to do yourself, but it is a little harder on Magento based sites and on bespoke sites.

Conversion tracking works by running a small script on the order confirmation page of your website that lets Google know that an order has been placed, Google then checks to see if the customer came to your site from Google using cookies placed on the users web browser by Google.

To add the tracking code to your Shopify store first get the code from your AdWords account

In your AdWords editor look at the top menu and select 'Tools' then choose 'Conversions' from the drop down menu

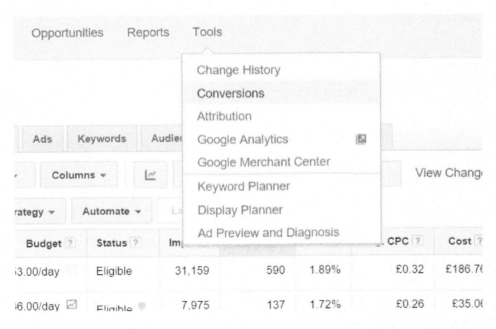

On the next page choose '+Conversion'

And follow the instructions to set up a conversion tracking code for an order placed.

Choose 'website' as the conversion type
Call the Conversion type 'Sale'
Set the Value to 'The value of this conversion action may vary (for instance, by purchase price)'
Leave Count, and the Conversion windows settings at default, change the Category of the conversion to 'Purchase/Sale' then save
You will then see your tracking code in a box like this

You need to select the code in the Tag box and copy it to your clipboard, Note that the code is longer than the box, but if you are using chrome it should all select when you click anywhere in the window. Press 'Control C' to copy the code then switch to your Shopify store Admin.

In your Shopify Admin select the bottom menu item 'Settings' then choose

'Checkout' from the slide out menu and scroll down until you see the box headed 'Additional content and scripts' shown below

Simply paste the tracking code into the box, click save and you are done.

I recommend that you set up Google AdWords conversion tracking on your website BEFORE you start running AdWords.

Chapter 78
Google Shopping

Now that you have a Google AdWords account set up with one Text Ad Campaign and a few Ad Groups under it we will add a second Campaign to your account using Google Shopping to run product adverts.

You need to use Google Shopping - there is no realistic alternative
If you want to sell anything on-line in the UK, USA, Canada or Australia then you should use Google shopping, it is the best way to get your products in front of potential customers.

Google Shopping is a part of the Google AdWords family of products, it allows you to advertise your product set using your product images and showing the current price of the item in your advert, these adverts normally appear in the top right hand side of a Google search results page - the best location and they are really powerful as they include a picture and a price to tempt buyers over to your store.

Google Shopping adverts allow customers to view pictures of your products and their prices alongside those of your competitors. Because of this they tend to attract people who are ready to buy things - so the conversion rates on shopping Adverts are much better than for standard AdWords.

Google automatically sets the shopping adverts up for you, but to allow it to do so you need to provide the information about your products, names, descriptions, prices, pictures and so on that Google Shopping needs to work. You provide the data by uploading it to an account with a Google service called 'Google Merchant Center', the data there will be updated every day by an App that we are going to install in your Shopify store, but first we need to set up an account in Google Merchant Center.

Create an account with Google Merchant Center
Login to your Google account - the same one that you use for your AdWords account and then point your web browser to https://merchants.Google.com/Signup. Fill out the form there to set up your account.

You will notice that you need to specify which country you are targeting - a Google Merchant Center account can only target one country and the listings that you use for that country should be in the appropriate language and use the correct national currency. If you want to target multiple countries through Google shopping you will need a separate account pointing to a different web URL for each country and to translate your web site - that is actually quite easy to do and it will be the subject of my next book!

However for now just choose the home country of your current web site. If you set up an account targeting a country that uses a different language or currency to your web site it will work for a while, but Google will eventually close the Merchant Center account until the content is translated.

When you put the URL of your store into the form, make sure that you include the 'http://' part at the start, otherwise you will see an error message 'URL must start with a scheme' when you try to save.

Next you need to tick the box and agree to Google's terms of service for Merchant Center, as usual these are a very one sided set of terms, basically Google takes your money and probably gives you a service for it, but they might not and if not you don't get your money back. And they can stop giving you this service any time for any reason at all! But frankly you have no choice but to accept.

Once you have agreed to the terms you lastly need to prove to Google that you really are the owner of your web site, obviously you do not want anyone else uploading fake product details for your web site and neither does Google. Google has a number of ways that you can prove to them that you own the site, for a beginner the best way to do this is to use the fact that you have already set up Google Analytics for your web store, click on the 'Alternative methods' box and then choose 'Google Analytics' as shown below

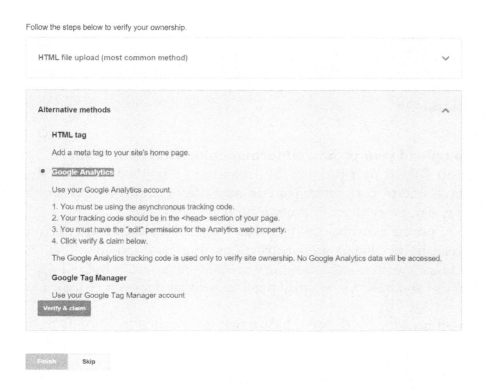

Click 'Verify&Claim' and your account set up will be complete.

Google may have already verified you when you set up Analytics - if so you only need the 'Claim' the website - once that's done you will see the Merchant Center dashboard for your new account

Note the account number which is shown in the top right of the page - you will need this later

109707831, Steve Horse and Tack
steve@steveshorseandtack.com

Set up a feed to upload your product information to Merchant Center
The next step is to upload your product information to Google Merchant Center. Because stock levels and prices change your ad needs to be regularly updated. You can update it every day, every week or every month at your choice.

You can choose to create a manual product data feed as a spreadsheet in Excel or in Google Spreadsheets, there are instructions on how to do that here https://support.Google.com/merchants/answer/188494?hl=en, but I don't recommend it unless you have a very small product set that does not change a lot.

The best way to set up a feed is to use the App that was written by Shopify to do it for you, by doing it that way you can be sure that your Google Merchant Center feed is always up to date, you just need to keep your product data up to date and that information will automatically be copied over to Merchant Center every day.

Add the Google Merchant Center Feed App to your Shopify Store
Open up a new browser tab, leaving the Merchant Center dashboard open in the current tab. In the new tab Login to your Shopify Store Admin and select 'Apps' from the left hand menu.

Apps

Then select 'Visit the App Store' from the top right of the screen

The App store will open in the same window of your web browser. Go to the search box in the top right and type in 'Google Shopping' a drop down list of suggested Apps will appear as below

As you can see there are a few choices of feed generator App, once you have been running your store for a while you may want to consider one of the paid Apps with extra features, but to get started the standard App provided free by Shopify is good enough, this is the icon for that App

Select that App and this page will appear

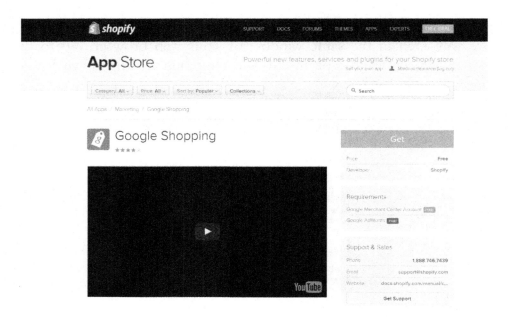

Select the big green 'Get' button on the top right to install the App in your store.

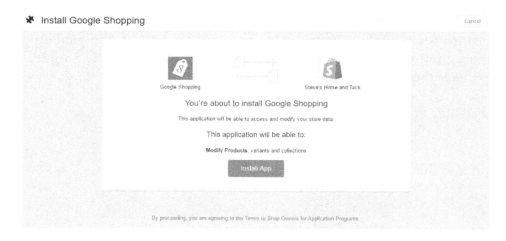

Press the blue 'Install App' button and the app will begin to be installed

Google Shopping / Getting Started

You need to sign into your Google Account from Shopify to let Google know that you are authorized to post to the Merchant Center account, press the blue 'Sign into your Google Account' button to do that and Allow the link.

Next you will need to enter your Merchant Center Account ID - you should have a note of it from when we set the account up.

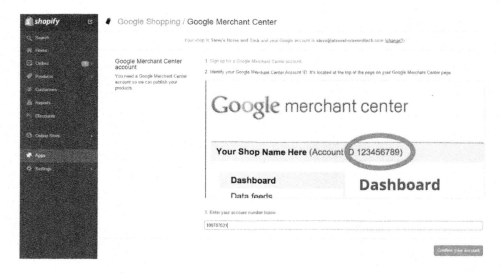

Type it in and press the blue 'Confirm your account' button

You will now need to set the tax and shipping rates for your products in Merchant Center.

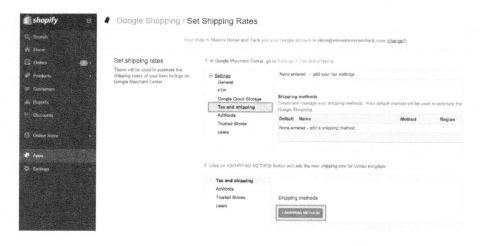

To compare your prices with other retailers in a fair and transparent way Google needs to know what you charge for shipping and taxes. To set these up click back on the Merchant Center Dashboard in it's own tab and select 'Settings' from the menu on the left

Select 'Tax' from the drop down menu

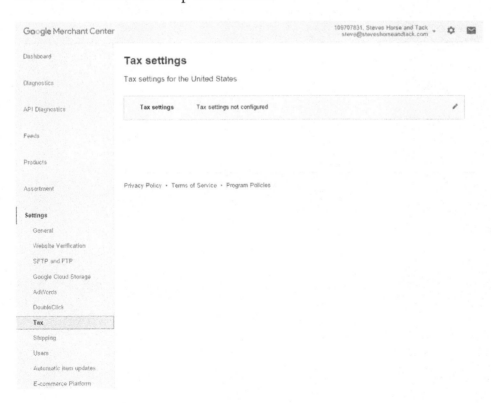

Google only needs tax rates for the USA at the moment, but even if you are not selling there you need to tell Google so press the Tax settings bar to open it out.

If you are based outside the US you can leave it set to 'Don't charge taxes in the United States' and hit save, if you are based in the USA then select 'Specify taxes for individual states' and set the states where you need to charge sales tax and the rates then press the blue 'Save' button.

Next click on the 'Shipping' menu choice under 'Settings'

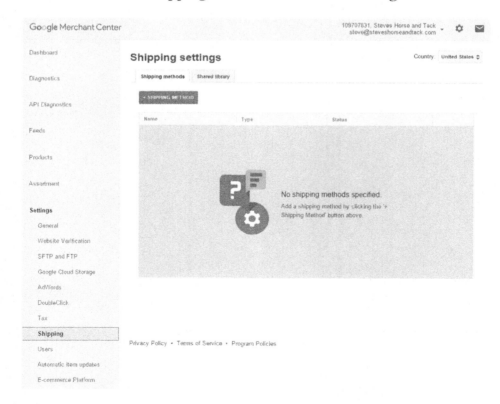

First choose your target country from the drop down in the top right.

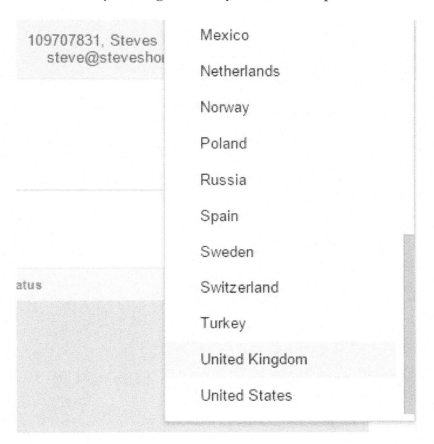

Next press the big red '+ SHIPPING METHOD' button

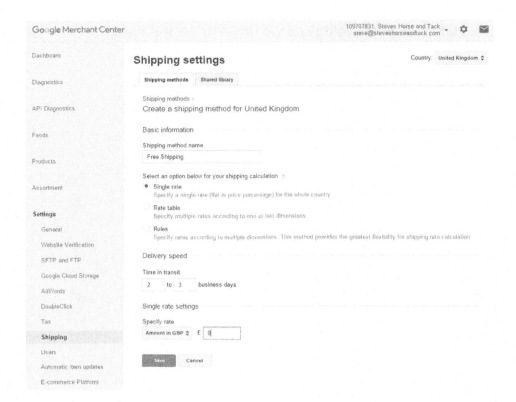

Fill out the details of your cheapest shipping method then press the blue 'Save' button.

You have now done the minimum required to allow the system to activate. Go back to the Shopify Admin window.

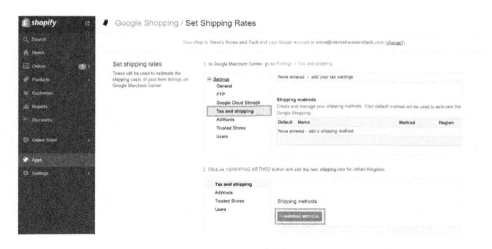

Scroll down to the bottom of the page and press the blue 'Test shipping rates' button

Shopify will go off to check that the configuration of Tax and Shipping rates has been done properly and then it will complete the set up and ask you what products you want to publish.

As long as you are happy to put all your products on Google Merchant Center just hit the blue 'Publish products' button. Alternatively you could select just a single collection to publish from the drop down.

Your products will now be published, if you have a lot of them it could take a few minutes.

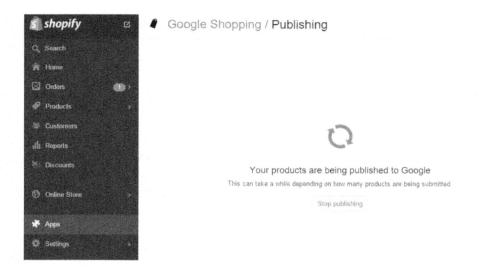

Don't worry - but the first time you publish all of your products will fail to publish because before they can be properly published you need to allocate them to Google Shopping categories, you should see a screen like this after the first try

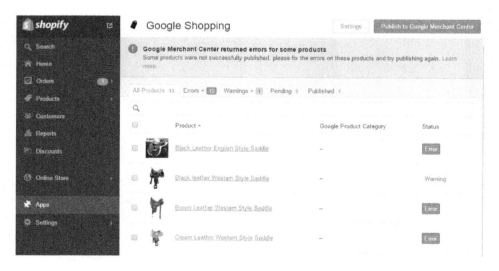

You can set the Google category for each item individually or you can set it for several items at the same time. For individual items just click on the item name and you will be taken to the Shopify product editing page where you will see that there is now a new field, installed by the Google shopping App. You can set the Google category here.

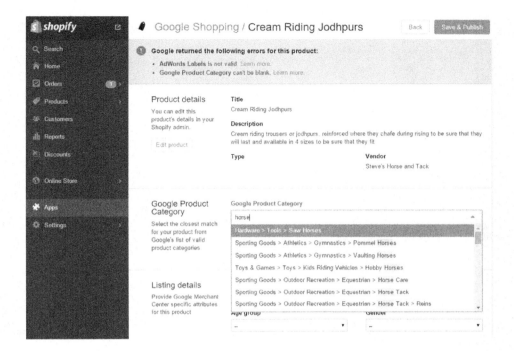

Just start typing the category name for your product and the matches from the Google taxonomy will pop up in the window, select the one that looks best and then press the blue 'Save & Publish' button.

Setting the category for every product in a whole store one by one would be really time consuming, so you can set multiple items at the same time, to do that go back to the App by selecting Apps and then clicking on the icon for the Google shopping App.

Multi select items from the same category by ticking the boxes to the left of the product images.

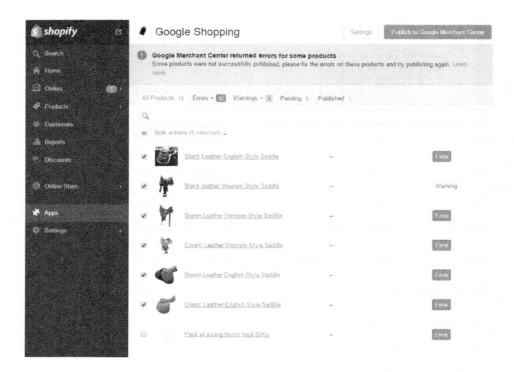

Then select the 'Bulk Actions' menu choice and select 'Set Google Product Category' a box will pop up where you can select the new category for all of the selected items.

Just type part of the category name and then select the correct category then press the blue 'Apply in bulk' button

The App will then try to publish the items to Google and you should see that the items have been published. Google has many complex rules about the data required for items in Google shopping, if there is other data missing the app will tell you and you can fix that in the same way. Normally you will need a Manufactures Part Number (MPN) or EAN code for most items.

Once the item is successfully published you will see a green tag to the right of the item to say so like this

Go through your products and make sure that they are all published and then you can move on to link your Merchant Center account to your AdWords account and set up a shopping campaign.

Link your Google Merchant Center Account to your Google AdWords account

To use your Google Merchant Center data in your AdWords campaign you need to link your Google Merchant Center Account to your Google AdWords account. To do that you create the link from your Merchant Center account and then accept it in your AdWords account.

Log into your Google Merchant Center account and on the left hand menu select 'Settings' and then from the drop down menu select 'AdWords'

Google may have already filled in your AdWords account details - if so you can just click the button to 'Send Link Request' if not select the red 'LINK ANOTHER ACCOUNT' button and enter the AdWords ID for your AdWords account.

You can find your AdWords client account ID on any page when you are logged into AdWords, it is a ten digit number that looks like this

Once you have clicked on the red 'LINK ANOTHER ACCOUNT' button you can enter the number into the box that opens up as shown below.

Link another AdWords account to this Merchant Center account

An AdWords customer ID appears at the top of every page in AdWords

AdWords customer ID

302-388-6714

Send link request   Cancel

Then press the blue 'Send link request' button.

To complete the process you need to accept the link in AdWords, to do that go back to your AdWords account and select 'Tools' from the top menu, then 'Merchant Center Account; from the drop down menu.

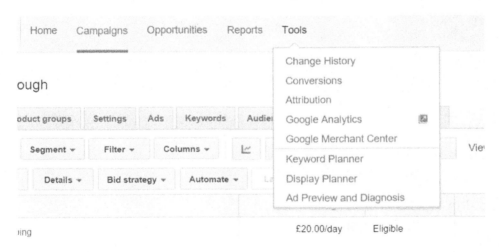

You will then be told that your Merchant Center Account has requested a link to your AdWords account. Accept it and the accounts are linked.

Set up a Google Shopping campaign in AdWords using the data from your Google Merchant Center Account.
The next step is to set up a Google Shopping Campaign in your AdWords account and start your Ads running.

To do this we need to set up a new Campaign in your AdWords account that will be dedicated to your Shopping Ads. Go to your AdWords account, select the

'Campaigns' tab and then the red '+ CAMPAIGN' button

There are a number of different types of Campaign that you can set up in Google Shopping, as we are trying to create a new Shopping Campaign, From the drop down that appears when you hit the red '+ Campaign' button you should select 'Shopping' as your new Campaign Type.

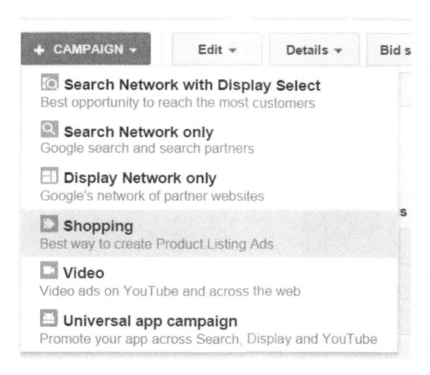

This will bring up a new page where you create the initial setting for your new shopping Campaign, the settings are very important so I will go through them one by one.

First you need to give your campaign a name

The name can be anything you like, I like to be obvious with these things…

The campaign type should be pre-set as shopping, leave that alone

Your Merchant Center ID should have been pre-populated

Next you need to decide on the country that you will target, you select that from a drop down menu.

It is VERY important that you target your campaign at the same country that you targeted your Merchant Center account towards or your ads will not run.

Next you choose which web sites will run your Ads. You thought that you were just advertising on Google - Right?
Wrong, Google Ads run on a huge range of sites, some very reputable, some less so and some are downright dodgy. I have found that Google search partners give you a much lower conversion rate than Google's own site does and as a result they offer very poor value for money.

Networks ? To choose different networks, edit the campaign type above, or create a new campaign.
✓ **Google Search Network** ?
☐ Include search partners

As default Google will have ticked the 'Include search partners' box, I recommend that you un-tick it to avoid paying for Ads on sites outside Google.

Next you will choose where the people that Google shows your adverts to are located

Locations ? Which locations do you want to target (or exclude) in your campaign?
○ All countries and territories
○ Hong Kong
● Let me choose...
[Enter a location to target or exclude] Advanced search
For example, a country, city, region, or postal code.

This setting crosses over with the country that you set as your target in the setting above - not everything in Google makes sense, but this can be a very useful feature to make sure that you don't waste money if you set it up correctly.

You can use this feature to avoid showing your Adverts to people who you can't sell to.

First select the 'Let me choose…' box as above.

Then enter your country name into the box marked 'Enter a location to target or exclude.'

Once you see your country name pop up under the box select 'Add' next to the name

Page 413

If you leave it like that your adverts will be shown to everyone in the whole of the country, but perhaps there are parts of the country that you can not ship to? - If you are a furniture retailer and you don't want to advertise to people who live on islands offshore because you can't ship to them economically you can exclude them from ever seeing your adverts. To do this type in the name of the place that you want to exclude or it's post code, then select 'Exclude' from the blue options next to the name when it appears in the pop up.
You can exclude as many regions as you like from your Ads

You may be surprised that Google knows the postcode for the Shetland isles - but maybe not, Google knows everything...

Once you are happy with where your Ads will be shown move on to the next section. Here you define what you mean by 'location' in this section. First open out the Location Options (advanced) section by clicking on it

Location options (advanced)

Target	○ People in, searching for, or who show interest in my targeted location (recommended)
	● People in my targeted location
	○ People searching for, or who show interest in my targeted location
Exclude	○ People in, searching for, or who show interest in my excluded location (recommended)
	● People in my excluded location

The best settings for anyone selling physical products are shown above, they are NOT the defaults.

You may want to use the recommended settings if you are selling some kinds of services like tourist trips but if you are selling physical products you should switch them as shown above.

Next you will set the default bid per click and the budget for your adverts in this campaign each day

I recommend setting a low but realistic value for the default bid per click as you can easily increase it on a product by product basis, but if you set it too high you may make uneconomic bids on some items. Set the default at the lowest value that you think makes sense for a click on any of your items. If you are unsure about what you should be bidding check the 'AdWords Bidding Strategy' section below.

Next you will decide when your Ads will run

Page 415

Advanced settings

⊟ Schedule: Start date, end date, ad scheduling

       Start date   Dec 6, 2015

       End date   ● None
                    ○

     Ad scheduling   **Show ads all days and hours**
                          + Create custom schedule

Click on 'Schedule: Start date, end date, ad scheduling' to open up the section above.

If you like you can use this section to set a start and end date for your campaign, this is great for campaigns selling tickets for events or for campaigns around product launches.

You can also use this section to restrict the times that your adverts run you may get a better return on your investment in adverts at one time of the day than you do at others, if so you can schedule your Ads here - if you don't know yet just leave these set to the default to 'Show ads all days and hours'.

Ignore the last option 'Campaign URL options (advanced)' as this is not needed in a shopping campaign and then press the blue 'Save and continue' button.

You will then go on to the next page to create your product Ad. Even though Google will automatically create the ads from your product data you have to have an Ad group for the Campaign. You can also add up to 45 characters of unique promotional text to the bottom of your ads.

I recommend leaving the Ad Group creation option set to the default 'Start with one product group with a single bid for all products'

Give your Ad Group a sensible name and if you like add a promotion phrase like 'Great Service and Low Prices' - make it realistic so don't promise great service and low prices if you don't offer them, but it can help to highlight your business USP here.

Then press the blue 'Save and continue' button and you have set up a new Campaign in your AdWords account dedicated to Google Shopping Ads - nice work !

How to set product by product bids or category or label based bids

Once you have completed the set up of your Campaign and your product data has synchronized over to AdWords from Google Merchant Center your Ads will be live, but they will all be using the default bid for clicks that you set up for the whole account. If you followed my Advice and kept the bid relatively low but realistic then that should not be too much of a problem, your Ads will run and you will start getting traffic and hopefully a few orders that you can use to assess how that bid works for you. However if you made the bid too low then you may not get any traffic on some key items or even get any traffic at all so you need to change your bids.

One of the great things about Google Shopping campaigns in AdWords is that you have a lot of control over your bids for clicks you can even change the bid for each item if you like, find out how in the Google Help files.

There is a huge amount to learn about Google AdWords - try to read as much as you can about it and work on your campaign a little bit each day.

Chapter 79
Notes about Google Shopping

NOTE: Google Shopping started to be available in 2012 in the USA and UK, since then it has been extended into other territories, it is now available in the following countries. The USA, the UK, Australia, Germany, France, Japan, Italy, the Netherlands, Brazil, Spain, Switzerland and the Czech Republic, it is also available in a reduced form in Austria, Belgium, Canada, Denmark, India, Mexico, Norway, Poland, Russia, Sweden and Turkey. So you can use Google Shopping to address markets across a very wide geographic footprint.

NOTE: The products that you advertise on Google Merchant Center and the way that you advertise them must comply with Google's policy principles which say that

- Product listings should provide a positive experience to users.
- Product listings should be safe for all users.
- Product listings should be accurate and truthful.
- Product listings shouldn't violate users' trust or privacy.
- Product listings should comply with laws and regulations.
- Product listings should be compatible with Google's brand decisions.

What this means in practice is;

- Your site needs to be secure and to work properly for Google to send you traffic through Google Shopping.
- You need to report accurate pricing to Google in your data feed.
- There are some products that you can not sell through Google Shopping at all these vary from country to country in line with local laws but they include things like legal highs, some supplements, cigarettes, and guns.

Chapter 80
AdWords bidding strategy

When you start running a new AdWords account the most difficult thing to do (once you have figured out the AdWords interface) is to decide what price you should bid for a click through to your on-line store from a Google Shopping Advert, this section is here to give you a clear strategy on how to calculate what you should bid for clicks.

The basic formula for what you should bid is;

(AVERAGE PROFIT PER ORDER)*(RE-ORDER FACTOR)*(CONVERSION RATE)*(Google SHARE)

This can be used across your whole portfolio to get an average bid or on a product by product basis to define a product level bid for each item that you sell.
I strongly recommend that you take the time and trouble to calculate these numbers for your store.

AVERAGE PROFIT PER ORDER = (ORDER VALUE - COST OF GOODS - TAXES - REVENUE RELATED COSTS)
You should be able to calculate this for each item in your product portfolio, it is a very important number. This is the one number in the calculation that you can not use an assumption for.
Revenue related costs are the costs of credit card processing etc (assume 2.5% of the full sale price including tax), the cost of returns, any unrecoverable shipping costs including the cost of delivery into your warehouse and the cost of storage if applicable.
If your products are often sold on batches of more than one unit then this number is based on the average order batch rather than one unit.

RE-ORDER FACTOR = The number of orders that were placed by existing customers in the last 90 days divided by the number of new customers who placed their first order in the last 90 days plus 1.
So if you had 10 orders from existing customers and 100 orders from new customers in the last 90 days then your re-order rate is 1.1

This is an attempt to include the 'value of a customer' into the calculation for

advertising spend, obviously it is not a very scientific measure the way that I have defined it above. You may have a much better way to work out what your re-order rate is, if so use that to calculate an appropriate re-order factor for your business.
If you are not trading yet assume 1.1 to get started and then re-calculate it every week or so to try to get a better understanding of what this should be.

Normal values for re-order factor will be between 1 (meaning that nobody ever re-orders) and 5 (meaning that on average new customers place 5 orders in the 90 days after their first order) Don't use a number over 2 unless you are 100% sure that it's correct.

CONVERSION RATE = The number of people who order after clicking on your AdWords adverts / the number of people who click on the advert.
Once your AdWords account has been running for a while Google will give you this number as long as you have conversion tracking working properly.
For a new on-line store this will normally be a very small number, outstanding accounts get a conversion rate of about 0.05 (5% of clicks result in an order = one in twenty browsers buys) to 0.005 (0.5% of clicks result in an order = one in 200 browsers buys). If you have no historic data assume that this number is 0.01 (one in a hundred browsers buys)
The best conversion rate I have ever seen in real life is 0.1, although Amazon claim that they achieve 0.3 at Xmas…

Google SHARE = The percentage of the profit on your AdWords related sales that you want to give to Google for using their services. So for example if you want to give Google 90% of your profit then this would be 0.9. Google would love you to hand over all of your profit on the things that you are selling to them, or even more - you would be amazed how many otherwise sensibly run businesses do this without knowing that they are doing it, but I recommend that to start off you offer Google two thirds so set this to 0.66

Worked Example
A business makes furniture, their best seller is a coffee table priced to sell at £99

Cost of goods is £40, Tax is £17 and they cost a bit more to ship than the company can recover due to damages in transit and returns so considering credit card charges etc The profit on each item is £33

However one customer in ten buys two units together so the average profit per order is £36.3

Conversion rate on AdWords clicks is 0.012 and the 90 day re-order rate is 10% - which is pretty good

The furniture business is competitive so the company is happy to hand over 50% of the profit to Google to get new orders.

Their cost per click maximum bid is calculated as

36.3 * 1.1 * 0.012 * 0.5 = £0.24

Mobile Bid Adjustment
Google allows you to alter the amount that you bid for clicks from mobile devices relative to the amount that you pay for clicks from desktop devices. You can increase the bid or decrease it, however I would recommend that you only reduce the bid as while placing orders from a mobile device is becoming more common it is much more common to research on a mobile and then order from a desktop - since you want to catch buyers just before they order you should be bidding less on mobile - I recommend a bid of 50% less to begin with.
Once you have conversion data for mobile browsers you can adjust this up or down accordingly.

Chapter 81
Google Analytics & AdWords

Linking your AdWords account to your Google Analytics account will help you to get more data about the performance of your AdWords campaign that you can use to improve your sales and that's always a good thing.

It's very easy to do, from your AdWords home page select the 'Settings' cog from the top menu, then choose 'Linked accounts' from the drop down.

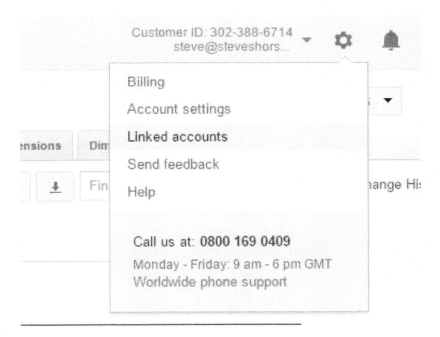

This will take you to the 'Linked Accounts' page on AdWords, once there choose 'Google Analytics' from the menu on the left hand side of the page.

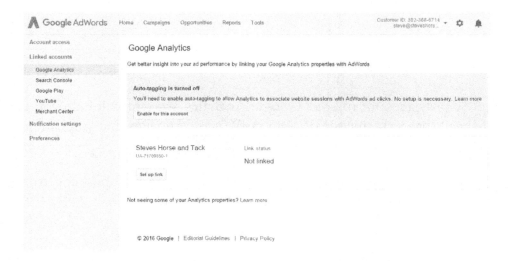

Google should have pre-filled in your Google Analytics account number so you can just press the grey 'Set up link' button, if it has not done that then you can just enter your Analytics account number to get the same effect.

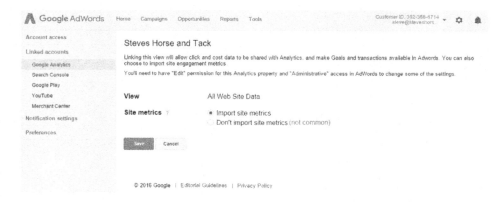

Leave the radio button selected for 'Import site metrics' and press the blue 'Save' button

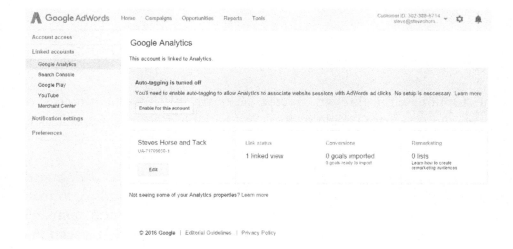

Next Enable Auto-tagging by pressing the 'Enable for this account' button

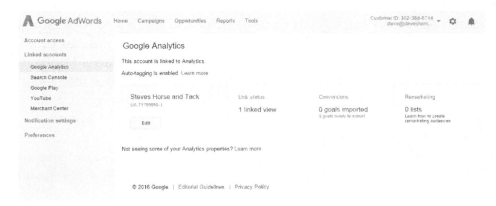

Your accounts are now linked and can be used to share goals that you can track as well as remarketing lists - all of these functions are outside the scope of this book, but there are lots of resources in AdWords help if you want to learn more.

Chapter 82
Search Engine Optimization (SEO)

Search Engine Optimization (known by the acronym SEO)is the process of making your web site easy for Google to read and making it clear to Google what you do and how you do it.

In the past Search Engine Optimization was considered a dark art, people used hidden links and specially created blog pages to point to web sites and try to make them look more important than they really were, all of these tactics ultimately failed as Google responded to this 'Cheating' and punished sites that engaged in it with lower ranking than they would otherwise have had.

If you want Google to recommend you as the best place to buy your products then you ultimately have two choices, on the one hand you can try to fool Google into believing that you are the best place to buy even though you are not or you can put your time and effort into actually BEING the best place. Fooling a company with the resources of Google is pretty tough and even if you manage it I doubt that you will manage it for long - trying to be the best place is much easier in the long run and it has added commercial benefits on top of the SEO benefit.

It's also worth noting that in this image for a Google search that I used earlier, the natural search results occupy 30% of the page and provide 22% of the results none of which are selling pages, what the SEO fight is over?

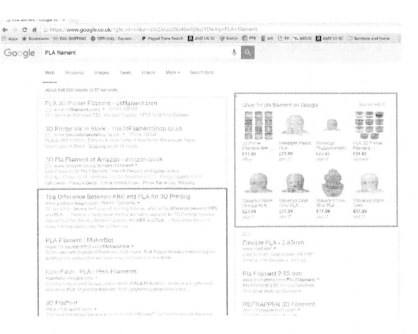

However being listed in Google natural search is helpful and there are a few things that you can do to make sure that Google knows that you are there and gives you some traffic.

Simple SEO Recommendations

Do the following simple things to make sure that Google knows who you are, what you do and what you sell, and if anyone tries to sell you 'Search Engine Optimization' services on top of that treat them in the same way as you would treat someone who was offering you diet pills or some money from the account of 'the former finance minister of the democratic republic of Shafiristan'

1. Make sure that your site has a valid site map available to Google's web crawlers. Shopify does this automatically, for Magento based sites and bespoke sites it needs to be specified in the requirements for the build.

2. Use Google webmaster tools to check how your site looks to Google, log into your Google account and go to https://www.Google.com/webmasters/tools/, you should see your site listed.
The link will look like this link for a site I manage if you are in the right place.

Page 427

Click on 'View details' in blue to enter webmaster tools for your site

The most important link on the whole page is the bottom one - the one to 'Search Console', A detailed explanation of how the search console works is beyond the scope of this book, but the Google supporting documents that you can see at the bottom of the image above are very helpful and I strongly recommend that you read them and get to grips with the search console.

These pages show you how Google crawls and indexes your site, they tell you if Google is having problems indexing your site and allow you to check the search queries that drive traffic to your site, as well as any links to your site from other web sites.

3. Make sure that the meta data is properly completed on all of your products, images and blog posts - and see how that makes a difference in webmaster tools (it can take 24 hours for changes to update to webmaster tools so be patient)

Once you understand how Google sees and ranks your site you will be in a much better position to decide if you want to try to do extra SEO work, but be realistic about what can be achieved in SEO for an on-line store.

Chapter 83
Bing

Bing (www.bing.com) is Microsoft's alternative to Google search, it's a fully featured search engine at the front end and behind that it has a system very, very similar to AdWords that you can use to advertise through Bing.

Bing has about a 5% share of web searches in the western world so it only really deserves about one twentieth of the time and money that you devote to Google, but the share that Bing takes is growing, partly because of the way that the new Windows 10 operating system and the Microsoft Edge web browser work, so I think that it's worth having a Bing account with a few ads running and keeping an eye on it for the future.

Bing has a similar system to Google Shopping called 'Bing Product Ads'. At the time of writing (January 2016) Bing Product ads are only available in the United States.

It may be worth investing in setting up Bing Shopping for your store once you have some free time, especially if the market share of Bing in search continues to grow. It will be less competitive than Google shopping so there may be some bargain traffic to be had in the short term. The people who used Google shopping before their competitors caught on got great deals for a while and the same thing could happen on Bing if Microsoft are able to drag users away from Google in sufficient numbers.

Chapter 84
Facebook Marketing

Facebook as a Platform for Finding Customers
If Google is the gateway to the Internet for most customers, Facebook is the world's social network of choice. The average American or UK based smart phone owner spends more than 40 minutes a day on Facebook. According to CEO Mark Zuckerberg in an earnings call in late 2014, Facebook accounts for one out of every five minutes spent using a smartphone.

In 2015 across both mobile and desktop, Facebook's share of Internet minutes was 19.3%, or about 6.3 times the amount of time spent on competing services.

There are potential customers for your store on Facebook.

Minimum level of engagement with Facebook
As well as using Google Shopping for advertising, you should probably also use Facebook as a part of your marketing strategy for your on-line store. The amount that you use it is up to you but at a minimum you need to set up a Facebook profile page for your store and manage it by checking every day for new comments.
Reply to all reasonable posts, if they are positive leave them there for all the world to see, if they are negative, like a complaint about a faulty product then reply, deal with the issue professionally and then delete the post a day or so later.
Delete any posts that are offensive or derogatory but never get involved in 'flame wars' with people who post that kind of thing, it's normally what they want and there is no benefit in that for your store or for you.

Other options of using Facebook
There are a number of ways that you can deepen and extend your store's use of Facebook to drive buyers to your web store, I'll separate them into things that you pay cash for and things that are payment free but cost you time.

Cash free ways to get more out of Facebook
Before you start using Facebook in more than the minimum way, you need to decide what you want from it. You can use Facebook to make sales directly for some items like costume jewelery or some home and fashion items, you can use it to collect newsletter subscribers or you could just collect Facebook likes to

broaden your reach.

Deciding what you want to achieve will inform the kind of activity you undertake

Here are few ideas for ways to use Facebook to deliver sales without paying anything.

- Regularly update your cover photo, doing so creates updates in your network. You can Change your Facebook cover to reflect a time of year or for a new product release, it helps to stay relevant.
- Don't worry about posting too much on Facebook as long as your posts are spaced evenly through the day there will be no problem. Less than 20% of your contacts will see each post because news feeds easily become over populated so the more you post, the better your chances are of being seen, but the quality of posts is important too, try to post a lot, but don't post rubbish just to post something.
- You can arrange posts on Facebook in advance and have them publish at a specific time, think about trying to engage regular customers with an update on a predetermined subject at the same time every week, provide useful information every week, for example if your store sells football kit for school kids you could publish match schedules and results sheets.
- Competitions are a great way to grow your likes and newsletter subscriptions, make a product or even a cash voucher the prize and insist on sign up for your newsletter and a Facebook like to enter, try partnering with a blog site or an influential group in your target market to advertise the competition. I have seen offers like that deliver hundreds of entries in just a few days. In the past you had to use a third-party application for Facebook contests, but Facebook recently changed their policy and now allows contests to be hosted directly on Facebook. Asking for users to provide a caption to an exciting or laugh-worthy photo is another smart strategy to drive interaction and engagement. A great example of a successful Facebook competition is the cover picture competition run by Dunkin Donuts. They ask fans to send in photos of themselves enjoying Dunkin Donuts and then choose their 'fan of the week' for their cover. It helps make customers engage with their brand and it encourages people to check back to see if they won the weekly contest. It's an ingenious use of free marketing space to engage fans and promote new products at the same time.
- Shopify stores include a free extension that allows you to sell directly from your Facebook page, it's easy to set up and looks great, and works well for

low value 'impulse' purchases like costume jewelery, low price clothing that Facebook users can share with each other. You can see the Facebook store app here https://apps.shopify.com/facebook-store, it is quick and easy to set up, but it does have a few special requirements such as square product photos.

- Facebook allows you to hide valuable content behind a 'like barrier' requiring users to like your page in order to get access to the content. Doing this with good quality content will get more likes to your page and engage more potential buyers. It helps to include an image and a nice call to action graphic.
- When you share a blog post or article use a large photo instead of the article box generated by Facebook, attach your own large (600 pixel wide is best) image to the post and add the link to the blog post using a URL link. A larger image can do a better job of capturing attention. You don't have to use a shot of your business, product or service, it helps if the image is relevant but the most important thing is that it will catch people's eyes and have them read your ad.
- Videos have much higher engagement rates than images which in turn have higher engagement rates than text only posts, so use your product videos in your Facebook posts to get some extra attention. Make sure to link them back to your product pages and add text captions to the videos to tell users where they can buy. Redbull has a huge following thanks to their high-quality, visually captivating content and while a start up store may not be able to make content that good at the start you can still get great attention for your site with video.
- Write short concise posts. They get more attention than longer articles, that's just the nature of Facebook, it's a short term medium. Trim down your posts to somewhere between 100 and 250 characters for optimal engagement through the News Feed of Facebook users on the go.

Try to link your posts to other organizations or people using Facebook tagging: Including tags in your posts is a great way to broaden your exposure, especially when working with other organizations. If you run a promotion giving away free dog treats from DOGGYCO tag the post with '@DOGGYCO'. With any luck DOGGYCO will see the tag and share your post with their fans, multiplying your reach. Tag as many friendly people and organizations as you can, tag conferences you're attending, tag businesses whose articles you're sharing, tag your best clients. Facebook has Hashtags, they are not very popular yet but they will get more popular. Use them to connect Twitter and Facebook marketing campaigns. You can also search Hashtag terms to discover fan conversations you may want to participate in, find your direct and indirect competitors, generate ideas, monitor customer conversations and find new product ideas.

Share good customer reviews on Facebook. Positive customer comments are always powerful, if you get a thank you note by e-mail why not share it on Facebook? Get the customers permission if possible and tag them in the post with a big thank you or make the comments anonymous. If you can incorporate photos, videos, or other media in the post then so much the better.

It's also a great idea to share customer created content on Facebook. Sharing like that can help turn customers into fans and build a sense of community among your users. It shows that you care and makes customers feel appreciated.

And one last Big tip - use Facebook Insights.
Facebook offers a service called Facebook Insights https://insights.fb.com/?. You can use Facebook Insights to measure your performance on Facebook in a similar way to the way that Google Analytics and conversion tracking works for AdWords. Insights lets you see your most popular and successful posts in terms of link clicks, shares, and likes. You can use the data in Facebook Insights to see what you're doing wrong, but more importantly to see what you are doing right - and then do more of it.

Paying for Facebook Advertising
As I have said above I think that setting up a Facebook page for your store is an important part of the start up process, setting up and trying Google AdWords and Google Shopping Ads are also important parts of start up, but I think that you should wait 3-6 months before you start to pay for Facebook ads. In this time you will gain a much better understanding of your margins, your costs and what kind of return you should expect from your on-line marketing activity.

Facebook advertising is more complex and potentially more expensive than Google AdWords, which quite honestly is saying something! So it helps to master AdWords first.

If and when you are ready to start paying for Ads on Facebook you can sign up here. https://www.facebook.com/business

Facebook offers a wide choice of different advertising options, you don't even need a Facebook Page to create a Facebook ad. You can create an ad for a website by choosing a 'Clicks to Website objective' or the 'Website Conversions objective'. However Facebook ads not connected with a Facebook page will appear exclusively in the right column, not in the News Feed as well - when it's so easy to set up a Facebook page and it's free, why not?

Just like other forms of advertising it's important to go into a Facebook advertising campaign with a clear objective. There are tons of ways to use Facebook to advertise and some of them cost a lot of money for very little reward. Paying to only get 'Likes' is never a good idea in my view. When you do decide to stump up and start advertising on Facebook here are a few tips and suggestions to consider;

Prioritize your spend carefully
If you have a limited budget (and you should) then you need to make sure that you address the easiest conversions first.

Your top priority targets are potential customers who are in 'buy mode', the best place to find these people is on Google Shopping, which is why I recommend using that channel first. My experience is that clicks from Google Shopping convert about twice as well as clicks from Facebook adverts.

Your second priority will be users who know you but are not yet customers, you can reach these people by using re-targeting which I will discuss later as it's complex to set up or by targeting Facebook Fans, people from your Email Lists and people who are Friends of Your Fans Who are Fans of Competitors.

Thirdly look at Facebook lookalike targeting, lookalike targeting takes a list of people that you know because they are customers or because they subscribe to your newsletter and then finds demographic data about those people and uses it to find other people who are similar working on the basis that they are quite likely to do the same thing, however this can be quite frustrating as when you give Facebook your list of 10,000 mailing list subscribers it can send back 2.5 million lookalikes. When Facebook provides you with a lot of potential lookalikes, combine it with another targeting method. You can target fans of competitors who are on your lookalike list for example. Combining these two kinds of targeting allows you to focus in on the precise people that you are looking for.

Offers work well on Facebook, Free offers work best..
Facebook Offers can work very well. Facebook Offers lets you promote a deal exclusively to Facebook users. Try using an offer to give away something with a very low cost like a digital 'how to guide' aimed at your target market or maybe a printed calendar in exchange for a like and a newsletter subscription but remember

these sign ups will have a significant cost so be sure that you have a plan to turn them back into cash. It can be a good ideas to target your first Facebook Offer to your existing fans only and then if it is a success you can widen your net to larger audiences.

Tell users what to do
Like all adverts Facebook ads should include a direct call to action. Include a clear call to action in the body text of your Facebook ad to encourage the Facebook users who see it to take your desired action. Good examples of clear calls to action are 'Buy Now' buttons or 'Click Here for more information' buttons.

Some features are not so great
De-activate Sponsored Stories as an add-on. When someone interacts with your Facebook page, offer, event, etc. the action triggers Facebook posts, or "stories," that the user's friends may then see in their News Feed. These "stories" are generated by the user and you can not control them, opting for sponsored stories basically means you are paying to increase the likelihood that these stories will be seen, that's a bad idea. You can opt out of sponsored stories in the left column of the ad creator tool.

Customize your Ads carefully
Facebook Ads offer a lot more customization options than Google Ads, you can add multiple images and customize your ad text and headline. Images are even more important than the headline, include as many images as possible in your ads and Facebook posts. When using an image keep any text content in the image under 20%, Facebook advertising rules dictate that image-based Facebook ads that are set to appear in users' news feeds won't get approved if any text included in the image takes up more than 20% of the image space. Facebook has a grid tool to help ensure that your image ad follows the guidelines.
Facebook recommends uploading an image that is 1200x627 pixels for your ads. You can use smaller images but try to always use images that are at least 600 pixels wide so that they look good when they appear in the News Feed.
When promoting a Facebook page, the automatic setup is for the ad headline to be the same as your page's title. I would recommend changing that for your own customized ad headline. Facebook ads with images get much higher engagement than those without, as they stand out much more in someones crowded news feed, you can upload up to six images to accompany your ads at no extra cost.

Bidding and Budgets

Facebook allows you to select from a range of different bidding options, you can bid for clicks, impressions, or some other objective such as page likes (bad idea!). If you choose the recommended (and selected by default) option of bidding based on your objective, your bid will automatically be set to help you reach your objective, whereas bidding for clicks or impressions allows for more customization. When using these options remember that Facebook wants your money, the recommendations are more likely to be good for them than good for you!

Facebook has the option to set a daily budget like Google AdWords for day to day campaigns or to set a lifetime budget for the activity which is useful for promoting events or short term deals. If you set a daily budget then your ads and sponsored stories will stop showing once you hit that level so think about what time of day your target users will be on the site and set the time frame for running your ads accordingly. Campaign lifetime budgets are spread over the entire span of time a campaign is scheduled to run. When you are budgeting for these campaigns don't forget that each campaign has a separate budget and it will probably all be spent.
You can edit your campaign's end date or budget anytime after the campaign has started running, however you can't change your minimum daily spend limit (it's set at $50). If you want to control your costs then change your daily ad budget that is ultimately how you can control the cost of Facebook advertising.

Targeting is Key
Facebook advertising has some very detailed targeting capabilities that can help to show your Ads only to your desired audience, you won't find options like the ones that Facebook has elsewhere. You need to take advantage of these tools to be successful running Facebook ad campaigns. Because Facebook has a huge amount of data on it's users you can target audiences by location, age, gender, workplace, work status, relationship status, language, education and so on.
For most small on-line retailers the best part of Facebook targeting is the ability to restrict your Ads to your ideal audience by using interest targeting. Facebook allows for some incredible deep interest targeting which you can use to get tremendous value out of your Facebook Ad spend, for some retailers the conversion rates achievable through interest group targeting alone can justify the use of Facebook paid advertising.

You can also target your Facebook ads exclusively to users who are already connected to your Facebook page, or you can choose to target them and their friends, or you can target people who aren't connected to you but who share characteristics of people who are, or who share characteristics with your existing customers which is extremely powerful.

Facebook allows you to target followers of specific brands. This is helpful when you are trying to sell to the same customer base as other well-known businesses or if you are trying to target the customer base of other non-competing brands in your market. Using this filter is a simple solution when you do not know anything else about your target audience. To become even more effective, create separate campaigns for each brand that you are targeting the followers of. That way you can create a more personalized and engaging message.

When you are changing your targeting methods keep an eye on your potential audience meter, as you change your targeting choices Facebook will update the approximate number of people in your target group on Facebook. This is just an estimate, but as you narrow or expand your audience it can help you make sure you're not targeting too many people or too few.
Note that by default when you select an interest group in Facebook and then add a second interest you are creating a larger group by combining the two groups with a boolean OR, most of the time you are looking to reduce the size of the group by targeting, for example people interested in Dogs AND Technology rather than Dogs OR Technology you can only do this through the Facebook Ads API. If you are not a developer, the only way to do that is to use one of the many applications that handle this for you. Ad Espresso and Qwaya are two of the big names offering this functionality. I recommend Ad Espresso, it allows you to hit the center of the Venn Diagram and accurately target the 15,000 dog technology enthusiasts in the UK.

If you're looking to build upon existing customer contacts through Facebook, you can add a custom audience and upload your mailing list directly to Facebook, enabling you to target users you have an existing relationship with. Taking advantage of the custom audiences feature often increases ad conversion rates. You can upload a mailing list or connect your Facebook account directly to MailChimp. Just click "Create New Audience" in the Audiences section. Having your ad appear in your existing contacts Facebook feed can help you look more professional and help a small retailer punch above his weight, but remember that you could address those customers more directly at a lower cost using e-mail.

Test different versions of your Ad text and Images
It's always a good idea to test several different versions of your ad text and different images. Try lots of different images with vertical and horizontal layouts.

Use Flickr or Freeimages.com to find free photos that you can use. Create 10 different ads and put a small part of your budget aside to test the different Ads and discover which ad is going to perform best and then run that Ad with the rest of the budget.

Measure the results of your ads right through the landing pages to the checkout on your site. You are trying to find messaging that both attracts attention and then converts into sales. Not all ads that get great click through convert well, your goal is to optimize the cost of customer acquisition, not just to maximize the number of clicks.

One last question - What is a Facebook 'Like' worth?

I have seen big companies spend tens of thousands of dollars to increase the number of Facebook likes on their page - honestly that is insane, a Facebook 'like' is worth very little so paying for them is nuts. If you search on Google you can find lots of articles that suggest a Facebook 'Like' is worth hundreds of dollars, but when you look into the source they are all written by marketing companies who want to 'sell' Facebook likes to big companies. A Facebook Like costs zero and takes 1/10th of a second create so it's worth nothing, period.

Chapter 85
Setting up a Facebook page for your store

To set up a Facebook page for your store you first need to have a Facebook account for yourself. The page for your store will be controlled through your personal Facebook account, you can add other people who can also use it, but you will be in charge

Log into your personal Facebook account and look closely at the top right hand corner of the page, you will see a small triangle pointing downward to indicate a drop down menu

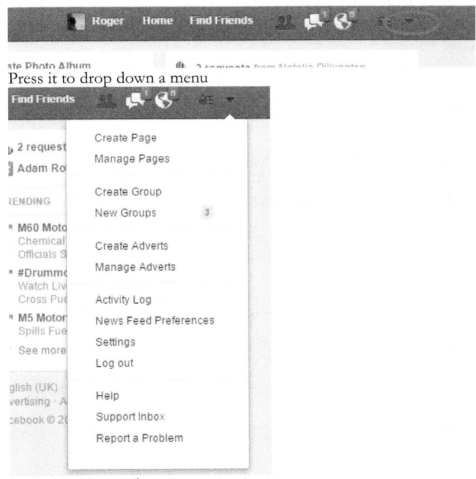

Press it to drop down a menu

Select 'Create Page'

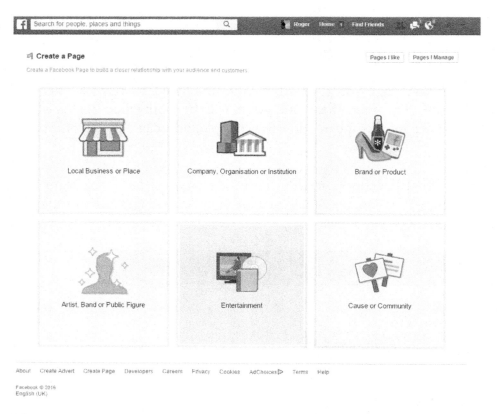

Then I recommend that you use either the 'Company, Organization or Institution' option or the 'Brand or Product' option depending on how you see your business.

If you are mainly selling your own brand items then choose 'Brand or Product' and if you are a store selling mainly other peoples items then choose 'Company, Organization or Institution'.

I'm using product or brand for my example store

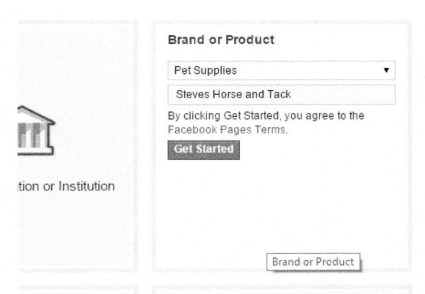

Fill out the profile details page

Then add a profile picture

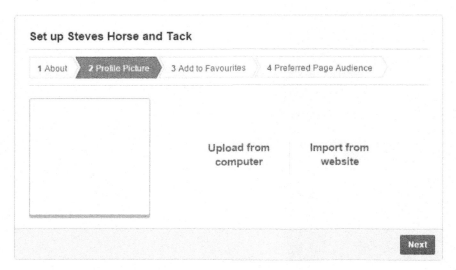

Click the green 'Add to Favorites' button, then click 'Next'

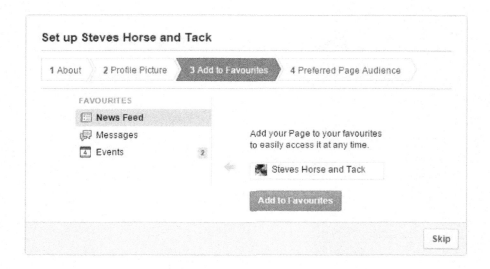

And then you get to the important bit - the last section where you tell Facebook who you want to see your page.

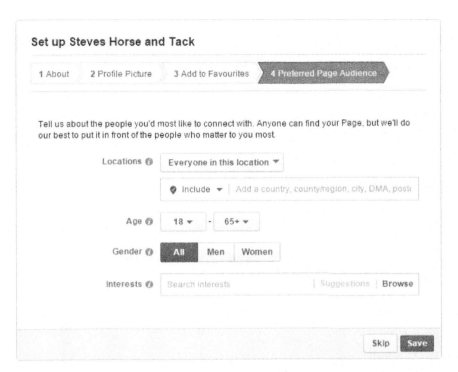

Start by selecting the location that you are interested in, you do that by typing in part of the country or location name in the box next to 'Include'

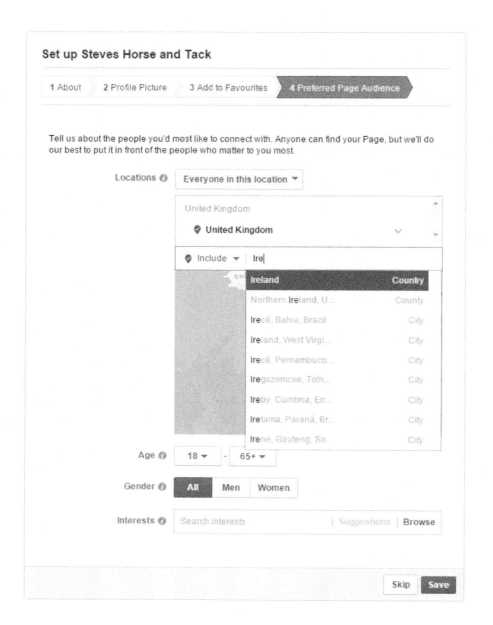

You can add multiple countries or locations - but be realistic, the more you add, the more expensive any marketing will be.

Then change the targeting using the drop down - I only want people who live in the location for my test store as visitors don't buy saddles.

Lastly you can select the age group that you think your customers will come from and the gender and add all of the interests that you think your potential customers may have.

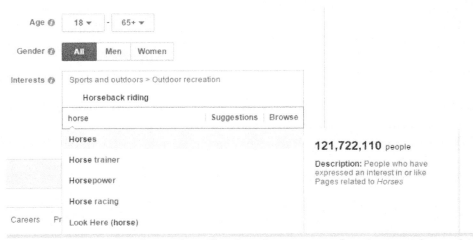

Note the huge numbers that Facebook pops up for the number of potential users in each category - these groups overlap and they are for the whole world so they are more or less meaningless.

You can add as many interests as you like by simply typing in part of the name and then selecting from the drop down.

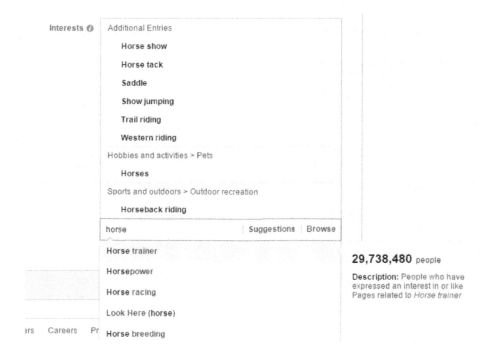

Finally, press the blue 'Save' button and your stores Facebook page will be set up

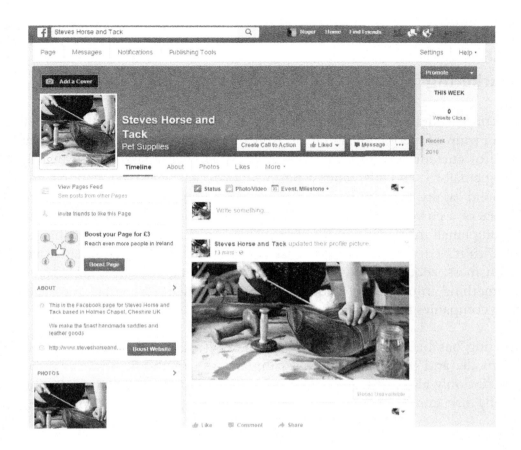

Chapter 86
e-mail marketing

Email marketing is defined in Wikipedia as 'Directly marketing a commercial message to a group of people using email. In it's broadest sense, every email sent to a potential or current customer could be considered email marketing. It usually involves using email to send ads, request business, or solicit sales or donations, and is meant to build loyalty, trust, or brand awareness. Email marketing can be done to either sold lists or a current customer database. Broadly, the term is usually used to refer to sending email messages with the purpose of enhancing the relationship of a merchant with it's current or previous customers, to encourage customer loyalty and repeat business, acquiring new customers or convincing current customers to purchase something immediately, and adding advertisements to email messages sent by other companies to their customers.'

Email marketing has been widely expected to die out as a result of competition from social media and other alternative communication methods, however email marketing is not only alive, it is the number one direct communication channel in terms of daily use and consumer preference for both personal and marketing messages.

Email is thriving because it is easy to use, flexible and more or less everyone has one or more e-mail addresses. You can get your email on your PC, on your tablet and increasingly on your smartphone the suggestion that email is dying is simply laughable. It is evolving and developing, but is is not dying, in fact Email should be the number one way that you market to your existing customers and prospects who are engaged with you enough to subscribe to your email marketing list.

You can send marketing emails using your regular Google email account, but creating good looking emails with good quality images is very difficult using Gmail and once you have more than 50 or 100 e-mail addresses to send your messages to it is difficult and managing subscriptions and un-subscribe requests is almost impossible.
Instead of struggling with email marketing from your regular e-mail address I recommend that you sign up for a professional eMail marketing service as soon as you establish your store and use that from day one instead.

The two services that I can recommend from personal experience are MailChimp and Constant Contact. http://MailChimp.com/ and http://www.constantcontact.com/uk/index.jsp respectively.

Both are great services, but I recommend MailChimp for a start up as at the time of writing (January 2016) they offer a free service to users with up to 2,000 subscribers who send less than 12,000 emails per month. Both systems can be easily integrated into any web site including those based on Shopify and Magento as well as completely bespoke sites so subscribers are added automatically and they manage un-subscribe requests for you which is required by law in the European Union and the USA.

Signing up for MailChimp is really easy, and then integrating it with your Shopify store is pretty straight forward too, you can get instructions on how to do that in the chapter called MailChimp eMail Marketing.

eMail Marketing Tips
Writing and sending your marketing e-mails is beyond the scope of this book, but I do have a few tips for how to run a good quality e-mail marketing campaign that delivers sales results. A good email marketing strategy includes how you build your mailing list, manage your subscribers and turn their interest into orders.

Build your list relentlessly
Make sure that customers ordering off your web site opt into the email marketing list by default and add a mailing list sign up box to your store. Consider running a monthly draw for a discount voucher for new mailing list subscribers. Make converting Facebook likes into newsletter subscribers an objective of your Facebook marketing.

Optimize your mails for mobile
MailChimp can help you to create e-mails that read well on a mobile phone which is where more than half or your readers will get the mail, make sure that you take this seriously. 63% of US consumers delete emails immediately if they are not optimized for mobile. Offer an elegant mobile experience from the start. Remember that your audience is made up of both smartphone users and desktop PC users so make sure your emails look good to both groups.

Your message should always be fresh and relevant
Subdivide your lists if you can and send really relevant offers to small groups, never be tempted to send a sub standard campaign just because 'we always send

out a mail on Fridays' Customers will respond much better to a targeted mail sent at a random time than a regular mail full of irrelevant fillers.

Don't be afraid to re-use the same promotional messages on social media that you are also using in email and vice versa, your average customer will see between 10% and 25% of what you put out so the chance of cross over between channels is actually quite low.

Use email to drive customers from mobile to desktop
People are more likely to browse on a phone and more likely to buy from a PC where they have faster Internet access, larger screens, full keyboards.

Smartphones and tablets replicate much of the desktop messaging experience but try to give customers a reason to mark the mail and come back to it on their desktop to buy. Email remains a powerful channel for it's ability to bridge the three-device environment of smartphone, tablet, and PC.

Never send Spam
Spam is email that is sent without the users explicit permission, never buy lists, never cross lists over from one shop to another without permission and never, ever send mail to random lists.

Always get permission first

Email is all about deals
According to the 2012 Channel Preference Survey, people prefer email to Facebook for deals because it's harder to miss deals in the inbox than it is in the huge number posts in a Facebook News Feed. Make sure that the deals and special offers that you send out by eMail really are special.

Use social networks primarily to spread the word about your offers, and push consumers to your website for email sign up.

Automate your post-purchase messages
Automate a set of e-mails to be automatically sent by Email a week, a month, and 90 days after a customer has bought from your store, you can do this with Helpscout.

Chapter 87
Using Videos

OK - this is a huge tip. - The best way by far to promote your product and sell more of it through your website is to make a video explaining the best features of the product.
The quality does not need to be brilliant, you can shoot a pretty good information video with your smartphone with a little practice and there are lots of free or very cheap video editing software packages about now so you can shoot a lot of video and cut the best bits together to produce a nice video that will really help customers decide to buy your product.

You can post the video on your product page as part of the product description and you can also post it on YouTube and Facebook where it will help bring in new customers as well.

The only downside of producing videos for your products is that it can be quite time consuming, shooting the video will take a few minutes, but editing a 1 minute video can take up to half an hour to complete so you may not be able to produce a video for every item in a big product set. Regardless, you should be able to create videos for your top 10 items with just a day or two of work and the benefit that you get from them will be well worth the effort.
Like anything else you do you will get better at making videos with practice, try starting by shooting on your cell phone and edit using the free software on your PC or Mac. I use Windows Movie Maker which is a free download from Microsoft http://windows.microsoft.com/en-gb/windows/get-movie-maker-download it's included with some windows PCs and free to download for others. It has basic editing functions and it is quite easy to use.

Here are a few tips for producing product videos that sell.

Plan your video
Write a list of the most important features and benefits for your product and use them to create a script. Read the script out loud and time how long it takes. A good product video will be under 1 minute, you can make it longer but people will switch off at about a minute unless it's really compelling so be sure to get the best features covered at the start. A good way to structure the video is to start with an overview shot then zoom in on key details and features before demonstrating any

important functions and the going back to the overview to wrap up and summarize.

Remember that you can include photos in your video, it doesn't all have to be live action.

You can record the voice over while you shoot or record it separately (unless you can be seen talking in the video - that has to be recorded live).

A really good product video can be made by thinking about how you would explain the product and why he should buy it to a friend, remember the key objective is to explain the product to a potential buyer.

Use a tripod or stand

Even when you are recording on your phone you should use a tripod or stand to hold the camera(phone) steady for recording. Especially if you are demonstrating products. Video recorded on handheld cameras is just awful with camera shakes and other distracting movements which ruin the effect.

Learn to use your editing software

Watch a few YouTube videos explaining how to use the video editing software that you plan to employ and read the documentation carefully. The more you know about what your video editing software can and can not do the better your videos will be.

Copy what works

Watch lots of product videos on YouTube or on your competitor websites before you start recording you own. Don't be afraid to copy what works best for products like yours. This will help you plan out your video recording approach before you begin.

Consistency helps

Try to film your videos in the same place each time with the same backdrop and lighting, if you can use the same place that you use for product photos that will help as well.

When you demonstrate your products try to do it in the same way each time.

Simple is best

Some of the best product videos are just a series of different shots of the product from different angles with a good voice over explaining the key features and benefits. You can use 'Zoom-in' shots to show product details and record from several angles then edit them together to blend a better product video together.

Never zoom out in a product video, it just looks wrong, cut from the close up to a wide shot again.

Practice makes perfect
Set a half day aside to practice shooting and editing video and don't be upset if you get nothing usable out of it just use the time to see what works best and what doesn't work, experiment with the shooting and editing until you have some experience. You can get too close to the project so it is a good idea to have someone else check the video that you produce and give you some constructive feedback.

Organize your hard drive
Video files take a long time to make and they are quite big, you may need to upgrade your PC to store them or consider putting them in a cloud storage service like Dropbox. Create file folders for each product category you sell and sub folders for each product.

Don't use background music
You are trying to sell the product, no background music will help with that unless you are selling a musical instrument keep it professional.

Chapter 88
Integrating videos into your Shopify store

You can embed videos into product descriptions, content pages or blog pages in your Shopify store, as the editors for these content pieces are the same you can use the same process for all three.

Shopify does not host video files on the Shopify store servers because video is very demanding for bandwidth and storage space, as a result you need to set up an account with a video hosting service to host your videos for you.

I recommend that you use Vimeo https://vimeo.com/, you can also use YouTube, but Vimeo videos do not contain adverts which is much better. Vimeo has a free option that allows you to stream up to 500Mb per week and a Pro package for £15 ($23) per month that allows you up to 20Gb per week, you can see the options here https://vimeo.com/upgrade

Once you have set up an account you need to edit your video and get it ready for use, I recommend using Microsoft Movie Maker or similar to edit the video, doing so is beyond the scope of this book, but once it is uploaded you will have a URL for your video.

To embed the video on your Shopify store go to http://embedresponsively.com/ to get the embed code for your Vimeo video you need to do the following

Open the embedresponsively web page

Switch to the 'Vimeo' section

And simply cut the URL for your Vimeo Video into the box on the page, the site will load a preview of your video below the box and give you your embed code

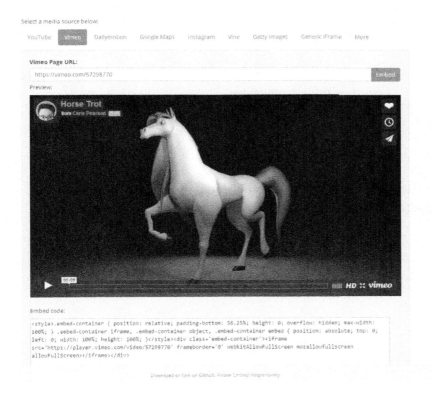

Double click on the embed code to select it all and then press ctrl+V on your keyboard to copy the code

Switch back to your Shopify store admin on the page where you want to embed the video, make sure that your cursor is at the right point in the text and press the 'insert video' button

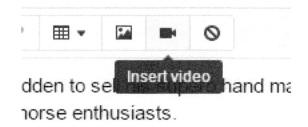

A box will pop up where you can paste the embed code

Paste the code into the box and then press the blue 'Insert video' button, the video will appear in the space that you selected

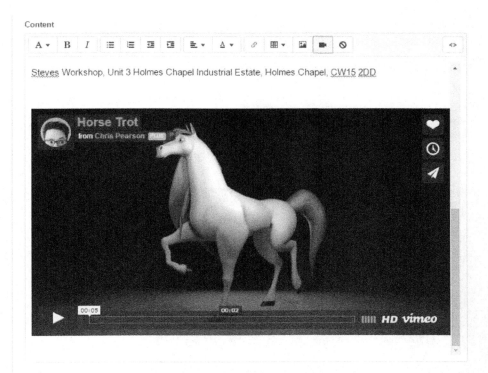

Press the blue Save button and then the View button to see how the video looks on your web site.

Callers are always welcome at the workshop, just call first to make sure that we are here - 01575 123456

Steves Workshop, Unit 3 Holmes Chapel Industrial Estate, Holmes Chapel, CW15 2DD

Chapter 89
YouTube channel

A YouTube channel gives you a place to post your videos for general viewing, and of course, as YouTube is a Google property YouTube videos rank very high in Google search results.

You can post your videos to both your Vimeo account and your YouTube channel and link to either from your Facebook page.

To set up a YouTube channel, first log into your Google account and go to your email inbox. In the top right hand corner you will see the symbol next to your name that looks like nine dots

Click on it to show the list of apps

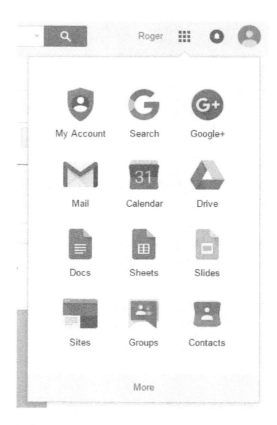

then click 'More' to show extra apps

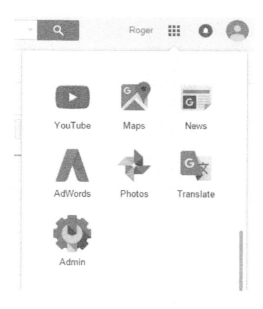

Choose the YouTube icon

You may need to confirm that you want to use YouTube under your business account.

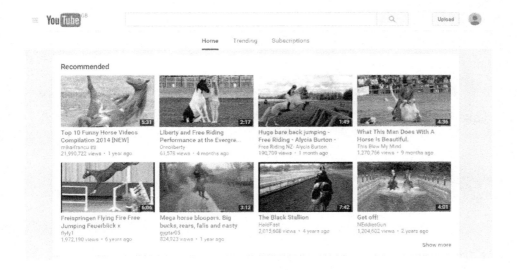

YouTube will show you your home page.

Click the menu button in the top left and select 'My Channel'

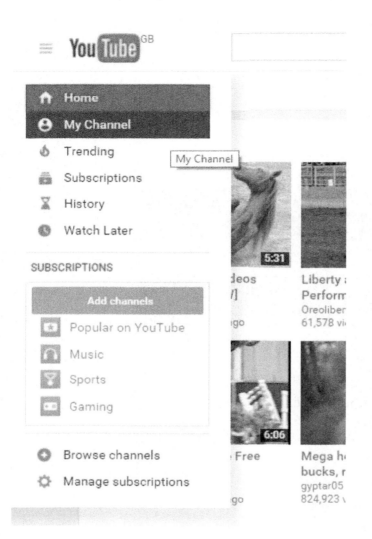

You will see a pop up asking you how you want your channel to be represented

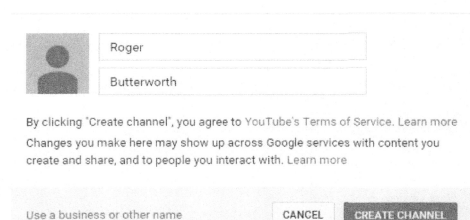

Click on the 'Use a business or other name' link

Fill out the Name and select 'Product or Brand' as your category then agree to the terms

Then click the blue 'Done button' and your channel is set up ready to upload your first video

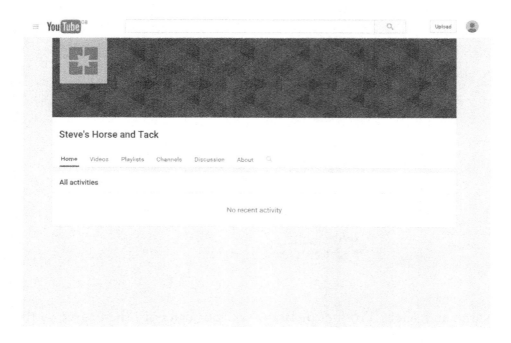

The last task is to link your AdWords account to your YouTube account

In a separate tab, open your AdWords account (https://AdWords.Google.com)

In the top right of the screen you will see the settings icon
Click on it to bring up a dropdown menu

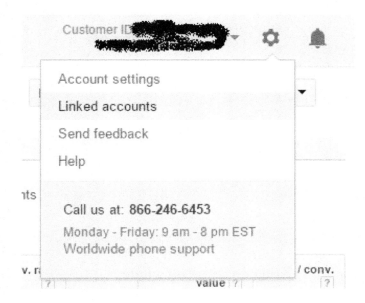

Select 'Linked accounts'

Linked accounts

Optimize your campaigns even more effectively by bringing valuable data from other Google services to your AdWords

Google Analytics

Gain greater visibility into how people behave on your site after they've clicked your ad, such as the average number of pages they view and how long they stay, by importing site engagement metrics from Google Analytics.

View details »

Search Console

See how your ads and organic search listings perform (both alone and together) by importing organic search results from Search Console

View details »

YouTube

Access your video view statistics as well as add call-to-action overlays to your videos. Show ads to people who visit and interact with your channel. Measure the impact of video ads by tracking visitor behavior on your channel.

View details »

Google Merchant Center

Use product information from Merchant Center in your AdWords campaigns. You'll be able to run Shopping campaigns and set up dynamic remarketing. Account linking can only be initiated from Merchant Center.

View details »

Click on the 'View details' link under 'YouTube'

Click on the red + CHANNEL button to bring up a pop up window

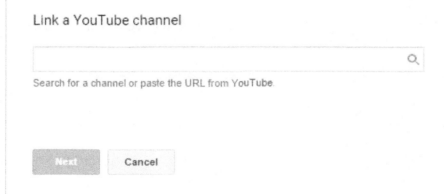

Type the name that you gave to your YouTube channel into the box and then select it from the drop down that appears.

Note that you may have to wait a couple of hours for your channel to be available for linking - Google services do not sync in real time.

Remarketing to YouTube viewers with AdWords
You can show tailored ads to potential customers based on their past interactions with your videos or YouTube channel. This is known as "video remarketing" and it works a lot like regular remarketing.
Remarketing lists are created by linking your YouTube account to your AdWords account. Once you link accounts, you can create remarketing lists that reach people who have performed the following YouTube actions:

People who watch any of your videos
People who take an action (like, dislike, comment or share) on any of your videos
People who view your video as a TrueView in-stream video ad
People who visit or subscribe to your YouTube channel

You can then use these lists in your targeting settings for new or existing video campaigns. Manage your lists at any time in the "Audiences" section of the AdWords shared library.

Chapter 90
Pintrest

Pinterest is a website that allows you to "pin" things Online, just as you would pin them on a real life bulletin board, but instead, Pinterest saves all of your pins on your account so that you can access them easily. Plus, you can follow friends on Pinterest and "repin" things that they have already pinned on your Pinterest boards or browse a live feed of items that are being pinned by strangers when you're searching for inspiration.
People use Pintrest for all kinds of different things, from saving recipes to saving articles for research to creating mood boards for a room re-modeling project, Pinterest can be whatever the user wants it to be.
A majority of Pintrest users are female.

Since it is mainly a visual medium Pintrest is mostly useful for shops that have striking looking images - if your store sells items for home design or clothing and accessories then you should use Pintrest.

For stores that are based in the USA you can sell the items in your Shopify store directly on Pintrest using the Shopify - Pintrest integration.

Chapter 91
Instagram

Instagram is a photo sharing site that works mainly from your cell phone based on an app. Similar to Facebook or Twitter, everyone who creates an account has a profile and a news feed, then when you post a photo or video on Instagram, it will be displayed on your profile. Other users who follow you will see your posts in their own feed. Likewise, you'll see posts from other users who you choose to follow.

Instagram is available for free on iOS, Android and Windows Phone devices. It can also be accessed on the web from a computer, but users can only upload and share photos or videos from their devices.

Small stores can use Instagram to share photos of products or products in use which can help to drive users towards your site to buy your products, it works best for unique brands and items that are visually striking, if your products fit this description then you should set up a company account and post as much as possible, it is quick and free so why not?

Chapter 92
Twitter

Twitter is a great platform for communicating with friends or with the whole world if they care to listen to what you have to say.

It is a dreadful platform for selling things, don't try to use it to sell things it simply does not work.

Some companies use Twitter for customer service, but the public nature of every complaint on there makes this problematic, I'd advise against using it this way too.

Advertising on Twitter has the lowest conversion rate of any advertising I have ever seen, it's almost immeasurably small.

Thats all I have to say about Twitter.

I recommend that you Register a twitter account in the name of your store to avoid people impersonating you and then never use it.

Chapter 93
Discount Vouchers

Discount vouchers (or coupons if you are on the US side of the pond) are a very effective marketing tool, digital versions can be used in e-mail campaigns, in printed form they can be used as a box stuffer or you can send them by post as a way to revitalize your relationship with a former customer.

They can be shared on social media or they can be handed round among friends and you can hand them out through partners and dedicated on-line sites so they can be used as part of your customer retention efforts and as part of your customer acquisition.

But the best thing about discount vouchers is that they are a very low cost marketing method, setting them up is quick and easy, and even if you print them the cost of doing so is very low. The main cost is of course the discount that you give on goods which is a price that you only pay on success.

I recommend that you make the use of discount vouchers a significant part of your marketing campaigns, using the right strategies, vouchers can be used to directly drive customer behavior and increase revenue, profitability and loyalty without devaluing your brand.

Here are a few ideas on ways to use vouchers

Get new customers with a first purchase discount
Offer new customers a first purchase discount when they set up an account but be careful how good a deal new customers are given as if your existing customers feel they are missing out, they may try to leave or sign up again with a new account to qualify for the voucher.

Increase your average order value
To increase the amount a shopper spends you can add a voucher to your site that gives the customer a benefit when they reach a certain spend threshold. The secret here is to make sure that threshold is higher than what they would already spend, so you are raising the average order value. You should include the cost of the benefit you're giving away in the additional amount added so to keep the deal profitable.

For Example: If the average order value for your site is £30, then you could look to offer £5 off if the customer spends £50, you are giving away 25% of the extra spend in the worse case, but that is probably worth it.

Use vouchers to introduce new items

A voucher can be an good way to test out a new product. Offer a free sample of your new product to customers who buy a related item or spend over a minimum. This can help to build up positive reviews for your new product.

Increase repeat purchases with personalized offers

Offer vouchers redeemable against the purchase of key, profitable items to customers who have purchased related or compatible items in the past, for example my example store could offer discounts on leather care products to customers who have purchased riding boots.

Use existing customers to bring you new customers with referral vouchers

The "refer a friend" voucher can be a brilliant business generation tool because it gives your current customers an excuse to shout about your store and help others to come on board as customers. It is a very cheap way to acquire new customers.

Partner with similar, non-competitive stores

Why not try to find a partner who has a store selling non-competitive items to similar customers, offer to send your customers their voucher in return for them sending your voucher to their customers, it's a great win-win deal that costs almost nothing but time to implement if the vouchers are sent by e-mail.
Trade show organizers or event promoters are often open to the same kind of deal.

Tips for how to use vouchers effectively

There are some best practices to follow when you use marketing vouchers and a few common pitfalls to avoid. Follow these do's and don'ts and voucher marketing can be a great, low cost way to developing your retail store

- Always give discount vouchers a cash value rather than a percentage value. $10 is a nice gift, 10% is a small discount.

- Put a minimum spend on the voucher, but keep it low, say £10 off any order over £25 - if your margins are right the worse case is that you break even and gain a customer…

- You should give your vouchers a short expiry date, vouchers with a short expiry date give shoppers a sense of urgency, buy now or miss out is a powerful motivating message.

- If a shopper receives a product with a £50 discount, psychologically, they'll see the saving as money they can spend, regardless of if they intended to buy the product initially. This means shoppers will often buy items alongside the product so maybe suggest a few add on purchases as part of the voucher presentation.

- Personalize your voucher offers. Personalized offers with specific vouchers targeted to certain customers make the shopper feel valued, and the more accurate and appropriate the personalization, the more likely a buyer is to act.

- Track the success of your vouchers carefully, monitor the results of your voucher campaigns and adapt future campaigns to optimize the results that you get from them. There is no shame in repeating a successful campaign, it's not lazy, it's smart!

- Always make the user type in a voucher code to receive the discount, as opposed to auto-applying any discounts. This way you can be sure it was the offer that converted the sale, and it prevents you giving away unnecessary discounts.

- It can also pay dividends to compare the performance of a voucher against different customer segments and other factors: such as does the voucher/offer perform better in the morning or late at night?

- Avoid 'guaranteed targeting' don't send vouchers to customers who buy every week regardless, that's just money down the drain. Better to send 'come back' vouchers to previously loyal customers who have stopped buying.

How to set up discount vouchers in Shopify

Shopify has a very flexible system for creating discount voucher codes, you can use them in e-mails, give them direct to customers one on one or you can print them onto nice slips of paper to hand out at shows or to include in your parcels.

To access the discount voucher tool go to 'Discounts' from the main menu of the admin system

Then press either of the two Blue 'Add discount code' buttons

You can create you own codes that are easy to remember and type in like '£20-OFF-FOR-BILLY' or press the blue 'Generate code' link to have Shopify create a random 12 letter code like 'C5WJY8YO5I6U'

If you leave the 'No limit' box checked then the code can be used any number of times, if you un-tick it you can set a maximum number of uses, I'm setting mine to a max of 100 uses.

Next set the date range - I recommend that you always set an expiry for your vouchers - no more than 90 days in the future, 30 days is best for the reasons mentioned above.

Lastly you need to configure the nature of the discount using the three settings in the 'Details' box, I'm going to set up a £10 voucher to be used on orders over £25 so these are my settings

You can give percentage discounts as well or free shipping (both bad ideas if you ask me!) and you can restrict the use of vouchers to items in a specific collection, for use with a single product or to a group of customers.

Once you are done press one of the blue 'Save discount' buttons to see the voucher set up

You can add as many as you like, they can always be seen here and they can be disabled or deleted from here using the buttons on the right hand side of the page.

Customers who want to use the voucher can simply enter it into the box provided on the checkout page to get the discount.

Chapter 94
In the box marketing

When you sell on-line a large number of your customers will only 'touch' your organization and get the opportunity to form an opinion of your professionalism through your web site and when they receive the parcel that you send them. So try to make sure that the parcels you send are as good as the web site.

If your product is expensive and easy to sell once stolen then it's probably not such a good idea to brand the outside of the parcels, but they can still look professional and high quality.

Inside each box always put a printed advert or discount voucher - they work really, really well to drive re-ordering. Always give discount vouchers a cash value rather than a percentage value. $10 is a nice gift, 10% is a small discount.

Chapter 95
Understanding Remarketing

Have you ever noticed that sometimes after you visit an on-line store you see their ads pop up on other web sites trying to drag you back? That does not happen by accident, it is an on-line marketing practice called 'Remarketing'

Remarketing is the process of selectively advertising to consumers who have already visited your web site. You can change the message that you show depending on the page that the target visited or the products that they viewed which can make this advertising a very effective way to keep your web store in mind and bring them back to your site for eventual purchase.

Remarketing has become an important tactic for improving the process of converting people browsing your web site into customers because it allows you to stay connected with your target audience, even after they leave your site.

Remarketing is something that you can only use once you have significant web traffic, so it is not a process that you need to know a lot about when you set up your store, but you will probably want to use remarketing in the future so it's worth learning about it and doing some preparations now to make sure that you can take advantage of the opportunity in the future.

To use remarketing you need to build lists of people who have visited your web site pages so that you can then run ads based on the potential customers website activity. This is extremely effective from a cost and performance perspective you can target or exclude customers who made purchases so that you can offer the appropriate messaging and you can offer different ads to people who have looked at different products.

The two platforms that offer remarketing tools are Google and Facebook, they both work in the same way. The customers that visit your site are tracked through a piece of code, also known as a remarketing tag which you add to your Shopify web store. We need to add two separate tags to use both Google and Facebook as the systems are separate, once both tags are properly installed Google and Facebook will be able to recognize every web browser that has visited your site. The tracking is done using 'cookies' which are small pieces of code passed to the customer web browser to track activity, but the cookies do not store personal information, they simply 'tag' the web browser so that Google and Facebook can see that the browser has been used to view your site when it is subsequently used to look at Facebook or to look at a site in the Google Display network.

Google AdWords Remarketing

Google AdWords remarketing is done through ads placed on the Google Display Network which are only shown to web browsers that are tagged as having visited your site. Once you have tagged enough visitors you can then use your AdWords account to create a remarketing campaign and Google ads tailored for each of your key product groups, visitors to your site will then see targeted ads across the huge number of Google partner sites in the Google Display Network. You pay Google a fee based on your bid for each click on one of your Ads by a visitor. Your bids need to be high enough to make it worthwhile for Google to show them of course.

The Google display network is huge with over 2 Million sites included (according to Google) Google can also show remarketing ads on YouTube and in mobile Apps which have much lower conversion rates. You can control where your ads are shown and it is vital that you restrict your ad placement or you will find that your budget for remarketing will be eaten up quickly.

When you remarket on the Google Display Network, you have the option of creating display ads that incorporate text, images, videos, or rich media. For help making customized Google remarketing banner ads, try using the free Google Display Ad Builder. You can choose from a number of pre-existing templates and then customize them for your business, selecting from a variety of Google remarketing banner sizes and formats.

Facebook Remarketing

Facebook remarketing works in a similar way to Google remarketing, but it uses a completely separate system and of course the Ads that are shown to people who have visited your web site are only shown on Facebook, you need a separate tracking code to be installed on your site to set up Facebook remarketing and the list of users is separate although most users will be on both lists so you need to make sure that your messages are consistent.

Facebook remarketing is paid for through your Facebook marketing account, for many items in fashion, jewelery and similar items targeted to younger people Facebook remarketing is very effective, although it can be a bit more expensive than Google remarketing.

Facebook has one big advantage over Google in remarketing, it allows you to market not just to people who have visited your site, but also to people who are like them on the basis of the data held by Facebook. This can help you to use your remarketing list to target appropriate new customers as well as existing web site visitors.

Prepare now to use remarketing in the future

We have already set up an account with Google Ad words and if you are going to use Facebook you should have set up a page for your Store there as well so to get ready to use Google and Facebook remarketing we just need to add the tracking code for each to the web site, the next two chapters will show you how to do that.

Remarketing Cost and Effectiveness

Both Google and Facebook recommend that when you are starting your first remarketing campaign, you begin by targeting everyone who viewed your website. Just remember, that will increase the number of times that your ad is shown a lot, and if you have a limited budget that will reduce the effectiveness of the campaign as your ads are being shown to more individuals

It is much better to target more narrowly both in terms of who you show Ads to and where you put them, that will increase relevancy. In time you can create some useful remarketing lists for targeted campaigns.

You'll see even better conversion rates when you start to combine remarketing campaigns with additional targeting methods, such as targeting by demographics.

Carefully restrict where your Ads are placed, it's best to use only relevant web sites that have some kind of link to your business or industry. Never place ads in mobile apps - it simply does not work.

Your remarketing costs will largely depend on the bids that you set, the budgets that you set and the places that you allow Google to place your remarketing adverts, these are all controlled through settings in your Google account. The broader your remarketing campaigns, the lower the returns will be. To keep costs low, use remarketing in combination with contextual targeting, conversion filtering, frequency capping, and so on. This will enable you to create highly targeted remarketing campaigns and increase your ad relevancy.

Keep in mind that users can opt out of seeing your remarketing ads by adjusting their settings in the Google AdChoices program, this normally only becomes a problem if your Ads are really annoying but you should also note that Ad blockers are becoming more and more common and they will block remarketing ads as well as regular banner ads - this does not cost you any more, but it does reduce the reach and effectiveness of your campaigns, it's also worth noting that it is higher value users who tend to use ad blockers, leaving you to advertise to lower value users.

Chapter 96
Google Remarketing Tags

Set up Google Remarketing Tags on your Web Store
To set up Google remarketing tags on your Shopify web site you simply need to get the code from Google AdWords and install it on your web site. For this to work you need to have set up both an AdWords account and a Google analytics account as explained in chapter Google AdWords

First log into your Google AdWords account

Click the 'Shared library' option on the bottom of the left hand side menu.

In the Audiences section, click 'View'.

Click the 'Set up remarketing' link under 'Website visitors'.

Tick the box next to 'Use dynamic ads' and a new drop down will appear, select your business type from the drop down, this will normally be 'Retail'

Then click the blue 'Set up remarketing' button and a pop up window will appear

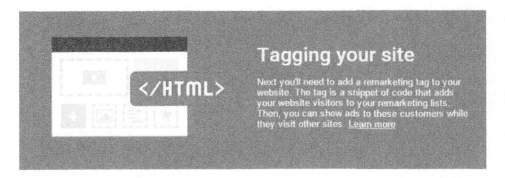
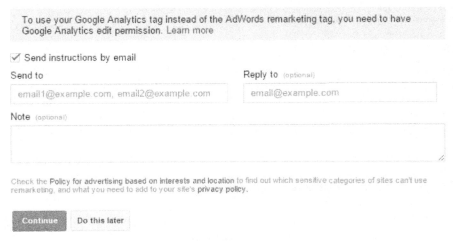

Click the 'View AdWords tag for websites' link and the window will open up to show the code

Send tag instructions

▼ View AdWords tag for websites

The tag should be placed on all pages and includes custom parameters for each business type, which enable the dynamic creative and bid optimization. Some parameters must match the values from your feeds.

Add this code to all your webpages, right before the `</body>` tag and see the insertion guide for how to fill in the custom parameter values for each business type.

```
<script type="text/javascript">
var google_tag_params = {
ecomm_prodid: 'REPLACE_WITH_VALUE',
ecomm_pagetype: 'REPLACE_WITH_VALUE',
ecomm_totalvalue: 'REPLACE_WITH_VALUE',
};
</script>
<script type="text/javascript">
/* <![CDATA[ */
var google_conversion_id = 972479869;
var google_custom_params = window.google_tag_params;
```

Check that you've added the tag and custom parameters correctly to your website using Tag Assistant. This is a browser extension that you can install on the Chrome browser.

Leave this window open in the AdWords tab and then switch back to your Shopify store admin page in another tab.

Navigate to 'on-line Store > Themes' and then click on the menu button in the top right, (it looks like this and when you click it a drop down menu pops up)

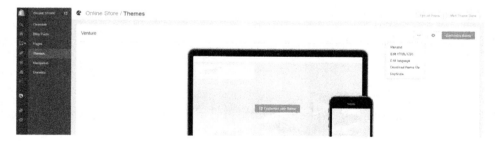

Click the 'Edit HTML/CSS' menu choice

Page 484

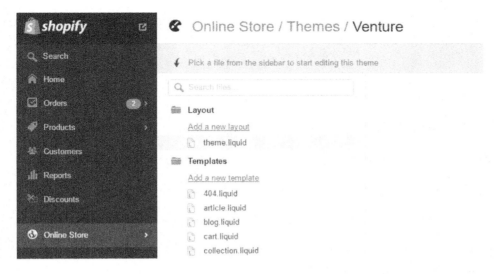

Select 'theme.liquid' from the menu, this will open up a window to the right of the menu showing the code that defines your theme.
Be very careful not to modify this by mistake.

You need to scroll the code window down all the way to the bottom as the Google tag code needs to be added at the bottom just above the </body> tag
Place your cursor to the left of the </body> tag and select it.

Page 485

Then press the enter key twice to add two empty lines and move the cursor up to the line just above the </body> tag.

```
522            <span class="icon_
523          </button>
524        </div>
525      {% endif %}
526
527    |
528    </body>
529    </html>
530
```

Go back to the Google AdWords window and select the Tag code, right click on the window and select 'Copy' from the drop down that appears to copy the tag text to your clipboard

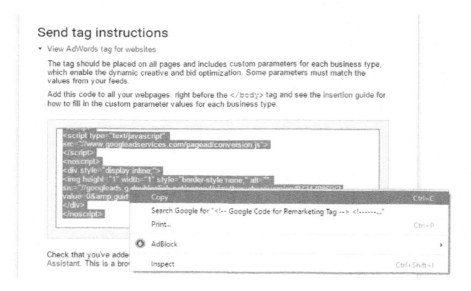

Go back to the Shopify admin window and right click on the line above the </body> tag.

Page 486

Select 'Paste'

Click the 'Save' button in the top right hand corner of the screen, a message at the bottom of the screen will tell you 'Asset saved successfully'.
But you are not finished, you should be able to see three lines at the top of the code that you have inserted that contain the words 'REPLACE_WITH_VALUE' These three lines should be changed to read

ecomm_prodid: '{{ product.id }}',
ecomm_pagetype: '{{ template }}',
ecomm_totalvalue: '{{ product.price_min | money_without_currency }}',

One more time click the 'Save' button in the top right hand corner of the screen, a message at the bottom of the screen will tell you 'Asset saved successfully'.
Back on the Google AdWords tab you can install the Google Tag Assistant in your chrome web browser which can be used to check that the tag has been properly installed.

```
ecomm_pagetype: 'REPLACE_WITH_VALUE',
ecomm_totalvalue: 'REPLACE_WITH_VALUE'
```

Check that you've added the tag and custom parameters correctly to your website using Tag Assistant. This is a browser extension that you can install on the Chrome browser.

Click on the 'Tag Assistant' link to go through the process.

Chapter 97
Facebook remarketing 'Pixel'

Setup a Facebook remarketing 'Pixel' on your web site
Adding the Facebook remarketing code to your site is very similar, first log into Facebook and get the code, then copy it into the theme HTML of your site.

To get the code, first log into Facebook, then select the small triangle icon in the top right of the page to open up the menu as shown below

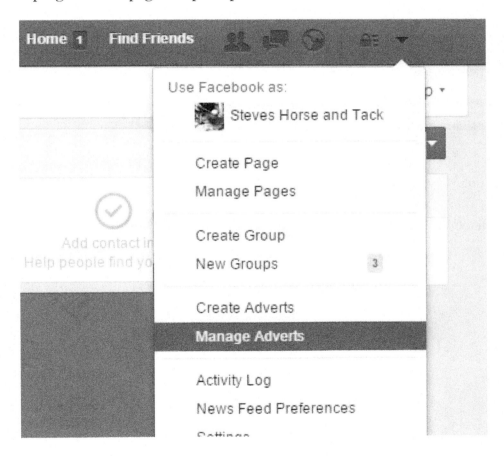

Select 'Manage Adverts' from the drop down menu to open up the Facebook Adverts Manager

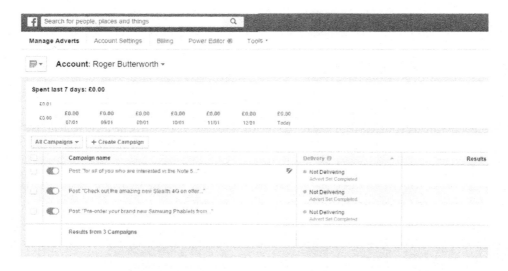

Choose the 'Tools' Menu

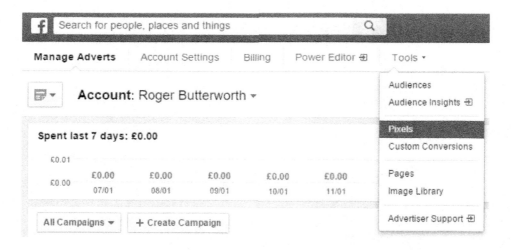

Then select 'Pixels'

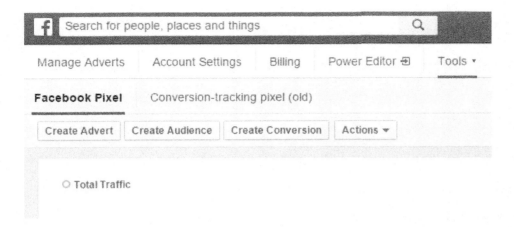

Select the 'Actions' drop down menu

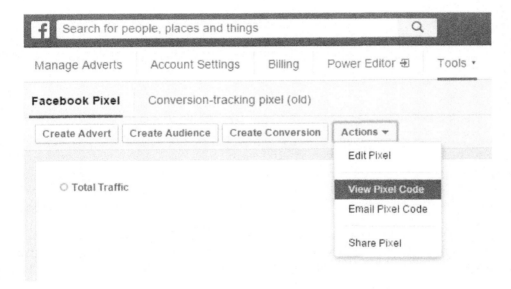

And choose 'View Pixel Code' from the drop down menu to open out a pop up that contains the code

Right click anywhere in the code box at the top of the pop up to select it all and bring up a menu

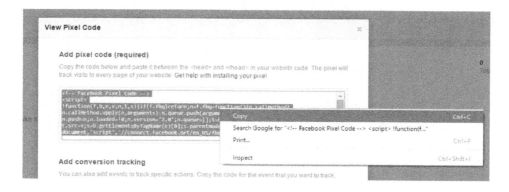

Page 492

Choose 'Copy' to copy the tracking code to your clipboard.
Then go back to the Shopify admin page

Click on the blank line above '</body>' and then right click in the same place

Select 'Paste' to paste the tracking code into your HTML between the end of the Google code and the '</body>' tag

Then press the 'Save' button in the top right of the page, a message at the bottom

of the screen will tell you 'Asset saved successfully'
Go back to your store home page and refresh it a few times, then back to the Facebook 'Manage Adverts' page and click the 'Tools > Pixels' menu to see that your pixel is getting traffic

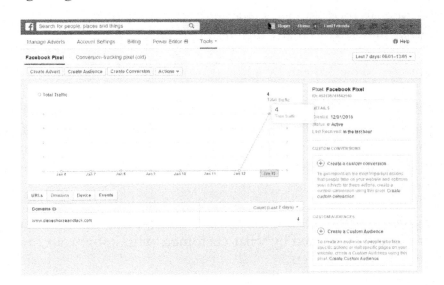

Chapter 98
Thoughts on Branding

Branding is one of those subjects that generates a lot of talk because it means so many different things to so many different people.

The definition of what I mean by a brand is this;

Your brand is the name, logo and design that identifies and differentiates your store or product from other stores or products that have similar offerings. Your brand is your promise to your customer. It is a shorthand for what they can expect from your store and products, it underlines the difference between you and your competition.

If you are going to run a store then you are building a brand, whether you want to or not. Your brand is defined by what customers who know your brand expect to get from you or your products.

Lots of commentators say things like 'Building your brand should be a top priority for any small business' and then use that exhortation to go on to explain why you should spend a ton of money with their company to 'Build your brand' - frankly that's just rubbish.

No matter what you do you will build a brand, simply by opening a store and getting products out in to the world you will start to define a brand around your name and logo because a 'brand' is just the perception that people have of what to expect from your business.

But here is the problem, 'people' as a group are both risk averse and pretty dumb. (Not you and me, obviously - the rest of them). People typically just expect to get the same thing over and over again, and expectations which are transmitted from one person to another are re-enforced in the transmission. If I tell you that I had a great experience with XYZ store, then you will probably just assume that you would have a great time too and maybe you will try them. If that's good and you report it back to me then for me and you XYZ has developed a positive brand value. We will both be more likely to shop at XYZ even if they are a bit more expensive than the next guy and that difference IS brand value - the bit extra that we will both pay in anticipation of the better experience that we have come to expect from XYZ.

Of course this story works the other way too, reports of poor experience will propagate a negative brand value, even more powerful in some ways as it does not require personal experience at all. I simply would not buy a Fiat car, I have actually only ever known two people who owned one and that was 20 years ago, but the experience, as reported to me was so bad I simply would not take a chance on buying one (so maybe I am one of the risk averse dummies after all).

If you get the image of your brand right then it will be a fantastic asset, a real asset worth actual money, your customers will be more loyal, your gross profit margins will be higher, you will get free customer recommendations and viral marketing The valuation of your company will be much higher if you have a good brand.

So how do you go about making sure that the brand you are building is a positive one?
Firstly you need to decide what the values of your brand will be, if you are setting up an on-line store in a market sector that is covered by big supermarkets then you need your customers to be people who are looking for something different that they can't get at a big store. You can't compete with the big stores on price, so go for differentiation through products and customer experience.

You need your store to have story that can position you and your products as a unique proposition in the minds of your customers. Research your potential customers and figure out what you want your brand to mean to them.

Brand development rules
- Good customer service and good quality products are the heart of a good brand, don't lose sight of that.
- Be prepared to say no to bad products and stick to your strategy, inconsistency will kill your brand.
- Develop your message to customers about your product as soon as possible, good service and good products will get you started, but the sooner you have a clear message the better and once you have your story and you start marketing it you need to stick to the message and make sure that it permeates everything you do.
- The design of your on-line store, packaging, marketing e-mails, logo, business cards, print adverts - everything that you can change should be in line, supporting your story. Thats why you need your basic story to be set before you start selling, you can develop it a bit over time, but you need to

have the basics in place before you start.
- Don't be afraid to tell a story or invest your business in a lifestyle, but be sure that it has long term prospects, fashions change and you don't want to be selling mustache wax once facial hair is out of fashion again.
- Make sure that the same, consistent values go right through everything you do, when you attend trade shows, or put on parties you need to keep the same image that you have on-line.
- And lastly remember a single serious slip up can damage your brand and lose all the hard work you've done to build it, you can kill your brand in weeks after spending years building it up, As Steve Jobs said - "Deciding what not to do is as important as deciding what to do."

Chapter 99
Making your web site sell

Getting customers to come to your site is half of the process of getting them to buy from you - the other half is persuading them to actually put their hands into their pockets to buy from you, to do that you need to consider why customers make purchases and do your best to meet their requirements.

Why do customers buy?
There are 5 factors that will effect the decision that a potential customer will make about whether they buy from your site or not once they have arrived on your site. You may be surprised by the order that I put them in, in my opinion in order of importance they are;

1. Perceived Product Quality
2. Product Availability
3. Price
4. Vendor Reputation
5. Website content

Perceived Product Quality
The customers perception of your product's quality is the most important factor in deciding whether they buy it or not.

Product quality is one of those things that is difficult to explain but 'you know it when you see it'. Most business books define product quality as the degree to which the product or service being sold meets the customer's expectations. In fact the aspect of product quality that influences a customers buying decision is better described as the customers perception of product quality rather than the actual product quality.

Video, images and product description can play a part in improving the perception of your product's quality in the mind of potential customers but the number one influencer of customer perception of product quality is customer reviews preferably word of mouth reviews from people that the customer knows or trusts. It can be really dangerous to get the perception of product quality too far ahead of the actual quality because there are always customer service problems after the sale if the perception is higher than the actual product quality as customers will be understandably disappointed with their purchase when the product is not as good as they thought it would be.

You can do a lot to help improve your customers perception of the quality of your products with your video, images, product specifications and description and since this is the most important part of the customers buying decision it's very important that you do this. Since your customers can send back any product that they are disappointed with it is best to be completely honest and focus your efforts on making sure that a potential customer understands your products what they can and can't do or be used for.

Preventing a customer who will send the product back from purchasing the product in the first place is just as important as persuading customers to buy, it will save you a lot of time and money in the long term.

Product Availability

Product availability is a very significant factor in most purchasing decisions, in my experience it is the second most important factor in the majority of on-line sales after the customers perception of product quality.

What most customers want from product availability is predictability, delivering goods as fast as possible is obviously helpful but many buyers have a hard deadline like a birthday in mind when they buy and they want to know when they will get their purchase for sure more than they want to get it right away.

Obviously the easiest way to improve your product availability is to hold stock but that costs a lot of cash and there is always the risk that customers will not buy your stock especially if it is an item with fast moving changes like technology or fashion where old stock can devalue quickly.

Efficient logistics processes and close relationships with supplier can both help give you faster and more predictable product availability.

Price

You may be surprised to see price come this far down the list of buying decision factors, but it is not as significant a factor as you may think - obviously availability and quality are the same from two different vendors then price is the next most significant factor in the purchasing decision - but if you are offering a better product for a customers needs with better availability you will usually be able to charge more for it. Thats why it is always better to have your own unique products for your web store.

Vendor Reputation

Your reputation as a vendor will factor into the customer's purchasing decision as well, you need to make sure that you do all you can to protect and enhance your reputation on-line and off line.

Website content

The last thing that influences customer purchasing decisions is the content on your web site. This is most effective when it is used to change customer perceptions of product quality where your products are unique, however it can also be used to improve your reputation.

There is a hierarchy to product content.

1. Video
2. Images
3. Specification
4. Descriptions

By this I mean that video is much more influential than images which in turn are more influential than text based content like specifications and descriptions. Bear this in mind when you set your products up, put more time into your product videos and make them more prominent. Do images next and bear in mind that detailed specifications are more important than flowery descriptions. Knowing that a table is 180cm long and 45cm wide is much more helpful than having it described as 'large'.

Chapter 100
Photography

The old adage that a picture is worth a thousand words is very true in on-line retail (and for that matter a video is worth at least 20 pictures)

When they shop in your on-line store, customers can not touch your products, they can't pick them up, feel the finish or try them on. That is what makes product photography so important in the process of turning a browser into a buyer. Your images, along with your product video need to give the browsing customer a clear understanding of your product in order to help them decide whether to buy or not. As a result of this, product photography is pretty much compulsory for an on-line store, a store using only text or even only video to exhibit products would be brave, but I'm not sure that it would work very well.

When you first come to set up your store it will help a lot if you take a few decisions about your product photographs that you will stick to in the long run to keep your site consistent and professional looking. Even if you intend to get your product photos from a supplier or another third party it's important to decide how you will present them as a part of your site.
While it is great to get some of your product photos from elsewhere, it is a good idea to still shoot some of your own and to make your own product videos.

The things to consider with regard to your image standards are as follows;

Image Shape or aspect ratio
The most important issue to decide about your product photos is the shape that they will have. Actually when I say 'shape' what I really mean is 'Aspect Ratio' as almost all images will be rectangular in shape.
The best shape for your images is definitely a square (1:1 aspect ratio), if you can accommodate a square image in your site then you should use that as your default, it is clean and works everywhere, on product pages, in grid systems, on Google Image search, Pintrest and Facebook. In fact the Shopify Facebook store can only work with square images.
The main reason that you would not be able to use a square image is if your product is long and thin, but even then you could still manage it with a little creativity.
Regardless, it is really important that you pick an aspect ratio for your product

photos and stick with it, if you absolutely can't use a square image then 4:3 works well, but I would not use anything less 'square' than 16:9 as images more 'wide screen' than that can look odd in grids.

Image Size
There are two things to consider when you look at the size of the images that you will have on your web store. The first is the resolution of the image, the number of pixels that the image has in it, the second is the image file size in kilobytes.
As a rule of thumb higher resolution images are better, but smaller file sizes are also better as they load faster, especially on a mobile device. These two considerations work against each other so you need to find a happy medium.
I have found that square images of 1,000 pixels x 1,000 pixels give a happy medium between file size and image detail when saved as a .jpg file they should be less than 400 kilobytes.

The background behind your images is really important
When it comes to the way that your products look on-line and in fact to the way that your whole site looks the choice of background for your product images is key, and keeping the background of your images consistent throughout your site really helps to make it look professional.
Many people choose to display their products on a pure white background, this is the default for a lot of sites including industry leaders like Amazon. If you plan to sell your unique items on Amazon you will need images on a plain white background to set them up in line with Amazon's guidelines. If you are using a lot of images supplied by third parties you may find that images on a white background are easier to get especially if you mainly sell small, dark colored products a plain white background is clean and simple with no distractions.
Even if you can't take or acquire images of your products on a plain white background, they are easy to edit using Photoshop. If you don't have the skills to do that yourself you can contract with freelancers through www.fiverr.com and www.elance.com who will do it for you at very good rates. Budget US$0.50c or £0.30p per image to get that done.
Sometimes the look and feel of your store demands images showing your product in use with a real-life background. Many cutting edge fashion boutique stores use this kind of look. It can be harder to keep the focus on the product if there is a lot going on in the background so you may need to add extra closeup pictures so your users can see the product in more detail.
Don't be afraid to mix white background images with real life backgrounds in your product records as long as the main images (the ones that appear on category

pages and are the default for the product page) are consistent across the whole site. Real life images for the product main image combined with white background images to show off the detailed features on the items often work nicely.

Colored backgrounds, especially black backgrounds are best avoided, they just look wrong.

Taking your own photos

If you can produce your own product photos then there are huge advantages to doing so. Unique images set you apart from the competition and help you stand out on social media and in Google search.

Learning to take your own product photos and edit them for use on your web store can be very satisfying and it need not cost very much so it's well worth a try. If you do decide to take your own photos there is a lot to learn to make them perfect and that's outside the scope of this book - but here are a few tips to get you on the right track.

- You CAN take good quality product photos with a modern cell phone camera, you really can but you need to secure it on a tripod or other mounting system to avoid camera shake and to get the lighting right.
- If you choose to buy a camera, buy the best that you can afford. A compact camera will be no better than a cell phone, buy an SLR with manual control of the aperture, exposure and focus if you can afford it. For most product photos you will use a lens between 20mm and 35mm. Lenses smaller than 20mm start to get 'fish eye' distortion, longer lenses make you get too far away from the subject to be practical.
- Lighting is important to good quality product photos, natural light can be a good choice for some products, but for smaller items and those with a lot of detail you can get better results by using artificial lights to highlight small details on products like watches and jewelry or similar.
- Small items benefit from a light box or special photo table, this is a perfect solution for your small items and, combined with 2 or 3 low cost photographic lights it will give you complete control over shadows and highlights in the final image.
- If you don't have a light table photographing small items in a white bathtub can be very effective. Bluetac works well to hold them in place.

More is - more

You can never have too many product photos, use different angles to show details, show everything that you can about the product. If it comes in multiple sizes and colors photograph then all, show everything that you think is important about the product. You should never have less than three images and more is always better as long as they each show something extra and worth seeing, for a complex product like a car 30 or 40 images is not too much.

Summary
Taking the time to have top quality, unique product images for the products in your on-line store can have a big payoff. Good pictures answer customers questions much more effectively than text descriptions and lead to more traffic more sales and an often overlooked benefit - lower returns.

Getting the most from Images and Videos

Use File Names for SEO benefit
It is really helpful to name your images and video files descriptively in plain English so that you can get full SEO benefit from your images. It's easy to take lots of product shots and keep the default file name that your camera gives them, but that's not such a good idea. When Google checks your site it will record all of the image names and then make them available for people who perform Google image searches using keywords contained in your image names. On top of that, the more relevant keywords that Google finds on your site the better

When it comes to SEO, it's important to use acceptable keywords to help your web page rank on search engines. Creating descriptive, keyword-rich file names is absolutely crucial for image optimization. Search engines not only crawl the text on your web page, but they also search for keywords within your image file names.

Use ALT tags for SEO benefit
As well as a file name, every image or video on your site will have an 'Alt Tag' It is important that you also use these carefully to improve the ability of customers to find your products in search.

Alt tags are a text alternative to images that are shown when a browser can't properly render the image for some reason. They also provide the text that you see when you hover your cursor over the image when the image is properly displayed.

Using carefully chosen, descriptive alt tags is the best way for your products to show up in Google image search which is a surprisingly effective way to sell some products, especially home decor and fashion items. However you should not use alt tags for decorative images on your site like 'on sale' banners etc as Google can see this as you trying to game the system.

You can check the Alt Tags on your images by viewing the source code of your web pages.

Which image editing software should I use?
The industry standard tool for editing images is Adobe Photoshop. Photoshop is a very complex and powerful image editing tool that can take years to learn to use properly, but if you want to have the ability to really make your images sing and dance then Photoshop is the default choice. Adobe recently switched their licensing model to Photoshop to a monthly rental arrangement which is very helpful for small business cash flow.
If Photoshop is too complex or too expensive for you there are lots of other on-line tools you can use for image editing.

PicMonkey - has been described by experts as a "staggeringly great photo editing tool".
Pixlr - is super user-friendly, and also comes with a 100% free app for your smartphone, so you can edit on the go.
FotoFlexer- is another fairly advanced on-line image editor. FotoFlexer even allows you to work with layers.

Google offers a free photo storage and editing tool with limited functions called Picassa, but it has the benefit of being very easy to use.

And if you prefer open source software GIMP is the open source version of Photoshop. GIMP can be run on Windows, Mac or Linux and it can do everything Photoshop can do, but tends to be a bit less user friendly. However it's free and that pays for a lot of not so friendly!

What type of images should I use
This one is easy the 'JPEG' image format with extension .jpg is always best for product images.

A good rule of thumb for eCommerce images is to try to keep your image file size below 70kb. That can be difficult sometimes, especially for larger images, but I'll get into that in a minute...

Be careful when you use decorative images
Websites often use large decorative background images, some of the best looking Shopify themes use this kind of image.

Although decorative images can add a lot of aesthetic appeal to a web page, they can often result in a really large combined page size and contribute to slow load times. You need to optimize the files of this kind of decorative images so that they don't slow your site down so much that they impair your web site's ability to convert visitors into customers.

Check the file sizes of all the decorative images on your web pages and use a service to optimize them if necessary to reduce the file size, there are great on-line services that will do that for you for free like http://jpeg-optimizer.com/

Chapter 101
Text Content

The two main types of text content on your web site will be product descriptions and product specifications, you will also have static pages and blog entries but the majority of the text that your customers will actually read will be the specifications and descriptions that you post on product pages.

Product descriptions and specifications
Before I go on to talk about how you can write good product descriptions I just want to point out that for most products, maybe even for all products specifications are more important than descriptions.

The difference between specifications and descriptions
Descriptions are prose, text explanations about the features and benefits of the product, specifications are facts, the dimensions of the product, it's technical make up. Specifications help a customer to understand the product, to see if a bookcase will fit in the gap that they have in their living room or to know if the seat that you are selling is compatible with their bicycle.

I recommend that you make sure that the specifications of your product are clearly displayed before staring work on the descriptions.

Writing Product Descriptions
Writing product descriptions is a difficult task, a product description is basically a sales pitch, and just like a sales pitch it is important that you explain the benefits of your product in the description, not just explain the features - the features belong in the specification.

If you read the descriptions on your competitors web sites or even on the sites of big retailer like Amazon you will see that even professional copywriters sometimes write product descriptions that simply describe products, that's an opportunity missed, product descriptions should sell your product not just describe it.

Here are some tips to help you write product descriptions that are sales pitches, not just feature lists.

Focus on the benefits of the product

A benefit is the reason that a customer will buy your products, it's the thing that they think about when they buy.

For example if a pair of shoes are made from soft leather, that's a feature. The Benefit is that the shoes are comfortable and will not rub your feet even when they are brand new. A new laptop having a 3Ghz processor with 4Gb of cache memory is a feature - the fact that it can run Photoshop without any delays or pauses is a big benefit if you spend all day waiting for Photoshop to load new images.

Make sure that you mention the benefits as well as the features of your products to give customers reasons to buy.

Go beyond benefits and tap into your customers aspirations
Scientific research has proved that if people hold a product in their hands, their desire to own it increases.

Your on-line store can't let people hold products. Good quality videos and big clear pictures of your product really help, but there's also a technique that you can use in your product descriptions to increase desire to own a product, write text that encourages the reader to imagine what it would be like to own the product.

Start the first sentence of a description with the word imagine, and finish your sentence by explaining how the reader will feel if they buy and use your product.

For example; Imagine how you would feel if you had a handmade saddle perfectly fitted to you and your horse, no worries about chafing on long rides and complete comfort.

Try to use sensory words where they are appropriate
Sensory words increase sales because they engage different parts of the brain.

If you describe chocolate as 'dark and sweet that's OK, but what else would you expect of chocolate? But when you say that it is 'crunchy and smooth' you help the customer understand what it is like to eat a piece.

Use words like velvety, smooth, soft, lush, sharp, and tangy.

Think about your perfect customer and write the description for him or her.
When you write a product description that you think will appeal to everyone you

can end up writing bland and wishy washy text that does not appeal to anyone at all.

Explain how the product can be used, what it will do for the buyer and if you think it's important tell the customer what it will not do as well. Try to put yourself in the shoes of the buyer - what would you want to know? List the top 3 features and construct sentences using this kind of structure.

The product has this feature, which gives this benefit for the user.

Tell your prospective customers what your product will not do
Explain the limitations of your product, remember not making sales that turn into returns is important.
Never write anything negative about your product, but you can use some product limitations as an opportunity to up-sell your customer with phrases like.

Please note that this saddle does not come with a storage bag, however our slightly more expensive premium saddle does. Link the up-sell reference to the product page for the better item.

Avoid filler phrases and pointless superlatives
Your potential customers will simply not read over long descriptions, so anything that makes the description longer without adding any sales power to the description is a waste of effort and counterproductive.

Adding bland phrases like "excellent product quality" or unjustified superlatives like 'excellent', 'superb' and 'unbelievable' makes your description read like 'blah, blah, blah' to the customer and can sound insincere.

As soon as a potential customer reads 'excellent product quality' or 'unbelievable performance' he blanks it out so you wasted your time writing it and you become less persuasive.

If your product is really the best, provide specific proof or better still quote a customer or an independent reviewer who uses those words about your product instead. 'This saddle is the best that I have ever owned' said by a customer is much more meaningful than your opinion that the saddle is the best ever.

People move in herds, you can exploit that...

Some potential customers who are not sure about which product to purchase look for suggestions in what other people are doing. They are often swayed to buy a product with the highest number of positive reviews but there are other ways to add 'herd effect' into your product descriptions.

You can say things like 'this is our most popular saddle' or add reviews, press cuttings or links to on-line reviews or even to stories about how you sold out or sold 1,000 items in a really short period always try to highlight the products that are customer favorites.

Chapter 102
Reputation Management

Maintaining and enhancing your on-line reputation is a big part of making sure that you sell more to the people who come to your store. Managing a good reputation on-line is a bit like getting good rankings on search engines, you have two choices, either try to fool people into thinking that you do a good job and that you treat customers well when you in fact do not - or be as good as you can possibly be and hope that your reputation reflects that.

Honesty is a big part of developing a good reputation on-line, remember that although customers really care about when they will receive their order, they tend to care more that you tell them before they place their order how long delivery will take - accurate predictions are more important to customers than faster deliveries. The same is true of total cost of order, product quality and product usability, honesty in these things is really important to maintaining a good reputation overall.

Review Sites
For any on-line store starting out today the management of customer reviews is a major part of making sure that your business is seen as credible by your potential customers. Sites like Trustpilot, Google reviews and Trip Adsvisor allow potential customers to see a selection of stories about your business posted by customers or even by people pretending to be customers.

Managing on-line reviews can be one of the most stressful parts of running a business for an owner / manager. When you work long hours making your business deliver for customers getting a bad review can be devastating. And no matter how hard you try to satisfy your customers you will get bad reviews.
There are really only two kinds of reviews on-line, Bad reviews and reviews that were paid for or organized by the retailer. Unfortunately customers simply do not go out of their way to offer good reviews.

The main web sites used for reviews of on-line stores in Europe and the USA are Google Reviews and Trustpilot. Both claim that they check reviews to make sure that they are legitimate. My experience is that they do not do that at all, both sites allow more or less anybody to post a review of any kind.
The Trustpilot model is particularly nasty, they encourage negative reviews and then charge companies who want good reviews in order to solicit good ones to

balance them up. Check the reviews for John Lewis and Marks&Spencer to see how bad the reviews that they get are simply because they refuse to pay Trustpilot. Check the reviews for Amazon.co.uk - they ship over 1 million parcels per week in the UK and more than 99% are delivered fast and effectively, but more than half or their reviews are negative, they too refuse to pay Trustpilot.

How to deal with Trustpilot.
You really have only two choices to deal with Trustpilot, you can either pay them for a service to manage the reviews about your site or you can try to manage the process outside of Trustpilot using other resources.

If you decide to pay for the review collection service on Trustpilot it will cost you between US$6,000 and US$10,000 per year (£4,000 to £6,500). If you do that you will have the opportunity to collect reviews directly through your site which are then posted to Trustpilot and to Google shopping in the form of stars next to your search results. This does not guarantee you a five star rating, but I have never seen anyone who pays them who does not have a very good ranking even when their customer service is dreadful. However the costs of paying Trustpilot are beyond many startups so they have to manage the issue by alternative means.

You can sign up for a free account with Trustpilot which will allow you to respond to reviews on their site as the business owner and to upload a logo etc to the site, be mindful however that when you do that you are agreeing to their terms of service which are very one sided.

No matter how good your customer service and products are you will get bad reviews on Trustpilot, you need to accept that fact up front, it just goes with the territory. So I recommend a pre-emptive strike to set the right tone. As soon as your site is up and running get everyone who you know to post a positive on-line review of your site, friends, family, anyone you trust who has an e-mail account or a Facebook profile, get them all to post as quickly as possible to start you off with a nice buffer of 5 star reviews, aim to get ten in place within a week or so. The reason for this is that the number of stars shown next to your ads on Google is the average review score from Trustpilot and a buffer of ten 5* reviews will mean that even if you get two new 1* reviews you will still have 52/12 = 4.3 stars overall. You should note that doing this is a violation of the Trustpilot terms and conditions (if you agreed to them) but I personally think it's quite justified when you are faced with the alternative of paying them thousands of dollars.

What to do when you get a bad review

When you get a bad review the first thing to do is not to take it personally.

Who am I kidding? Of course you will take it personally! But you need to put that to the back of your mind and try to treat every negative feedback as a learning experience is can be hard, but you have to do it.

The first thing to do is to read the review carefully and dispassionately - Ask yourself or even someone else who is less emotionally committed to the business 'Is the customer right to be upset?' and 'How would you feel in the same position?'. Investigate the case, not to try to disprove the customers points but to really find out if there is a problem.

If the customer is right to be upset then your course of action is clear.

1. Identify the problem in your systems, products or processes that caused the customer to get so upset and fix it, document what you did to fix it.
2. Write directly to the customer by e-mail. Apologize, explain in detail what went wrong and what you have done to stop it happening again, apologize again and offer some sort of fix or compensation if you think that it's appropriate. Lastly, ask the customer to update their review in light of the fixes that you have put in place. Post a shorter reply on the site where the review was left, do not mention compensation directly through the review site.

If the customer review looks fake or abusive

If you think that the review is not from a real customer or if they are abusive then you can usually report the review to the site where it is posted to ask for it to be taken down, although my experience of the results that you get when you do this, even in the most obvious cases is mixed. You can usually add a reply to reviews like that asking the reviewer to contact you directly and saying that you don't recognize them or the details of the review.

If the customer is real, but the complaint is not serious here are some tips for handling them.

It's important to take what you can from reviews to try to improve your services and your products, some reviews can really help, try to turn the negative comments into ways to improve your service.

The best solution that I have found to counteracting poor reviews is to buy some good ones, you can buy reviews from third parties at www.fiverr.com just search for 'review' most reviewers there are happy to post on Trustpilot or Tripadviser for

$5-$10 (£3 to £7) per review, I recommend buying 5 fake ones every time you get a bad review, it's still cheaper than paying Trustpilot unless you get a lot of bad reviews - in which case you should probably change a few things.

When you reply to a review, provide a business email that the reviewer can use to contact you directly, this will help to take the conversation 'private' while you resolve it and ask the customer to improve the review. You will be able to go more in depth with the customer through an email, depending on the severity of the problem that can help a lot.
You could say something along the lines of, "I apologize for the problem that you have had, we would like to learn from your experience to improve our service in the future. Please contact me at xxx@yourstoreurl.com to help us resolve this issue for you."

You simply can not please everyone all the time, some people are nasty and some people are stupid and some people just have unrealistic expectations. I have seen reviews of mountain top skiing lodges that complain that the approach was 'too hilly' and a review of a Samsung phone charger that gave it one star because it would not charge an iPhone. When you get one of these complaints over something that is completely out of your control, explain the situation patiently in your reply, but don't take on a condescending, sarcastic or negative tone toward the customer just explain the situation.
For example, a customer leaves a horribly negative review after receiving their delivery from your store a day late because they were out when the courier first called. You can apologize for the inconvenience, but explain that things like this happen occasionally. Apologize and explain that the timing of the courier delivery is out of your control and explain that the customer has some responsibility to be in when the courier calls. Be direct, but not offensive or confrontational. This is an example of when you should not offer any compensation or provide a contact email address because there is nothing else that you can do to help.

In fact you should NEVER offer gift cards or other compensation for a negative review directly on the review site where other people can see the offer. If you think that the customer experience is serious enough that you think that you need to compensate them, then do it through e-mail. Offering repayment or gift cards publicly can be seen as bribery by an outsider reading reviews, it also attracts other bad reviews from people who just want the compensation.

And a few general tips about reviews

Even if you are confident in your product and service you should never add blanket invitations to your customers to leave reviews, don't add review site links to your order confirmation e-mails and never link to them from your web page or Facebook page you will attract ten times more negative reviews than positive ones I'm afraid that's just the way it works. Instead have a very obvious way for customers to complain directly to you through your web site, making it easy for unhappy customers to bring their problem to you directly makes it much easier to deal with problems in private which gives you more flexibility.

If you have good feedback from customers ask them to post it on Trustpilot or Tripadviser - but only ask customers who have already expressed positive feelings towards you to do this.

Chapter 103
Product support

It is important to have as much support information and documentation on your web site as possible to improve customer satisfaction and to make servicing customer requirements easier for you. Obviously you should have things like
Drivers for IT products that you sell available to you, but you should also try to collect digital copies of these kinds of document;

- Manuals
- 'How to' guides
- Customer testimonials and customer usage stories
- Newspaper Stories about your business or products

If you can get original documents as '.pdf' files from the people who made the products, if you generate them your self you can save from Word or any publishing package as a '.pdf'. If you have paper copies of the documents it can help to invest in a good scanner to digitize them.
Once you have the documents as ',pdf' files you can upload them to your site as follows.

Navigate to Settings > Files

From this page you can upload as many files as you like, to get started click the blue 'Upload files' button, this will bring up a file selector window showing the files on your computer, you can select one or many items to upload using the normal file select method for your computer.
For windows press Ctrl + Alt and select the files required individually, or if they are together in a list then you can press Shift and select the first in a group then

while holding down the Shift key select the last file of the group to select all of the files in between.
Then press 'Open' to upload the files to Shopify.

You can upload files up to 20Mb per file so most .pdf files and images should be fine - if your manuals or other documents are longer than that you can use on line services like 'Compress pdf' (http://smallpdf.com/compress-pdf) to compress them or split them into several parts.

If you upload a file that you decide to remove just press the delete button next to the file name.

Once the files are uploaded you can add them to the appropriate page of your store as follows.

Showing Files for download through your store

Navigate to Online Store > Pages

I'm going to add a new page to my store with down-loadable documents about my products, so I will press the blue 'Add page' button and create a new page called 'Manuals'

I add the title of the page and the first line of text, then I select the part of the text that I want to make into a link to download the document.

Then press the link button

A pop up will appear like the one below.

The link for the file that you uploaded can be found back in the Settings > Files page, to get it you can open up a new browser tab and navigate to that page

Select the URL next to the file that you want to link to and the whole URL should be highlighted, right click and select 'Copy' from the drop down menu or press Ctrl + C to copy the URL to your clip board, then go back to the 'Page' window and paste the URL into the 'Link to' box.

You can choose to have the link open in the same browser window that the user uses to click on the link, or in a new window. For the purposes of opening an instruction manual I like to make it a new window, so I will select that from the 'Open this link in' drop down, then fill out the Link title for SEO.

Then press the blue 'Insert link' button and you have created the link.

You can use all of the other functions to set the page out to look good and then add it to the menus on your site either at the page top or in the footer - remember that unless you add the page to a menu somewhere it will not be visible on your web site.

Chapter 104
Marketplace Web Sites

Selling through your own store is by far the best way to develop a long term income through on-line sales, when you own the domain, the brand and the customer list as well as the web store that you set up, you own the business. Even more so if you make or design the products that are sold through the store.

However it is also possible to develop sales through web stores owned by other people which allow smaller companies to offer products for sale through their own web sites, this kind of web site is often referred to as a 'Marketplace'. In the English speaking world the most prominent marketplace web sites are Amazon and eBay but there are lots of others all over the world.

Once you have set up your on-line store you can use marketplaces to add extra revenue to your sales and you can use them to develop your brand or even to promote your own web site, although the marketplaces try to restrict your ability to do that where they are allowed to.

Using Amazon or other marketplace sites can be a very effective way to start the process of expanding your reach into foreign markets because they already have all the appropriate payment methods, delivery services and appropriate customer service rules set up you can use them by simply translating your product details.

Chapter 105
Objectives

The main lure of the marketplaces is the opportunity to access their huge customer bases, when you use Amazon or eBay to sell your products you get access to millions of potential customers for your products.
In a lot of ways you can see Google Shopping as very much like a marketplace and you can see Amazon and eBay as types of search engine, on Google you pay for each click that a shopper makes on your advert, on Amazon and eBay you pay a commission on the sales that you make. The commission that you pay varies between 5% and 20% depending on the site, type of product and the volume of sales that you make, if your profit margins are 'normal' which I define as between 30 and 45% gross then the economics of selling on Amazon, eBay or using Google shopping are similar.

If you have a brand of your own and unique products then selling on Amazon is a great idea, if you are selling products from other people which carry their brand and which are widely available then you should probably not use Amazon at all as price based competition from other sellers will probably make it uneconomic. eBay is different, as price competition of eBay is not as severe as on Amazon - that is probably counter intuitive, but in fact eBay uses it's search function to share business between different sellers who have prices which are close to the best, while on Amazon the seller with the lowest price will take almost all of the sales.

Of course the big difference between Amazon and eBay is that Amazon is a retailer in it's own right while eBay only acts as a marketplace, it is almost impossible to sell anything on Amazon if you are in competition with the same thing or a similar thing that is being sold by Amazon themselves.

Providing your products are suitable Before you start selling or offering your products on Amazon, eBay or both you first need to decide what your primary objectives for using the marketplace are and you need to be sure that you have the time and resources available to do it properly.

The two things that you can use marketplaces for are

1. To develop awareness of your brand and your products that you will try to use to bring traffic to your own web site where you can make direct sales to customers.

2. To sell you product directly to the marketplaces customers at a profit.

Of course it's perfectly reasonable to try to do both, but the priority levels that you apply to these two different objectives will influence the way that you use your marketplace listings. In the simplest terms you can develop your brand awareness by simply listing your products on the marketplace at your recommended retail price - potential customers will see the product and price on Amazon which can be used to establish the value of the product, they may go on to search for your product and find your own site where you can make deals available.

eBay can also be used in this way, but it is less effective. eBay is essentially a kind of on-line 'car boot sale' so the typical eBay customer is expecting to buy second hand or deep discounted items making it a lot less effective for brand development, in fact appearing on eBay could harm a brand.

Both eBay and Amazon are great places to sell second hand items or to clear returned items as 'nearly new', they represent a huge market for refurbished or used products, they attract shoppers whose main concern is price and don't mind waiting on shipping.

Chapter 106
Amazon

Setting up a seller account on Amazon is very easy, a seller account on Amazon is an extension of a normal buyer account.

Amazon does not like you to have two seller accounts set up at the same time although it allows you to have as many buyer accounts as you like so if you have used Amazon to sell items using your personal Amazon account then you should stop doing that and remove your listings before you start running a business account for your on-line store.

I recommend that you set up a new account for your business using your business e-mail address, you can do this by going to Amazon, making sure that you are not signed in and then going to the 'sign in' page to set up a new account.

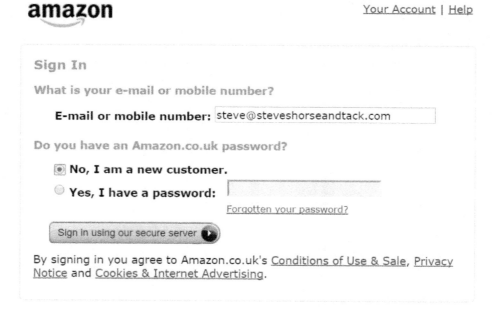

You will then need to set a password for your new account, it's another important account so make it a secure one.

Once you have done that you need to set up a seller account on this new address

Your Account

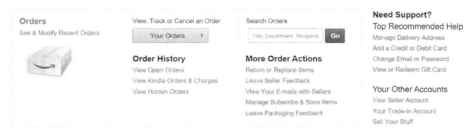

To add the ability to sell on Amazon to your new account Click on 'Sell Your Stuff' over to the right hand side of the Amazon 'Your Account' page.

A detailed description of how to sell on Amazon is beyond the scope of this book, but there are a few things that you should know about how selling on Amazon works to help you decide if you want to do it or not.

- Becoming a professional seller on Amazon will incur a monthly fee of about $US50 per month (£30).

- Amazon allows you to add items to it's catalog, for small retailers selling own brand or unique items just having your items listed on Amazon is a great way to validate your products to potential customers and help to develop your brand. To list an item you will need to allocate an EAN code to each item that you want to list, you can buy EAN codes for your items at www.gs1.org, 1,000 codes will cost about $500 (£300) per year.

- Setting up items on Amazon is just like setting up on your own site, if anything good quality images are more important on Amazon as the description is much less prominent.

- But remember that once you set up an item on Amazon there is nothing to stop other Amazon merchants offering the same item through the listing that you set up. You can help to prevent people selling copies or unauthorized versions of your items by joining the Amazon brand registry (https://sellercentral-europe.amazon.com/hz/catalog-brand-application/brand-application-wizard?) This will not prevent other people listing, but it will help you to police the site.

- If you are serious about using Amazon as a sales channel for your products then you should also consider using Fulfillment By Amazon (FBA). FBA is the Amazon fulfillment service, you can send your goods to Amazons warehouse to be handled by Amazon's own staff, this means that you don't have to do it and additionally Amazon gives priority to items that use FBA in customer searches.

- Amazon expects sellers to give a very high standard of customer service to people who buy through the Amazon site. When selling on Amazon you need to accept any return that the customer requests and refund in full regardless of the condition that the customer returns the goods in, after the cost of Amazon fees the cost of maintaining customer service is the most significant cost when selling through Amazon.

- If you want to use Amazon to open up business in overseas countries you will need to add seller accounts for each Amazon site where you want to list your items to your merchant account, you then need to set up separate, but linked listings for each of your items on each international site which can be very time consuming, but it is a great way to start building your brand overseas.

Chapter 107
eBay

Selling on eBay is very different to selling on your own store or selling through most other marketplaces. eBay started off as an auction web site for used items and this is still evident in the way that you set up items for sale.

A detailed description of how to sell on eBay is outside of the scope of this book, but here are a few points to consider while you decide it it's something that you want to do. It is a big commitment of time and it is not risk free - think carefully about it before you do it.

Does your brand fit on eBay?
Selling high end branded items on eBay could devalue the brand, think carefully if you are trying to develop a high end brand you should probably not offer it through eBay, but mid market brands will be fine there.
If you are re-badging items that are available elsewhere with other brands on them that can be a problem on eBay as you will be side by side with the other item.

Can you offer a discount and pay eBay fees and still make money?
Customers expect a deal on eBay, selling at RRP does not work well, but unlike Amazon the lowest price item will not always dominate the market - eBay shares revenue around between sellers with all sellers that have a price close to the best price getting some of the exposure in eBay searches and hence some of the orders. eBay does this because they do not want a small number of dominant sellers on the platform.
Ebay charges small sellers 10% in fees plus a small fixed fee per listing.

eBay customer service is important
eBay and PayPal enforce the highest standards of customer service on eBay, even for second hand goods so remember that anything that you sell on eBay can be returned for a refund in any condition and it could be the subject of a PayPal complaint at any time up to 180 days after dispatch.

You also need to respond to all buyer e-mails quickly, and eBay buyers love to send emails asking questions that may seem obvious and are covered in the product description or even name, some users can be rude or even abusive, regardless you need to reply professionally and quickly. This can take a lot of time and can be frustrating.

You need to issue refunds quickly on eBay, even if the customer is being unreasonable

eBay also requires you to issue a refund for any item that the customer reports as not delivered unless you have a tracking number and proof of delivery - some eBay users abuse this, but you need to live with it and refund quickly. If a buyer does open a return or refund request, reply quickly and address the buyer's concerns, refund as fast as possible.

You need to use a 'signed for' delivery service for eBay orders

if you sell on eBay you should send most items with a delivery service that collects a signature on delivery, factor that cost in as well.

Chapter 108
Other Marketplaces

If you find that you are doing well out of marketplaces then there are a lot of others to consider, most use a similar model and they are a great way to get into overseas markets quickly.

In the English speaking world the most prominent marketplaces are Amazon and eBay but there are lots of others all over the world and because of the success that eBay and Amazon have enjoyed there are new businesses using the same or similar business model popping up all the time.

Examples of businesses using very similar models to Amazon include Lazada in Asia, CDiscount in France and the Rakuten Group in Europe. Other sites with successful but different models include etsy, a marketplace for hand made goods and Kickstarter and Indigogo which are very similar marketplaces for new and innovative designs.

Here is a long list of sites that you might like to consider working with to address smaller markets around the world.

Multinational Marketplaces

Rakuten.com - Worldwide through many different brands
Rakuten is a Japanese based on-line retail business that offers a huge range of goods and a high quality partner program that allows you to sell through their various web sites around the world including Buy.com in the USA, Play.com in Europe and Rakiten it's self in Japan.

Newegg.com - USA
Newegg.com Inc. is an on-line retailer of IT products. It is based in City of Industry, California, United States, they have a well developed partner program and if you offer electronics they are a great choice to address the US market.

Tmall.com - Greater China
Tmall is a part of Alibaba, an offshoot of their Taobao marketplace, it is an on-line platform where Chinese locals and foreign brands can sell their goods to mainland China, Macau, Hong Kong, and Taiwan. TMall is the biggest B2C marketplace in

China and accounted for 57% of the total market in 2014. The website itself offers more than 70,000 official brands ranging from apparel, cosmetics, mobile phones, snacks, electronic appliances, and more. One advantage of shopping in TMall is that TMall only allows verified stores, so the products sold on-line are genuine. This is essential for building consumer trust and to increase conversion rates in China.

Jd.com - China
JD.com or Jingdong Mall, formerly known as 360Buy, is a Chinese on-line marketplace and one of the country's largest on-line retailers. It is second to Tmall for Western brands, but still worth considering if you product is appropriate to the huge Chinese market.

Yahoo shopping - Japan
Yahoo shopping died out more or less everywhere else in the world, but in Japan it's still a big thing and in combination with Amazon japan it's a great way to get your products in front of Japanese consumers.

Cdiscount.com - France
Cdiscount is the number one e-commerce site in France, ahead of even Amazon France. They sell a wide range of products including fashion, electronics, sports goods and of course CDs. They have a well developed partner program and are the best way to access the French market.

Zalando.com - European Union
Zalando specializes in clothing, shoes, accessories and sports goods, they have a partner program that you can use to sell items in these categories.

Lazada.com - South East Asia
Lazada is a newcomer to the e-commerce world as it was founded in 2012, it has spent a lot to become the "Amazon of Southeast Asia" with sites covering Indonesia, Malaysia, the Philippines, Singapore, Thailand and Vietnam. Popular Categories on Lazada include kitchenware, smartphones and tablets, appliances, beauty products, toys, sports equipment, laptops
You can sell through Lazada using your own stock or place stock with them.

Daraz.com - Bangladesh, pakistan and Myanmar
Daraz is a marketplace built in Bangladesh and also covering Pakistan and Myanmar (AKA Burma). The most popular products sold on Daraz are mobile

phones, clothing, tablets, cameras, and home entertainment goods.

Zalora.com - South East Asia and Australasia

Zalora is a fashion retail store with sites that cover Hong Kong, Taiwan, Brunei, Indonesia, Malaysia, the Philippines, Singapore, Thailand, Vietnam, Australia and New Zealand.

You can sell through their partner program and use their logistics service which is a very effective way to deliver to customers in this region.

Pixmania.com - European Union

Pixmania is a consumer electronics marketplace that covers the EU, they offer products ranging from cameras to laptops, you can sell products of this type through them using their partner program, PixPlace.

Groupon.com - Worldwide

Groupon is a global eCommerce marketplace that connects millions of subscribers with local merchants by offering discounted activities, products, travels and services. Selling on groupon is deal based and it tends to be very regional but it can work for some categories.

Livinqsocial.com - Worldwide

Almost exactly the same model as Groupon, living social is a worldwide deal site.

Souq.com - The middle east and Arabic speaking world

Souq.com is the biggest electronic commerce community in the Arab region. Founded in 2005, Souq.com has established itself to the point where 50% of UAE's population visits the site once a month. With categories ranging from consumer electronics to clothing and accessories, Souq.com is a place for merchants and buyers to get good deals you can sign up top sell on the platform in English and they offer logistics services.

Linio.com - South America

Linio is an on-line store with close ties to Lazada in south east Asia and similar systems and processes. It offers various products like cellphones, tablets, TVs, and other home appliances. Linio was launched in April 2012 and has enjoyed rapid growth since then. Linio welcomes marketplace sellers to it's stores but also sells direct to consumers.

Kaymu.com - Africa

Founded in 2012, Kaymu is part of Rocket Internet which also owns Lazada and Linio. Kaymu has expanded to cover the 23 biggest markets in Africa. Kaymu offer goods in a wide range of categories - from fashion to technology and everything else in between. The system is similar to Lazada and Linio.

MercadoLibre.com - South America

Launched in 1999 in Argentina Mercadolibre and was designed to be an eCommerce site for Latin American shoppers. Aside from fixed price deals, MercadoLibre also allows auctions on items. It has a similar model to eBay wherein customers can bid for an item that they want and the highest bidder after a specified date wins that product. However, the site is more focused on functioning as a retailer of items with fixed prices. Mercadolibre has a partner program that you can join to sell through their stores.

Allegro.pl - Poland

Allegro is the number one eCommerce site in Poland. It was founded in 1999 and has a wide variety of categories for customers to choose from including Electronics, Fashion, Health, Entertainment and Sports. Allegro has more than 12 million users and offers a great channel into Poland.

Country Specific Marketplaces

Flipkart.com - India

Flipkart is currently India's leading eCommerce marketplace. This website offers more than 20 million products in 70 categories which include books, digital media, clothes and jewelry. It was founded by a team of 2 former Amazon employees in 2007 and offers a way to address the huge Indian market.

Konga.com - Nigeria

Konga is a Nigerian third-party marketplace as well as a first-party direct retail store. Founded in 2012, Konga is an on-line mall. They currently have 8000 merchants and counting and are a great way to address Nigeria as a market.

Bidorbuy.co.za - South Africa

Bidorbuy is South Africa's localized answer to eBay. The site is a two sided marketplace that allows sellers of all sizes to list their products on the website. Similar to eBay, sellers can either list their goods in auction or fixed price format. All listing and transactions on bidorbay are in South African Rand, and bidorbuy facilitates electronic payments in the currency. Bidorbuy is one of the easiest ways for foreign sellers to get started selling in South Africa.

Cobone.com - UAE
Launched in 2010, Cobone is the biggest group buying site in the Middle East. This website is similar to Groupon. However, Cobone is culturally adapted to the middle eastern market. They offer deals in both Arabic and English they sell activities, concerts, the latest gadgets and clothing.

on-line-Shopping.gr - Greece
on-line-Shopping.gr is a network of categorized electronic retail shops serving customers in Greece. Holding shops from the famous Asos to home grown brands. The product categories range from clothing and jewelry to services such as travel & vacation, insurance, and energy.

Aukro.ua - Ukraneian auction market
Founded in 2007 by Allegro Group Ukraine. It is visited by 600,000 users with more than 300,000 auctions among 20 categories daily. Aukro is the most popular Ukrainian Internet auction site.

banqladeshbrands.com - Bangladesh
Built in 2010, this is the first and largest on-line marketplace in Bangladesh. It's popular categories include books, health and beauty, home and plastic. Bangladesh Brands offers sellers logistics help, customer service, payment gateway, and delivery services. They accept various payment methods and use mainstream delivery partners (DHL, FedEx, and Sundarban Courier).

OLX.UA - Ukrane
OLX (On-line exhange) is an on-line classifieds marketplace for used goods such as clothing, footwear, cars, furniture and household goods. Founded in March 2006 by Fabrice Grinda, 0LX.ua was acquired by Naspers, a media and digital company. OLX generates it's revenue through Google Ad- Sense banner ads.

shopinisrael.com - Israel and the Jewish diaspora worldwide
Shopinisrael is a marketplace site selling a huge range of goods to customers in Israel and spatiality Jewish items to the worldwide diaspora, you can sell through Shopinisrael by setting up a partner account.

Chapter 109
Accounting

Accounting is one of the least exciting, but most important parts of running an on-line store but without accurate accountancy you will not be able to understand how and where your business makes it's profits, and if you do not understand the profitability of the business that you are running then you will not be able to take sensible decisions on how to run your business let alone how to market, develop and grow your business.

Many new business owners are confused or even scared by accounting, but in reality accounting is just the process of keeping records of what your business owns, what it spends, what you are paid by your customers, what your business owes to other people and what they owe you. These are all things that you need to know - right?

30 years ago, before the invention of desktop computers most small business accountancy was done by keeping records in hand written ledgers, modern accounts kept on a computer system are much better as you can use them to get reports that tell you a lot more about how your business is doing, but the principle is still the same and it is not as hard to understand as many people think it is.

The simple fact is that if you want to run a successful business you need to understand accounts, you don't have to be an expert on all forms of accounting, but you do need to understand how your accounts are prepared and what the numbers in your accounts actually mean. The best way to understand your accounts is to set up the accounting system yourself, or have an expert set it up with you, it really isn't that hard once you understand the basic principles and what you are trying to achieve.
Once the business is running well and shipping more than 10-20 orders a day the day to day tasks of entering data into the accounting system may become more work than you are able to handle on your own and you will need to get someone to help with it.

I can't over emphasize that whether you set up and run the system yourself or get help but make sure it gets done and make sure that you understand the results.

For everybody running a web business using Shopify I recommend Xero accounts as an accounts package, it is an on-line system hosted for you just like Shopify and better still Shopify and Xero have partnered to integrate their systems so that data can flow from your Shopify store to your Xero accounts system without you having to transfer it manually. The integration is quite new (release in mid 2015) and while it has some limitations today (January 2016) I expect that it will improve over time.

Regardless of whether you will be doing your own accounts or having an expert help with the set up Xero is great because of the Shopify integration, low costs and because it is an on-line system you can get great value accountancy help to work remotely by hiring people from low cost regions like the Philippines or India to enter data into your system.

You can sign up for Xero at https://www.xero.com/ plans start at just £9 (US$14) per month although that system is too limited for all but the smallest retailers - the more realistic system is £20 (US$30) per month and for £5 (US$7.5) more you can have a full multi currency system, it's excellent value.
Xero also have a very useful and free on-line training system at https://www.xero.com/uk/partners/education/ which is well worth looking at if you need to understand more about accounts.

Accounting tips
As I said above it is really important that you fully understand your accounts and how they are prepared, put some time and effort into understanding how the accounts work and what they can tell you about where you business is making money and where it is loosing money.

Here are my top tips for running accounts for an on-line store

1. Make sure that all of your costs are posted into your accounts system as fast as possible, make sure that all costs are posted on the day that they are incurred without fail - if you are not recording your costs you have no idea where you stand and a huge backlog of invoices that need posting can build up very fast. If you can't post the costs yourself because you don't have the time, get help.

2. Understand the Profit and Loss Sheet(also know by the abbreviation 'P&L') or in the USA as an 'Income Statement' in detail, it is the key part of the accounts of an on-line store for making short term decisions about product pricing and small investment decisions.

You can lay out a P&L in many different ways to show different levels of profit, learn about them and what they mean.

Gross Profit, Earnings Before Interest and Tax, (EBIT) and Earnings Before Interest, Tax, Depreciation and Amortization (EBITDA)and finally Nett Profit on the bottom line of the P&L. Thats where the phrase 'The Bottom Line' comes from - the bottom line of the P&L shows the profit or loss that your business has made during a given time period after all costs have been considered and all taxes have been accounted for.

3. Alongside the P&L you need to fully understand your Cashflow statement, this will tell you both how much money you have in the business and where it came from (or where it went to) it's really easy to feel that your business is doing well because you have lots of cash in the bank, but if you owe it all to your suppliers and a bit more besides you have a problem - you can be bust with $1million in the bank if you owe $2million.

4. Learn to understand your Balance Sheet. The Balance Sheet for your business is a table of the assets, liabilities and owners investment in your business on a specific date, the balance sheet of a business is often described as a "snapshot of a company's financial condition" because it applied to a specific point in time only, unlike the P&L and Cashflow which are usually presented as a table that covers a period of time like a month, quarter or year

A standard company balance sheet has three parts, assets, liabilities, and owners equity, the name comes from the way that the table is usually presented with assets in one section and liabilities and equity in the other section with the two sections "balancing" because total assets in the business always equals liabilities plus owner's equity

The main categories of assets are usually listed first in order of how easy they are to turn into cash. The difference between assets and liabilities is known as the net assets or 'equity' of the company the net assets in the business is what you own if you are the sole proprietor of the business.

Looking at the balance sheet can tell you how the assets of the business were paid for, either by borrowing money (which shows as liabilities - either to suppliers, the bank or to customers) or by using the owner's money.

5. Understand Depreciation and Amortization, they are the way that you account for the cost of items that you pay for in one payment that will benefit you over a

long period. For example if you paid for 3 years domain registration when you bought your domain name you would charge one thirty sixth of that cost to the P&L for each month in the 3 year period, that's Amortization, depreciation is the way that you recognize the way that assets like laptops, packing benches and machinery reduce in value over their lifetime.

6. Reconcile your bank statement to your sales ledger every working day - this is the process of making sure that you have been paid for all the orders that you have shipped, it is vital because if you have not been paid it is much easier to get paid if you find the error quickly.

7. Review your P&L and Cashflow every week, compare the actual performance of your business to the planned performance and then update the weekly forecast for the next 12 months. Consider what you need to do to maximize profits and avoid losses, do you have enough cash in the business, if you need to borrow money or raise investment it's always easier to do it if you don't actually need it yet.

Chapter 110
Business Considerations

When you set up any business you need to decide what legal form you want it to take. Depending on where your business will be located you will have a number of choices as to how you set up the business.

If you are based in Europe you will also have to decide if you need to register for VAT reporting with your local tax authority and with others in neighboring countries if you will be selling a lot there.

I am not qualified to give appropriate legal or tax advice, so the information that follows is just background to help you decide for yourself. It should be combined with appropriate research or professional advice.

To incorporate or not?
If you are based in the USA, Australia or any where in Europe including the UK I recommend that you incorporate a limited company before you start trading and make that the owner of your on-line store with yourself as the sole shareholder and a director (or officer) of the business. This will give you protection from creditors in the event that your business fails which you will not get if you are a sole trader. It also gives you flexibility in your business tax affairs if you start to make a profit and it allows you to easily sell the business if you choose to do so in the future.

VAT registration
For European businesses and businesses that sell a lot of goods into the EU you may need to register with your government to collect VAT on their behalf and pay it over monthly or Quarterly.

Each European territory has a threshold level and allows small businesses with revenue below the threshold to trade without registering or collecting VAT - if you can stay under the threshold then you should and in that way avoid registering for VAT. There is nothing good about acting as an unpaid tax collector so don't do it if you can avoid it.

Chapter 111
Overseas Staff

When you first set up your on-line retail store every penny counts. If things go well you will soon start to need extra staff to help with customer service tasks like answering customer e-mails, answering phone calls, chatting with customers on-line or admin tasks like posting bills to your accounts package and reconciling bank statements.

For a while you may be able to get family and friends to help but eventually you are going to have to consider hiring staff, when that time comes it is well worth considering using outsourced staff based in low cost parts of the world working from home over the Internet.

There are a number of on-line businesses that have set up to facilitate the relationship between employers and contractors who work in this way, including

Upwork (formed from the merger of Odesk and elance)
https://www.upwork.com/

Freelancer.com
https://www.freelancer.com/

Peopleperhour.com
https://www.peopleperhour.com/

I recommend Upwork as the market leader and a site that I have used for years, they make it easy to find staff, interview them and act as an intermediary to ensure fair dealing by both the employer and the contractor.

There are a number of advantages to using this kind of arrangement when compared to hiring local staff.

It's cheaper
Hiring people based in the Philippines or India, or Eastern Europe can be a lot cheaper than hiring people in your locality.

There are no extra overheads

Because the people that you hire through sites like these typically work from home using their own Internet connection, PC and desk you do not take on any extra overheads, for a UK staff member you can pay as much as 30% extra on top of salary for overheads. Normally you pay a flat rate to the contractor who is responsible for paying their own costs, local taxes etc.

Freelancers are more flexible than permanent staff
You can take on freelance staff for a few weeks to cover peak season, hire them for a trial or as permanent staff, they are much easier to terminate if things change or if the relationship does not work out with no legal requirement for notice or compensation payments.

Better educated
The kind of people that are available to take basic customer service jobs in the UK or USA are not as well educated as the people available overseas, you will probably be able to get staff with a degree level education based in the Philippines for around $US30 (£20) per day.

Most of the people available through the sites mentioned above speak good English and write it very well.

Downsides
However there are a couple of downsides that you should consider as well

Freelance staff can be unreliable
You will have a lot less control over overseas freelancers than you would have over staff based in your office, they are often based in parts of the world with unreliable electricity or which are prone to harsh weather events like typhoons which can prevent them from working. It is not uncommon for freelance staff in the third world to work two jobs at the same time without telling either of their employers.

I recommend hiring overseas staff in two's, and expect a 50% drop out over time.

No physical contact make training and supervision harder
All remote workers have this problem, regardless of whether they are based a few miles away from your office or on the other side of the world, but modern communications tools are available to make things easier. Your Google Apps subscription includes video conferencing and on-line chat through Google Talk.

I recommend that you take time to carefully document your processes for things like answering customer e-mails and calls so that you can share the documents with

new staff as a form of training.
The stored replies function in Helpscout really comes into it's own when you use overseas staff to reply to e-mails.

Accents

Overseas staff will usually have an accent which can be awkward if they are answering calls. Because of the history of the Philippines as a US colony Philippines staff have a US style accent that is more acceptable to most customers than an Indian accent.

The ethical dimension

There is an ethical dimension to hiring people overseas, the concern is always that people working for lower wages are being exploited in some way, but if they are earning more than they could in a local job and working in a flexible style that suits their other commitments it is hard to see how that is a form of exploitation.

Chapter 112
On-Going tasks

Now that your site is up and running you are committed to a range of tasks that will need to be done every day.

I can't over emphasize how important it is that you check your companies e-mail every day and ship orders every day, if you don't then it makes your store look like it's closed and that will seriously affect your conversion ratio as a lot of customers will e-mail before buying. If you are running as a small team or a family business it could make sense to have a rota to make sure that these jobs get done every day, if you can afford some help, these are the key jobs to be sure are done every single day without fail.

There are a few other on-going tasks that you need to make sure get done on a regular basis as well, some will become part of your daily routine, for the others you can use Google Calendar to create recurring reminders to make sure that they get done.

Daily Jobs
These are the jobs that should be done almost every hour, but at least once each day.

- As mentioned above the most important jobs are to check e-mail every day and to ship orders every day - and of course if you can you should do these many times each day.

- Check that the site is working.

Make your web site one of the homepage tabs in your web browser, that way you will check it every day just by opening your web browser.

- Make sure that the Checkout is working

Place a test order every morning, use a bank transfer order or a credit card with your payment settings set to authorize only.

- Check Facebook every day if you have set up a page there, more often if you are advertising there. You can set up alerts so that you can react quickly to new posts.

- Check AdWords costs and performance every morning for the previous day, just to make sure that everything is going as expected.

- Post all invoices and bills into your accounts package at the end of each day - you do not want that to get behind.

Weekly Tasks
Weekly tasks and monthly tasks are the jobs that you might like to schedule in your Google Calendar so that you get a reminder to do them. These are short term review jobs aimed at catching things before they go wrong

- Update your blog every week, if you have committed to writing one. If you have posted in the last 3 days there is no need to post again unless you have something really meaningful to say, but if it's been a week or more since your last post you should post something even if it's a bit empty.

- Pull a report from AdWords to check the performance of your adverts over the last week, check which phrases have been triggering your ads and update negative keywords where necessary, check conversion rates and adjust bids.

- Review your P&L against your plan, check each line and try to understand why they vary from plan (if they do) and either change what you are doing to get back on plan or update the future plan.

Monthly Tasks
Monthly tasks are a chance to review longer term, strategic issues.

- Monthly P&L Review

I recommend that you do a monthly P&L review, along the same lines as the weekly one but for a 4 week period. This is also a good chance to review your Shopify plan, if your revenues are likely to stay above $US 16,700 per month (£11,000) then you should switch to the 'Professional' plan, if they are likely to be above $US 25,000 per month (£16,500) then you should switch to 'Unlimited'. Don't be afraid to switch back down though if your sales fall for any reason.

- Competitive review

Check around the web for direct and indirect competitors. Look at sites you already know about and check for new sites coming on-line. Are there ideas there that you can copy - don't be shy! How does their pricing and market positioning compare with yours? Don't drop your price immediately in response to cheaper competition, think about how their store and reputation compares to yours, can you command a premium?

- Monthly AdWords Review

Every month you should complete a full review of your AdWords account, check data for the last 30 days and last 90 days, re-work your bids based on your conversion rates as they exist now and make sure that you have added all the negative keywords that you need to to avoid pointless clicks. For a shopping campaign you do not set keywords, the ads get triggered based on the title, category, and the description of the products. To see which search terms and phrases have triggered your ads you can look into the search terms report found in the dimensions tab. You can then identify the search phrases that are not relevant to your business and then add them to your negative keywords list to make sure that you don't waste money on them in the future.

- Facebook and Marketing Plan review

It makes sense to review your marketing plan monthly as well as your AdWords account, if you are doing Facebook marketing review the performance of that in the same way as AdWords and compare the two - should you move budget between them? Check the plan to see if you have done all that you thought you would in the last month and change the plan for the next month if you need to.

Chapter 113
Taking a Break

If you are going on holiday and there is nobody to manage the store while you are away you need to consider how you will manage that. The ideal is of course to keep the store working by having enough staff to cover for holidays, but for some small family businesses that can be problematic. If you are unable to keep the store open while you are away for any reason, here is a checklist of things that you should do before you go.

1. Before you leave, eMail everyone with a backorder in your system to let them know when their goods will be delivered, cancel and refund any orders from people who can not wait. Don't just ignore them and hope, that will generate lots of bad feeling and could lead to charge backs.

2. Turn off all of your advertising - no point in paying for traffic when you are closed

3. Put a message on your phone voice mail saying that you are closed and telling customers why and when you will reopen.

4. Put an auto responder on your email explaining that a reply will come when you will re-open and saying when that will be.

5. Put a note on your site to say when orders will be shipped, disable express shipping and collection options.

6. Set your payment system to authorize only, not to collect cash automatically, go through the orders and collect the cash manually when you get back, an authorization can not become a charge-back while you are away.

Chapter 114
Logistics system

The stock control in Shopify is basic, but it works quite well, as long as you are only selling on Shopify and only through one store.

Shopify are developing the stock control functionality of the system all the time and I expect that it will continue to improve over 2016 and beyond, however at the moment if you sell through multiple Shopify stores and through marketplaces like Amazon and eBay, then you should consider adding system to control your stock and synchronize your product listings outside of Shopify.

The detail on how to set that up is outside of the scope of this book, but I do have a recommendation for you to consider if you are in that position.

When you need to sync your marketplace stores and your Shopify stores I recommend that you use StoreFeeder (www.storefeeder.com). StoreFeeder is a great system, it is hosted on-line just like Shopify and integration is easy, it has a wide range of features to support multi channel retailing, but it is not cheap, plans start at £150 ($US225) per month and go up to £500 ($US750) per month so you have to be sure that you need it before committing.

Chapter 115
Processing your first Order

If you are following through this book while you are setting up your own store then congratulations are due, you have your first order - well done!

You should get an e-mail notification from Shopify to let you know that the order has been placed, the notification is sent to the address that you set up in Settings > Notifications. You can click on the link in the e-mail to go to the order processing page or you can go to the Orders menu choice from the main menu directly.

To see the order details click on the order number.

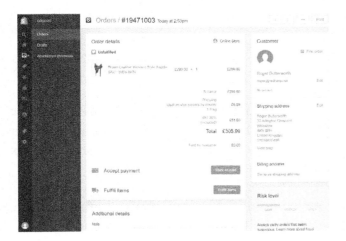

This is where you work through the fraud screening process that we discussed in the chapter on Checking Orders. Shopify helps you by giving each order a risk level rating - that's a big help, but you still need to go through a thorough evaluation of the order as well.

Another helpful tool is the 'View map' link under the shipping address, click on that to see the address on Google maps and street view.

If you are happy to ship the order then the first step if you have your payment settings set to authorize and then charge manually is to collect the cash by charging the card, if you are charging automatically then this will have already been done for you. The example above is a bank transfer order - be careful not to ship those until the cash is confirmed in your account.

Once you have the cash, the next step is to pick and pack the order, at the top right hand corner of the screen you will see the 'print' button, press it and print off a copy of the order. With that in hand find the stock and put it in the shipping box or bag, but don't seal it.

Next enter the customers delivery address details into your shippers system and print off a delivery label then press the 'Fulfil items' button.

Double check the shipping address against your shipping label, then re-check the items in the delivery against the printed copy of the order. If everything is correct put the printed version in the box with the goods as a delivery note, seal the box and put the shipping label on the outside.

Enter the tracking number from your shipping label into the box on the page, Shopify will try to identify the courier from the format of the tracking number, but the system for doing that is not perfect as many different couriers tracking numbers look the same. If it gets it wrong or can't tell, pick the courier from the drop down.

A nice tip here - if Shopify does not have your courier integrated add the URL for their web site to the end of the tracking number like this and select 'other' for the courier

That way when the customer gets the tracking number they will also see how to track it without having to call you.

Once that's done, press the blue 'Fulfil items' button and the order will be marked as shipped and your stock will be decremented one item if you are tracking stock through Shopify.

Part Shipping
If you do not have all the items on the order in stock you can part ship the order, I'd recommend only doing that if the items that you are shipping make sense (for example if the customer orders a main item and 3 accessories, it's OK to ship the main item and one accessory with the others to follow, but shipping the accessories without the main item is annoying for the customer)

To part ship an order you can simply change the number of each item that you are shipping in the Quantity field of the top section to match the number being dispatched.

Part shipped orders are highlighted in the 'orders' page so that you can see them to send the rest when it is possible.

Chapter 116
Taking orders over the phone

Once your store is up and running, if you have a telephone number you will get requests from customers to place orders over the phone. There are a few things that you need to know about taking telephone orders.

Firstly the risk of fraud through phone orders is higher than through the Internet, but if the telephone operator is alert it is easier to spot. I would recommend that you have your phone staff simply place telephone orders through the web site in the same way that a customer would do, but you must be very careful that you do not allow staff to write down or store credit card numbers as this is a breach of the credit card processing scheme rules (the Payment Card Industry rules also known as the 'PCI' rules).

If you have overseas staff answering your phones it is a good idea to have them transfer calls to you when customers want to buy in this way so that you can deal with these issues your self, you are liable for them, so it makes sense that you should be the one to do the transaction.

Appendices

Chapter 117
List of Courier Options

List of courier options with their strengths and weaknesses.

International Couriers

DHL - http://www.dhl.com/en.html

Strengths
Simply the best delivery service in Europe
Great import service in Europe

Weaknesses
A little more expensive than the competition

FedEx - http://www.fedex.com/gb/

Strengths
A great delivery service for US exporters
Great import service in the USA
Good service in Australia and Asia

Weaknesses
A little more expensive than the competition

UPS - https://www.ups.com/

Strengths
If you have to have one courier worldwide they have the best service
Good import service in Europe, USA and Asia

Weaknesses
A little more expensive than the competition

For UK based shippers

Royal Mail - http://www.royalmail.com/

Strengths
Covers the whole UK for a single rate
Customers like the service as it is easy to pick up parcels from your post office if you are not in
Low Cost for small items under 2Kg

Weaknesses
Inflexible service offering, no discounts unless volumes are HUGE
Very expensive for items over 2Kg

DPD - http://www.dpd.co.uk/

Strengths
Best rates for parcels over 2Kg and under 30Kg
Excellent tracking
Delivers in a one hour window

Weaknesses
Poor quality international service
Expensive for items under 2Kg
They do lose parcels from time to time

Parcelforce - http://www.parcelforce.com/

Strengths
Covers the whole UK for a single rate - best rates for Highlands and Islands
Customers like the service as it is easy to pick up parcels from your post office if you are not in
Low Cost for small items under 2Kg

Weaknesses
Inflexible service offering, no discounts unless volumes are HUGE
Very expensive for items over 2Kg

UK Mail - https://www.ukmail.com/

Strengths
Low cost offering
Very low Cost for small items under 2Kg
Low cost for larger items

Weaknesses
Poor brand image
Slower delivery than royal mail
No signed for options

Yodel - http://www.yodel.co.uk/

Strength
They are cheap

Weaknesses
They are awful, slow, unpredictable and they lose a lot of parcels

My Hermes - https://www.myhermes.co.uk/RWD/

Strength
They are cheap

Weaknesses
They are awful, slow, unpredictable and they lose a lot of parcels

For USA based shippers

USPS - https://www.usps.com/

Strengths
Covers the whole USA at a reasonable price
Customers like the service
Great for small items

Weaknesses
Inflexible service offering
Slow service

For Australian based shippers

Australia Post - http://auspost.com.au/

Strengths
Covers the whole USA at a reasonable price
Customers like the service
Great for small items

Weaknesses
Inflexible service offering
Slow service

Toll - http://www.tollgroup.com/onetoll

Strengths
Great for shipping to Australia, Singapore and Japan from Asia
Lower cost than FedEx etc

Weaknesses
Can be Expensive
Service not as good as FedEx

Chapter 118
Template fraud screening e-Mail

Template e-mail to send to customers for extra fraud screening info

```
Hi {Insert Customer Name},

Thanks for your order.

Unfortunately we are not able to verify your address with
the card processor or by other means. The credit card
company rules make us responsible for protecting ourselves
and our customers from the misuse of credit cards we
require some further information to confirm your identity.

Please could you reply with a copy of the following:

- a scan or picture of your photographic ID, with your
address

- a scan or photograph of the front of your credit card
(front only for your security)

If this can be supplied, we can process your order and
dispatch your goods as soon as possible.

If you are unable to provide the necessary further
information, we can cancel and refund this order, you can
re-order via PayPal or bank transfer which do not require
this kind of verification.

We sincerely apologize for any inconvenience caused by
these extra checks, but please understand that we suffer
the costs of all orders placed on our sites by people
using credit cards without the holders permission and we
make these checks to protect ourselves and our customers
from these costs.

Regards

Template Ends
```

Chapter 119
Checklist

Checklist of actions and links

1. Build a Financial model for your store
2. Build a written business plan for your store
3. Choose name for your store and buy domain or domains
    www.godaddy.com
4. Set up a Google Apps account with one user, using your domain
    https://apps.Google.com/
5. Confirm that Shopify will work for your store
6. Choose your Payment processors and set up your accounts with them
    www.paypal.com
7. Set up your Shopify store.
    www.shopify.com
8. Set up Google analytics on your web store using your Google Apps account
    http://www.Google.com/analytics/
9. Set up a Google AdWords account for your store
    AdWords.Google.com
10. Set up a Google Merchant Center account for your store
    merchants.Google.com
11. Connect your Merchant Center account to your AdWords account and start running Google Shopping Ads
12. Set up a MailChimp Account for your store
    www.mailchimp.com
13. Integrate MailChimp into your store
14. Set up a Facebook page for your store
    www.facebook.com
15. Set up a HelpScout account for customer service tickets
    www.helpscout.com
16. Set up a Voipfone account and Phone number
    www.voipfone.com
17. Set up an eBay account for your store
    www.ebay.com
18. Set up an Amazon Seller central Account
    https://sellercentral.amazon.com/gp/homepage.html
19. Claim your business name on Twitter

www.twitter.com
20. Set up an Instragram Account for your Store
www.instagram.com
21. Set up a Pintrest Account for your store
www.pintrest.com
22. Set up an account on your chosen reviews site
23. Create a Marketing Strategy
24. Create a Marketing Plan

CPSIA information can be obtained
at www.ICGtesting.com
Printed in the USA
BVOW09s0715260317
479466BV00011B/521/P